Richard II and the English Nobility

To my Father and Mother

Richard II and the English Nobility

Anthony Tuck

Lecturer in History, University of Lancaster

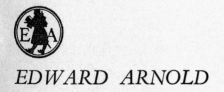

EDWARD ARNOLD

Printed in Great Britain by
Butler & Tanner Ltd
Frome and London

Contents

Acknowledgements

It is a pleasure to acknowledge the help and kindness I have received while working both on this book and on the thesis on which parts of it are based. I owe a special debt of gratitude to Mr Edward Miller, of Fitzwilliam College Cambridge, who supervised my research for my Ph.D. and who has given me much helpful advice since. Professor E. B. Fryde of the University College of Wales, Aberystwyth, gave me valuable guidance in the early stages of my research; Dr Roger Virgoe of the University of East Anglia, Dr Ralph Griffiths of University College Swansea, and Mr James Sherborne of the University of Bristol offered many useful comments on my thesis. Mr Sherborne was also kind enough to read several chapters of this book and offer invaluable criticism.

I have been helped by the staff of many libraries and repositories, but especially by those of Cambridge University Library, the Public Record Office, and the Literary and Philosophical Society of Newcastle upon Tyne. The later stages of my work on this book would have been much more difficult but for the generosity of the University of Lancaster in giving me a sabbatical term in 1972. To all these persons and institutions I offer my grateful thanks.

Transcripts and translations of Crown copyright records in the Public Record Office appear by permission of the Controller of HM Stationery Office.

Lancaster, 1972   Anthony Tuck

Abbreviations

These references are cited in their abbreviated or short form throughout the book.

Anon. Chron.	*The Anonimalle Chronicle, 1333–81* ed. V. H. Galbraith (Manchester 1927)
BIHR	*Bulletin of the Institute of Historical Research*
BJRL	*Bulletin of the John Rylands Library*
BM	British Museum
CCPRI	*Rotulorum Patentium et Clausarum Cancellariae Hiberniae Calendarium* ed. E. Tresham (Dublin 1828)
CChR	*Calendar of Charter Rolls*
CCR	*Calendar of Close Rolls*
CFR	*Calendar of Fine Rolls*
CIPM	*Calendar of Inquisitions Post Mortem*
CMI	*Calendar of Miscellaneous Inquisitions*
CPR	*Calendar of Patent Rolls*
EHR	*English Historical Review*
Evesham	*Historia vitae et regni Ricardi II a monacho quodam de Evesham* ed. T. Hearne (Oxford 1729)
Favent	*Historia sive Narracio Mirabilis Parliamenti* attributed to Thomas Favent, ed. M. McKisack, Camden Third Series XXXVII (London 1926)
Foedera	T. Rymer, *Foedera, Conventiones, Literae, etc.*, 2nd edition, ed. G. Holmes, 20 vols. (London 1704–35)
Froissart, *Oeuvres*	Jean Froissart, *Oeuvres* ed. K. de Lettenhove, 25 vols. (Brussels 1867–77)

GEC	*The Complete Peerage* ed. George Edward Cockayne, 12 vols. (London 1910–59)
Kirkstall Chronicle	*The Kirkstall Chronicle, 1355–1400* ed. M. V. Clarke and N. Denholm-Young, *BJRL* XV (1931), pp. 100–37
Knighton	*Chronicon Henrici Knighton* ed. J. R. Lumby, 2 vols., Rolls Series (London 1889, 1895)
NLI	National Library of Ireland
Nicolas, *POPC*	*Proceedings and Ordinances of the Privy Council of England* ed. N. H. Nicolas (London 1834)
PRO	Public Record Office
RDP	*Reports from the Lords Committees touching the dignity of a peer of the realm* 5 Vols. (London 1829)
Rot. Parl.	*Rotuli Parliamentorum: the Rolls of Parliament* 6 vols. (London 1783)
Rot. Scot.	*Rotuli Scotiae* 2 vols. (London 1814–19)
Sc. HR	*Scottish Historical Review*
Tout, *Chapters*	T. F. Tout, *Chapters in the Administrative History of Medieval England* 6 vols. (Manchester 1923–35)
Traison	*Chronique de la Traison et Mort de Richard II* ed. B. Williams (London 1846)
TRHS	*Transactions of the Royal Historical Society*
Usk	*Chronicon Adae de Usk* ed. E. M. Thompson (London 1904)
VCH	*Victoria County History*
Walsingham, HA	*Thomas Walsingham Historia Anglicana* ed. H. T. Riley, 2 vols., Rolls Series (London 1863–4)
Walsingham, *Annales*	*Annales Ricardi Secundi et Henrici Quarti* in J. de Trokelow et Anon., *Chronica et Annales* ed. H. T. Riley, Rolls Series (London 1866)
Westminster	*Polychronicon Ranulphi Higden* Vol. IX, ed. J. R. Lumby, Rolls Series (London 1886) (Continuation probably by a monk of Westminster.)

1

The Political Community in 1377

In 1327 a group of nobles deposed and imprisoned King Edward II. In 1399 another group deposed his great-grandson, Richard II, and the leader of the revolution then placed himself upon the vacant throne. These two events are sufficient in themselves to suggest that the most important problem facing English kings in the fourteenth century was their relations with their nobility, the group of twenty or so men with the rank of earl and above. These men were the wealthiest landowners, the traditional leaders in war, and the focus of the interests and ambitions of many barons and knights of lesser wealth and standing. These great magnates also claimed, by tradition and by virtue of their wealth and their social and military importance, a large share in advising the king and in shaping his policies. They expected the king to pay due regard to their interests and prejudices in his conduct of government. Providing he did so, they confined their political role to advice and military leadership. But if he did not do so, they might intervene more directly in government and attempt to impose measures of restraint upon the king. Naturally, the extent of a magnate's involvement in politics or war depended to a great extent upon his own interests, inclination, and capacities; but groups of magnates in the fourteenth century were capable of forming coalitions which, in the short run at least and with the support of the Commons in parliament, proved irresistible. Political stability therefore depended upon the maintenance of good relations between the king and the nobility; and an understanding of the politics of Richard II's reign requires some discussion of relations between crown and nobility in the reign of his grandfather.

It has been well said that the fourteenth century lies in the shadow of Edward I's legislation.[1] But it might be equally well said that the century—or rather the last seventy years of it—lies in the shadow of Edward II's deposition. After such a precedent, Edward III had not only to re-establish the prestige of kingship, but also to re-establish royal initiative in government and royal control over the nobility, without at the same time provoking another baronial revolt. For most of his reign he succeeded. His handling of the aristocracy from the outset of his reign reveals a sensitivity towards their social prejudices, their liberties, and their views on government which did more than anything else to ensure political harmony. For instance, Edward's grandfather had reduced the numbers of the titled nobles by allowing some titles to lapse and failing to create new ones,[2] Edward II's creations had been mostly short-lived—symbols of his favouritism. Edward III, however, set out deliberately to enlarge the number of the titled nobility. In 1337 the four senior members of his household were simultaneously promoted to the earldoms of Huntingdon, Northampton, Salisbury, and Suffolk.[3] In their patents of creation, the king stated explicitly that the number of titled nobles had diminished as a result of the extinction of families, and that by various accidents many titles had lapsed or come to the crown. Edward now proposed to increase the number of nobles by creating new titles and restoring old ones: there could hardly have been a more specific repudiation of Edward I's policy towards the earls.[4] But this was not all. Those families who had suffered forfeiture in Edward II's reign or in 1330 were restored to their lands and titles,[5] thus ensuring that there was no group of disinherited to act as a focus for political discontent. Edward also developed a more elaborate *cursus honorum* by making greater use of the title of duke. Before 1337 only the king as Duke of Aquitaine had borne the title; but in that year Edward conferred the dukedom of Cornwall on the Black Prince; in 1351 the most powerful and eminent of the magnates, Henry of Lancaster, became a duke; and in

---

[1] G. A. Holmes, *The Estates of the Higher Nobility in Fourteenth Century England* (Cambridge 1957) p. 2.
[2] K. B. McFarlane, 'Had Edward I a "policy" towards the Earls?', *History* 50 (1965) pp. 145–59.
[3] L. O. Pike, *Constitutional History of the House of Lords* (London 1894) pp. 75–6; PRO Exchequer Accounts, various, E.101/387/9. (I owe this reference to Dr E. B. Fryde.)
[4] *RDP* Vol. V, p. 29.
[5] These were the Earls of Arundel and March, and Lord Despenser. Lancaster recovered most of his inheritance in 1327, and the Kent inheritance eventually passed by marriage to the Holland family.

1362 the king conferred the dukedom of Clarence on his second son Lionel.

At the more practical level, the king interfered very little in the arrangements the magnates made for the disposal of their property.[1] The device of the trust developed rapidly in his reign,[2] and in many cases the crown's officials took no action to protect royal rights from erosion.[3] Furthermore, as McFarlane pointed out,[4] the king encouraged the nobility's tendency to develop into a more cohesive and more exclusive self-perpetuating élite by granting new or re-granting old titles and estates in tail male, excluding women from inheritance and thus making the fragmentation of estates and the lapsing of titles less likely. Social cohesion within the ranks of the nobility was reinforced by marriage alliances which, in the course of Edward III's reign, bound most of the comital families to one another and many to the crown. It is true that some marriage alliances generated feuds rather than friendship; and true also that Edward III's policy of marrying his children into the great aristocratic families has traditionally been seen as one of the reasons for subsequent political instability; but at the time his policy made for social harmony.

The ceremonial side of court life served a similar purpose. The order of the garter was granted to magnates who distinguished themselves in war. It also provided a means of rewarding men of equal military distinction who lacked the lineage and territorial power of the titled nobility. The garter was a symbol of the military ethos of aristocratic society. Edward created a court and a court ceremonial which attracted the magnates and affirmed the values by which they themselves lived. But Edward was not concerned merely with the social and ceremonial side of aristocratic life. He also ensured that the nobility received their due share of political power, and benefited in material as well as social terms from the exercise of royal patronage. In creating William Montague Earl of Salisbury in 1337, Edward stated that his intention was to increase the number of the nobility, 'by whose counsels', he

---

[1] J. M. W. Bean, *The Decline of English Feudalism 1215–1540* (Manchester 1968) pp. 212ff.
[2] G. A. Holmes, *Estates of the Higher Nobility* pp. 41–50.
[3] J. M. W. Bean, *Decline of English Feudalism*. The crown did not abandon its rights entirely. Some Chancery officials were efficient and diligent in safeguarding royal interests, but the crown usually interfered with trusts only to enforce them strictly or to break fraudulent ones; and its right to prerogative wardship in most cases went by default.
[4] K. B. McFarlane, 'The English Nobility in the Later Middle Ages', *12th International Congress of Historical Sciences* (1965) pp. 337–45.

said, 'the kingdom should be governed'.[1] And this principle was re-affirmed in other peerage patents later in the reign. It was a principle which Edward upheld and probably believed in. At no time in his reign were the magnates excluded from power; at no time could they complain that royal favour was being shown to, and patronage given to, 'men raised from the dust'. At no time—until perhaps his powers failed in the last years of his reign—could the magnates complain that his attention was being held by evil counsellors. Edward ensured that the political issues of his father's reign would not be raised again.

The career of Richard, third Earl of Arundel of the Fitzalan line, illustrates the benefits a magnate might derive from his enjoyment of royal favour. His father, Earl Edmund, had suffered forfeiture and execution in the reign of Edward II, but Edward III restored Earl Richard to the honour and most of the lands of the earldom in 1334. Through his mother, the sister and heiress of John, last Earl of Warenne and Surrey, Earl Richard was heir to the Warenne inheritance; but before his death Earl Warenne made several attempts to settle the earldom and lands on his illegitimate offspring, and only Edward III's active support of his claim ensured that the inheritance came to him in 1361.[2] Throughout Edward's reign, Arundel was high in favour at court. In March 1345 he married Eleanor, daughter of Henry of Lancaster, after divorcing his first wife,[3] and this second marriage consolidated his influence at court. The king allowed him at the time of his second marriage to carry through a re-enfeoffment of all his lands to a group of trustees, eliminating the inheritance's liability to feudal incidents.[4] The king's intervention had increased his territorial power, and the king's patronage increased his authority in other ways. In 1337, Edward granted him the franchise of return of writs within the honour of Arundel;[5] in 1339 he was appointed keeper of Caernarvon Castle and sheriff of Caernarvonshire for life; and in 1345 the king granted him the offices of Justice of North Wales and sheriff of Shropshire, also for life.[6] By the middle of the century, the king had enabled Arundel to extend his influence throughout North Wales

[1] *RDP* Vol. V, p. 320.
[2] F. R. Fairbank, 'The Last Earl of Warenne and Surrey', *Yorkshire Archaeological Journal* XIX (1907) pp. 193–264.
[3] *Calendar of Papal Registers, Petitions* Vol. 1, p. 75.
[4] *CPR* 1345–5, pp. 487–8. The Warenne inheritance was similarly re-enfeoffed in 1366 (*ibid.* 1364–7, pp. 237–9) and when he died in 1376 Arundel held nothing in fee simple.
[5] *CChR* Vol. IV, p. 402.
[6] *ibid.* p. 415; *CFR* 1337–47, pp. 412–13.

and the northern marches, and the offices he held must have been a source of considerable profit. It is impossible to estimate how much wealth these offices brought him, for the nominal fees were very small, and most of the income came in the form of douceurs and gratuities. But in 1348-9, probably an exceptional year but the only one for which any evidence survives, his deputies in his North Wales offices owed him £440-3-0 and the Black Prince owed him 300 marks.[1] Other magnates similarly enjoyed the benefits of royal favour and patronage,[2] and were not disposed to rebel against their beneficiary. Between 1341 and 1370 there were few, if any, serious political or constitutional disputes between king and magnates. The upheaval brought about in mid-century by the Black Death made little difference at the time, for the landowning class was united in its reaction to the new and much more unfavourable economic circumstances in which it found itself. The cumulative social and economic effects of successive outbreaks of plague showed themselves only in the longer term.[3]

By the early 1370s, however, the harmony of the middle years of Edward III's reign had broken down. In the parliament of 1371 the Commons launched an attack upon the clerical ministers of state, and with the support of some hotheads among the lords, including the young Earl of Pembroke, drove them from office. They were replaced by a group of lay ministers, behind some of whom the influence of John of Gaunt may perhaps be seen. This precedent for an attack on the king's ministers by the Commons and some lords was to be followed in the Good Parliament of 1376. There was evidently no longer any confidence or identity of aims between the magnates and the king's councillors and administrators, or between Commons and councillors, or even (as the events of 1375-7 were to show) among the magnates themselves. The fundamental reason for the breakdown of political harmony was failure in war. From the outset of the war with France and Scotland, Edward had been victorious in pitched battles. He had given the magnates and Commons what they most wanted and were most prepared to pay for—striking military success. The navy had won the battles of Sluys and Winchelsea, which

[1] Shropshire Record Office, Acton of Aldenham Collection (unnumbered).
[2] For instance, Thomas Beauchamp, Earl of Warwick, was made hereditary sheriff of Warwickshire and Leicestershire; the earls promoted in 1337 received substantial grants of land and office; and the alliance between Edward and the House of Lancaster was cemented with a series of grants of lands, liberties, and offices.
[3] G. A. Holmes, *Estates of the Higher Nobility* pp. 114-15.

appeared to ensure English domination of the Channel and the route to Gascony; and the army had won two spectacular victories in France (Crécy and Poitiers) and one against Scotland (the battle of Neville's Cross). The kings of France and Scotland had been captured, and the victories had given the illusion that the war was won. But Edward was unable to follow up his victories. The treaty of Brétigny, which followed the battle of Poitiers, provided for the cession to Edward in full sovereignty not only of Gascony itself, but also of Poitou, Agenais, Perigord, Quercy, Limousin, Thouars, and Belleville, together with certain areas of Northern France. But the transfers of territory were never carried out, and Edward found himself powerless to enforce the terms of the treaty. In Scotland, the English were gradually driven out of the lands in the south which they had occupied in the 1330s, and neither David II himself nor the Scottish regents were prepared to concede these lands, or to accept English suzerainty over Scotland as a whole, as the price of David's release from captivity in England.[1] English strategy and English war finance were well adapted to achieve set-piece victories, but they were much less suitable for the long process of attrition necessary if Scotland and France were to submit permanently. In the 1360s, therefore, the initiative in war passed imperceptibly to Scotland and to France, and this gradual erosion of the English position perhaps sapped English morale more than obvious and decisive defeat.

Diplomatically, too, England suffered several serious reverses in the 1360s and early 1370s. Perhaps the most serious, in the long run, was the formation in 1368 of an alliance between France and Castile. The formal alliance followed a long period of unofficial French support for Henry of Trastámara in his struggle for the Castilian throne against his half brother Pedro I.[2] The English intervened on Pedro's behalf, and the Black Prince's victory at Nájera in 1367 restored him temporarily to his throne. But Henry's murder of Pedro in 1369 ensured the triumph of French interests at the Castilian court for the next twenty years. English and French intervention in peninsular politics aimed at securing the support of the Castilian navy, and Franco-Castilian naval co-operation made a decisive difference to the course of the war in the 1370s. England had perhaps been unwise in any case to place too many

[1] R. A. Nicolson, 'David II, the Historians and the Chroniclers', *Sc.HR* XLV (1966) pp. 63–9.
[2] P. E. Russell, *The English Intervention in Spain and Portugal in the time of Edward III and Richard II* (Oxford 1955) pp. 3, 139–40.

hopes upon Castile. For, as recent Spanish historians have shown,[1] Castile's interest was to maintain her lines of communication from the Cantabrian coast ports to Flanders in order to transport her wool to Flemish weaving towns. Castile and England were, to some extent, economic rivals in Flanders, and Castile needed to keep the shipping lanes open and protect her commerce from attack. The Franco-Castilian alliance was based not only on the political victory of Henry of Trastámara but also upon Castilian economic interests.

In Flanders itself, too, England suffered a serious diplomatic setback. Louis de Male, Count of Flanders, had been well disposed to Edward III in the years after Crécy, but the maintenance of English ascendancy in Flanders after his death depended upon the marriage of his daughter and heiress, Margaret. Edward hoped for a marriage between Margaret and his fourth son, Edmund Langley, but intensive French activity at the Papal Curia at Avignon resulted in the pope's refusal to issue the necessary dispensation so that instead Margaret married Philip Duke of Burgundy, the brother of the king of France, in 1369. England could no longer count on Flanders as a base for operations against France, and she had lost one of her more valuable allies. By 1370, in fact, England had become isolated diplomatically. The Scots renewed their alliance with France in 1371; the Franco-Castilian alliance was for the moment unshakeable, and Flanders had moved into the French orbit. By contrast, England's alliance with Portugal and with various princes of the Low Countries and Germany seemed of little account. England had to fight the war alone.

These diplomatic setbacks partly explain England's military ineffectiveness in the 1370s, but equally important were lack of leadership, lack of money, and dissension over strategy. After Poitiers, the king, traditionally expected to lead the nation in arms, became less and less adequately able to do so. In the 1370s he declined into senility and fell under the domination of his mistress, Alice Perrers. After the resumption of war with France in 1369, Edward did not take the field in person again. In 1372 he planned to lead a naval expedition to revenge the Earl of Pembroke's defeat by the Castilians off La Rochelle,[2] but throughout the summer the winds remained unfavourable and he had to abandon the expedition. It was an inglorious and frustrating end to

[1] J. Vicens Vives, *Historia Económica de España* (Madrid 1966) pp. 159–62, 211–13; *Navegación y comercio en el golfo de Vizcaya. Un estudio sobre la política marinera de la Casa de Trastámara* (Madrid 1958).
[2] J. W. Sherborne, 'The Battle of La Rochelle and the War at Sea 1372–75', *BIHR* XLII (1969) pp. 22–3.

his military career. Leadership ought to have passed to the king's eldest son, Edward the Black Prince, the focus of enthusiasm and optimism after his victories at Poitiers and Nájera. But the Black Prince had returned from Spain in 1371 stricken with an illness which rendered him inactive until his death in 1376. The king's second son, Lionel Duke of Clarence, had died in 1368, and in the last years of his life he had been more occupied with the pacification and reorganization of Ireland than with military activity on the continent.[1] His fourth surviving son, Edmund Langley, created Earl of Cambridge in 1362, figured in the diplomatic and matrimonial schemes of his father and brothers,[2] but seemed to have neither the will nor the capacity to give an effective lead in war. Later events in both Portugal and England were to suggest that he would do everything in a battle except actually fight it. The chronicler Harding, writing in the early fifteenth century, said of him:

> When all the lords to councell and parlyament
> Went, he wolde to hunte and also to hawekyng.[3]

Neither of his marriages brought him large accessions of territory, and his father settled only a modest endowment on him. Throughout his career he avoided identification with the more extreme members of his family,[4] and for the most part he pursued a policy of moderation and compromise which has perhaps led to an underrating of his political importance.

The king's younger son, Thomas of Woodstock, created Earl of Buckingham at Richard II's coronation in 1377, was too young and inexperienced to play any great part in either politics or war in the last years of his father's reign. He made, however, a better marriage than his elder brother, for Eleanor de Bohun, daughter and co-heiress of the last earl of Hereford and Essex, brought with her half her father's inheritance and (if Froissart is to be believed) Woodstock tried to secure the other half as well by having Eleanor's younger sister, Mary, professed a nun. John of Gaunt intervened, and secured Mary's

---

[1] The most recent account of his career in Ireland is given by J. Otway-Ruthven, *A History of Medieval Ireland* (London 1968) pp. 285-95.
[2] *ibid.* p. 8. In 1372 he married Isabel of Castile, to reinforce the English connection with the legitimist line there.
[3] *The Chronicle of John Hardyng* ed. H. Ellis (London 1812) p. 340.
[4] He took no part in the attacks upon the king's favourites in 1388, nor in the condemnation of the former Appellants in 1397.

hand for his eldest son, Henry Earl of Derby. Woodstock and Derby shared the Bohun inheritance, and the arrangements for its partition led to a dispute between the two lords which smouldered on until 1395.[1] Woodstock inherited many of the more informal connections that had been formed by the Bohuns,[2] and by the time of Richard's coronation he had become a magnate in his own right, disposed to play an independent part in politics: though he may well have felt that his earldom and his admission to the Order of the Garter were unduly delayed.[3]

In view of the personal circumstances of the other members of the royal family, therefore, leadership came almost by default to the king's third son, John of Gaunt. In 1359 Gaunt had married Blanche, younger daughter and co-heiress of Henry Duke of Lancaster. But Duke Henry's death in 1360 was quickly followed by that of his elder daughter, and Gaunt thus acquired the whole of the inheritance—the dukedom of Lancaster, and the earldoms of Lincoln, Leicester, and Derby. He also held, in his own right, the earldom of Richmond, but this was transferred from time to time to the Duke of Brittany to persuade him to enter, or to reward him for entering, the English allegiance.[4] But in the 1370s Gaunt's interests centred not so much upon his inheritance as upon the rights in Castile, acquired by his marriage to Constance, the daughter and co-heiress of Pedro I. After Pedro's murder, Gaunt himself became heir of that line and, in 1371, Edward III allowed him to assume the title and arms of King of Castile and Leon. Gaunt's successful assertion of his claim to the Castilian throne would have been greatly in English interests, for it would have ended the Franco-Castilian alliance; but this was not Gaunt's sole or even main object in planning an expedition to Spain. No landowner, no king or magnate, in the fourteenth century, ignored the opportunity to acquire hereditary rights, and having acquired them, expected to uphold and enforce them. Gaunt undoubtedly wanted to enforce the right he had acquired by marriage and make himself king of Castile, but his success in so doing would also make English success in the war with France more likely. In 1372 Gaunt prepared an expedition to Castile, but Edward III ordered him to abandon it and join the attack

[1] PRO Duchy of Lancaster records DL.41/2/3; DL.41/5/1: Derby's demands on Woodstock and his reply to Woodstock's demands.
[2] PRO Ministers' Accounts SC.6/1156/18, SC.6/921/16, DL.29/680/11004-9.
[3] He did not become an earl until Richard II's coronation, and his nephew Henry of Derby was admitted to the Garter before him.
[4] M. C. E. Jones, *Ducal Brittany 1364-1399* (Oxford 1970) pp. 172-98.

being launched on northern France.[1] Castile, however, remained the centre of Gaunt's interests and it determined his position in discussions on military strategy for the next fourteen years.

The magnates traditionally looked to the royal family to provide leadership in war, and in the 1370s this leadership was lacking. But even if the royal family had provided vigorous and attractive leadership, the war might still not have flourished. Successful war requires not only leaders and allies but also money and a sound strategy. By the 1370s English financial resources were insufficient to support the war on the scale which both magnates and Commons expected. The financial difficulties of the crown in the 1370s should not be exaggerated. No medieval English king managed to secure a steady supply of money to finance a war; most of them heavily anticipated revenue, defaulted upon their debts, and thereby diminished their credit. Shortage of money had hampered Edward I's campaigns in Scotland, and inability to mobilize financial resources quickly and forcibly impeded Edward III even at the height of his success.[2] In fact by the 1370s the lay and ecclesiastical subsidies and the duties on wool and other commodities had become customary; the constitutional struggles over taxation which had marked the early stages of the Hundred Years' War had resulted in parliament's acceptance of the regularity of taxation in return for a monopoly of the right of consent. Edward could, therefore, count upon frequent lay and clerical taxes and upon almost automatic continuation from parliament to parliament of the taxes on exports. But in all probability, the yield from both sources of taxation diminished as the century went on. The subsidy assessment remained fixed at the 1334 figure; it thus did not reflect changes in the location of wealth, and more importantly, England's total moveable wealth was almost certainly lower by the beginning of Richard's reign than it had been in the pre-plague period.[3] The quantity of wool exported declined in the decades after 1360, and the few calculations so far made suggest that variations in the rate of duty, and the imposition of subsidies far heavier than the original customs did not prevent the monetary yield from wool exports declining in the second half of

[1] J. W. Sherborne, 'The Battle of La Rochelle', pp. 22–3.
[2] For instance, shortage of money impeded the land campaign which followed the victory at Sluys in 1340, and hampered Edward's war plans in the period between the truce of Esplechin and the truce of Malestroit, 1340–43.
[3] This has never been fully worked out. For a survey of the problem, see *Cambridge Economic History of Europe* Vol. III, ed. Postan, Rich, and Miller (Cambridge 1963) pp. 317–18.

Edward's reign.[1] But even though the yield from taxation may have declined, taxes still formed by far the largest item in the royal income.[2] The conduct of government and war was impossible without them, and their necessity ensured the summoning of frequent parliaments, for although consent was not withheld, it could not be foregone. The revenue from taxation came in slowly at intervals throughout the year; but to finance a campaign the king needed ready money quickly. His policy was to borrow on the security of the taxes. Throughout the reign, large-scale loans were negotiated with bankers and great capitalist merchants. By the 1360s Edward's credit had become so bad that he was having difficulty in floating the large loans necessary for full-scale campaigns overseas. The Italian bankers who had financed the king in the early part of his reign had gone bankrupt by 1346; the English merchant syndicates who succeeded the Italians as royal financiers were ruined by 1352, and Edward's treatment of two of the leading English merchants damaged his shaky credit still further.[3] In the 1370s, some London merchants were still prepared to lend him money, though evidently at a rate of interest as high as $33\frac{1}{3}$ per cent.[4] They played an important part in these years and in the early years of Richard II's reign in financing, supplying, and equipping naval and military expeditions. In addition to the large sums borrowed from the small group of London merchants, Edward and Richard borrowed smaller sums from a very wide range of people—magnates, prelates, corporate towns, religious houses, and country gentry. Loans of this kind, which may have been seen as an alternative to personal military service, were levied by commissions *de mutuo faciendo*; consent had to be obtained but could not be withheld, and no interest or other inducement was offered. These loans brought the crown into a financial, and therefore a political relationship with a wider range of people than any other royal activity, and those who made such loans could not but contrast the manner in which they were required to lend with the enormous profits made by the small group of merchants who had sufficient capital to make large, and apparently voluntary, loans to the

[1] *ibid.*; E. M. Carus-Wilson and Olive Coleman, *England's Export Trade 1275–1547* (Oxford 1963).
[2] *Cambridge Economic History* Vol. III, pp. 317–18. Figures provided by Dr G. A. Holmes.
[3] E. B. Fryde, 'The Last Trials of Sir William de la Pole', *Economic History Review* 2nd series XV (1962–3) pp. 17–30.
[4] K. B. McFarlane, 'Loans to Lancastrian Kings: the Problem of Inducement', *Cambridge Historical Journal* IX (1947) pp. 63–4; R. Bird, *The Turbulent London of Richard II* (London 1949) pp. 184ff.

crown. The ferocity of the attack by the Commons on the merchant Lyons in the Good Parliament of 1376 is more readily undestood when seen in this light.[1]

The king had few other sources of revenue to exploit. The hereditary revenues of the crown were not large: in 1374-5 they amounted to only £22,000 out of a total exchequer receipt of £112,000[2] and they, like the customs revenue and taxes, came in only slowly. In normal times—and even the most warlike of kings was not at war all the time —the hereditary revenue and the slow yield of taxes might be sufficient, for the king had no pressing need for ready cash. He lived by assignments of various kinds, leaving his creditors to collect the money due to them, though in so far as they failed to collect, the king's handling of his financial affairs might even in peace time become a matter of political controversy.[3] The crown, like the great magnates and professional captains, might hope to make money out of war, but as the war stagnated this source of money became intermittent and highly speculative. The ransoms of David II and John II were never paid in full, and no prizes of comparable worth were captured after the renewal of the war in 1369.[4] Profits from war were won with much more difficulty after 1369, and this perhaps explains the bitterness of the disputes over some of the ransoms that were available, such as those of the Count of Denia and John of Blois.[5] Parliament and the king's advisors considered other revenue-raising expedients, such as a hearth-tax or a sales tax; they cast covetous eyes on the property of the church, and fortified by Wycliffe's propaganda, considered disendowment.[6] They widened the basis of taxation by imposing poll-taxes in 1377, 1379, and 1381. But after the Peasants' Revolt the government abandoned this method of raising revenue, and the brief period of fiscal innovation came to an end.

English military failure, however, did not arise simply from poor leadership and a cumbersome financial system. Inadequate military

---

[1] G. L. Harriss, 'Aids, Loans and Benevolences', *Historical Journal* VI (1963) pp. 1-19.
[2] G. A. Holmes's figures in *Cambridge Economic History* Vol. III, pp. 317-18.
[3] G. L. Harriss, 'Preference at the Medieval Exchequer', *BIHR* XXX (1957) pp. 17-40.
[4] D. M. Broome, 'The Ransom of John I King of France', *Camden Miscellany* XIV (1926). Rather less than half was paid. The English government was still demanding the oustanding portion of David II's ransom in 1389 (BM Cotton *Vespasian, F* VII f.28).
[5] *Walsingham, HA* Vol. I, p. 376; Vol. II, pp. 150-51.
[6] *Rot. Parl.* Vol. II, pp. 361ff.

resources and strategy also played a part and was most clearly demonstrated at sea. England had never established a permanent naval force. When a naval expedition was projected, the government commandeered naval ships which it retained for the duration of the campaign and then returned to their owners. The ships were manned not by professionals but by men engaged for a particular campaign. Castile, on the other hand, had a permanent fleet of war galleys, stationed in the Cantabrian ports and manned by professional oarsmen. The use of oarsmen, of course, made the ships independent of the wind. The Castilian navy also displayed greater sophistication in the use of firearms. In both firepower and flexibility the Castilian navy appears to have been superior to the English in the 1370s, and the outlook worsened for England in 1374 when the French admiral Jean de Vienne began the construction of a fleet along Castilian lines.[1] The alliance with Portugal placed at England's disposal a fleet similarly organized to, though of course much smaller than, the Castilian fleet, and Edward III opened negotiations with Genoa in the hope of obtaining the help of her galleys;[2] but these moves made little difference to the situation in the English Channel.

On land, too, English strategy had become inadequate by the 1370s. Her military supremacy in Edward III's earlier years arose from the effectiveness of the longbow against mounted opponents in pitched battles. The longbow ended the domination in battle of the mounted warrior, but England had no effective answer to the tactics the French adopted after the renewal of the war in 1369. The French refused to risk defeat in pitched battle, requiring the English instead to lay siege to their towns. Du Guesclin's strategy was to whittle down English territory in France by attacks on small outlying garrisons, by subversion, and by the exploitation of local feuds and feelings. He intended at all costs to avoid facing the English in a pitched battle, though the price of such a policy was the infestation of French soil by large and destructive English armies, who could march through France unopposed and acquire the illusion of invincibility. The English had no effective answer to this strategy, and in view of the resources and the techniques at their disposal it is hard to see how they could have devised one. Siege warfare was long and expensive, and although by the end of the century artillery had become effective in attacking stone defences, the systematic use of cannon in sieges did not

[1] *Walsingham, HA* Vol. I, pp. 340–42.
[2] P. E. Russell, *The English Intervention* pp. 228–9.

become common until the middle of the fifteenth century. The alternatives to siege were localized raids, usually in coastal areas, or long marches through undefended country, such as Gaunt's march from Calais to Bordeaux in 1373; but both these expedients were costly and produced little long-term advantage for the English. In Scotland, the English faced a strategy similar in some ways to that of the French, and they had no answer to the Scottish policy of withdrawing in the face of an English invasion and slighting fortresses to prevent their capture or recapture by the English. Both English enemies had learned to avoid offering her pitched battle. In the last thirty years of the fourteenth century the only campaign which revealed any originality in strategy was Richard's in Ireland in 1394—a campaign which compels a reassessment of him as a military commander.[1]

These difficulties and inadequacies, then, may help to explain England's ineffectiveness in France and Scotland in the years after 1369. But the war did not merely stagnate overseas; England's enemies successfully carried it to the English coasts and border counties. England was thrown back on the defensive in the 1370s and 1380s, and to the parties advocating different strategies against France was added another which argued that the government should give first priority to home defences.[2] From the outset of the war, the south coast of England had been vulnerable to enemy attack. No power in the fourteenth century could hope to achieve complete and permanent domination of its seas. The balance might vary from area to area and season to season, and nothing could stop a small enemy naval squadron occasionally getting through to the coast.[3] As early as 1360, French squadrons had raided Rye and Winchelsea and an invasion had been expected that year.[4] But after the renewal of war, raids became more frequent, and Franco-Castilian naval strength was convincingly demonstrated. In the summer of 1369 a French fleet attacked Portsmouth and the government ordered a garrison to the Isle of Wight to defend it against invasion. Two years later a French fleet appeared off the coast of East Anglia, and the defeat of the Earl of Pembroke off La Rochelle the following summer (1372) led to renewed panic about coastal

[1] J. F. Lydon, 'Richard II's Expeditions to Ireland', *Journal of the Royal Society of Antiquaries of Ireland* XCIII (1963) pp. 135-48.
[2] See, for example, the Monk of Westminster's report of a debate in the council in 1385; Westminster p. 56.
[3] J. W. Sherborne, 'The Battle of La Rochelle' pp. 21, 28.
[4] E. Perroy, *The Hundred Years' War* (London 1951) p. 138.

defences. In fact, the defeat at La Rochelle was not, perhaps, as serious as has sometimes been argued.[1] The loss of a small transport fleet did not represent a serious set-back to England and its most serious effects were felt not at sea but on land (in Gascony), for the failure of Pembroke's forces to get through enabled the French to occupy most of Poitou and Saintonge without serious resistance.[2] The defeat stimulated a more aggressive attitude in England, and in the following two summers the English had the initiative in the Channel. But the English recovery was short-lived. In December 1373 Jean de Vienne had been appointed admiral of France, and he proposed to develop the French navy along Castilian lines, with vessels built specially for war. He began building warships at Rouen in 1374, and by 1377 he had thirty-five large men of war armed with up-to-date guns, and about eighty-five smaller vessels.[3] Thus equipped, the French and their Castilian allies launched the most serious and wide-ranging raids yet on the English coasts in the summer Edward III died. Throughout 1376, France and Castile were co-ordinating their naval preparations, and in the early summer of 1377 thirteen Castilian galleys under the command of Fernán Sánchez de Tovar set out to join the French fleets assembled under Jean de Vienne at Mont Saint Michel and Harfleur.[4] When the truce expired on the 24th of June, the Franco-Castilian fleet moved towards England. They took Rye and burnt it on the 29th of June, and then moved along the coast to Rottingdean, where the Abbot of Lewes put up vain resistance. In July other squadrons attacked Portsmouth, Dartmouth, and Plymouth; in August the French fleet took and occupied the Isle of Wight, abandoning it only on the payment of 1000 marks, and they then moved up the coast to attack Winchelsea and Hastings.[5] These were the most serious raids England had suffered during the war; the defences were inadequately prepared, and only the local levies put up any serious resistance.[6]

The south coast was not the only place where England fell back on the defensive in the 1370s. Her enemies also launched an attack on the Irish sea coasts and the English possessions in Scotland. The coasts of Wales and Ireland are not much further from the Cantabrian

[1] E.g. by A. B. Steel, *Richard II* (Cambridge 1941) p. 19.
[2] J. W. Sherborne, 'The Battle of La Rochelle' pp. 21, 28.
[3] W. L. Clowes, *A History of the Royal Navy* Vol I (London 1897) pp. 2, 5–7.
[4] Suarez Fernandez, *Historia de España* (Madrid 1966) p. 187.
[5] *Walsingham, HA* Vol. I, pp. 340–42.
[6] *ibid.*

coast of Spain than the coasts of southeast England, and after the renewal of the war in 1369, the English government expected French and Castilian raids on Wales, and ordered castles there to be fortified.[1] The expected attack did not come, but Owen of Wales's defection to France and subsequent command of a naval squadron, together with his issue of a proclamation in 1372 calling for the restoration of princely rule in Wales, must have intensified English fears of a French attack on Wales. French ships were undoubtedly operating in the Irish Sea, for in 1377 a squadron attacked Castle Rushen in the Isle of Man;[2] and in the North Channel, Scottish vessels were active, launching raids on northern Ireland and occasionally even penetrating as far as North Wales.[3] In 1375, Robert II recognized George Dunbar Earl of Moray, as Lord of the Isle of Man, and Scottish recapture of this important naval base had been clearly envisaged in a grant made by Robert II in 1372-3.[4] Scottish naval power has been seriously underestimated by historians, who have tended to concentrate on the landward aspect of the war with England. The possibility of French, Castilian, and Scottish naval supremacy in the Irish Sea was a grave threat not only to the coasts of Wales and northwest England, but also to the English position in Ireland. It perhaps explains why both Edward III and Richard II were so anxious to conclude an alliance with the Lord of the Isles, the only other power in the region with any naval strength.[5]

For much of Edward III's reign, the north of England was less directly exposed to enemy attacks than the southern and Irish Sea coasts. The devastation of the northern counties by Robert I in the second and third decades of the fourteenth century and the payment of enormous sums in blackmail and protection money by the local communities had not been forgotten.[6] Edward Balliol's cession to England in the 1330s of the border counties not only satisfied the territorial

---

[1] *CCR* 1369-74 pp. 61-2.

[2] *Monumenta de Insula Manniae* ed. J. R. Oliver, Manx Society Publications IV (Douglas 1860) p. 73. The Manxmen were required to buy the French off for 1000 marks.

[3] E. A. Lewis, *The Medieval Boroughs of Snowdonia* (London 1912) p. 245; NLI, Harriss Mss. IV, p. 29.

[4] *Registrum Magni Sigilli Regum Scotorum* Vol. I (Edinburgh 1912) pp. 201-2.

[5] Edinburgh University Library, Ms. 183 fol. 97; *Diplomatic Correspondence of Richard II* ed. Perroy, *Camden Third Series* XLVIII (London 1933) pp. 103-5.

[6] G. W. S. Barrow, *Robert Bruce* (London 1965) pp. 333ff.; R.M.T. Hill, 'The Labourer in the Vineyard: The Visitations of Archbishop Melton in the Archdeaconry of Richmond', *University of York Borthwick Papers* 35 (1968).

claims of some English magnates[1] but also provided a protective barrier for the northern counties. By 1370, however, the English held only Annandale, Roxburghshire, and Berwickshire, and in the 1370s and 1380s the Scots gradually pushed them back towards the border and once again began raids into northern England. The accounts of the Chamberlain of Berwick show that English rule in that county was confined by 1377 to the eastern part of the Tweed Valley and Fast Castle on the coast,[2] while the Earl of Douglas had recaptured much of Teviotdale and probably at least the northern part of Liddesdale.[3] English possessions in Scotland had been split into three separate parts: Annandale with Lochmaben Castle in the west, Jedburgh and Roxburgh in the central borders, and the southeastern part of Berwickshire. By the middle of Richard's reign, all but Jedburgh, Roxburgh, Fast Castle, and the immediate neighbourhood of Berwick had fallen. England fought few organized campaigns in Scotland in this period; the war was fought by raid and counter-raid, and to a great extent planned and led by the local magnates on either side of the border. But the local character of the war did not lessen its financial burden on the English exchequer. The wardens of the marches received money from the exchequer to maintain sizeable forces for the defence of the border and the English lands in Scotland in times of truce as well as war, and the cost of the custody of the royal castles of Carlisle, Newcastle, Berwick, and Roxburgh also fell on the exchequer. The defence of the north was a constant burden on national resources. And the concentration of political, military, and financial power in the region in the hands of the local magnates was to make them, by the end of Richard's reign, a weighty force in national politics.

These, then, were the circumstances which underlay the growth of political dissension in the last six years of Edward III's reign. The lead in criticizing the government and expressing political discontent was taken by a small group of great magnates who had a direct personal interest in the government's handling of the war. For, although some men of knightly rank played a notable part in the war,[4] the great magnates were second only to the royal family as leaders in war, and when in the 1370s members of the royal family took a much less

[1] R. A. Nicolson, *Edward III and the Scots* (Oxford 1965) pp. 98ff.
[2] PRO Ministers' Accounts SC.6/951/4–10, SC.6/1265/4.
[3] *Registrum Magni Sigilli Regum Scotorum* Vol. I, no. 586.
[4] E.g. Sir John Chandos, Sir Robert Knolles, Sir Hugh Calveley. On this subject see H. J. Hewitt, *The Organisation of War under Edward III* (Manchester 1966) pp. 28–49.

prominent part in the war, command of expeditions as well as recruitment of troops became the responsibility of those earls who had the
capacity and inclination for it. A magnate's prestige and popularity was
closely bound up with the success or failure of the expedition which he
led but which he did not himself finance and may well not have
planned. This alone is sufficient to explain the criticism of government
which followed unsuccessful expeditions. It was easy to blame military
failure on maladministration, speculation, and embezzlement by
government officials and tax-collectors; easy to blame an unsound
strategy for the lack of success of a particular expedition. But a
magnate had more than his own personal prestige at stake in war. It
also offered him the opportunity for sizeable profits from booty and
ransoms. Little information survives about the profits made out of war
by either the magnates or the knightly class in the fourteenth century:
there is no evidence comparable to that available for the study of Sir
John Fastolf's profits of war in the fifteenth century.[1] The Duke of
Gloucester undoubtedly exaggerated in 1391 when he said that the
livelihood of the commons of England depended upon war,[2] but the
prospect of profit certainly acted as an incentive to continue hostilities.
In the north, income from booty and ransoms might help to offset
the losses caused by the devastation of agricultural land and the carrying
off of stock.[3] Earlier in Edward III's reign, some magnates had certainly
made large profits out of the war with France. The Earl of Arundel,
for instance, spent almost £4000 on the purchase of manors in Surrey
and Sussex between 1336 and 1376. He was one of the most successful
war commanders during the most successful phase of the war, and
these purchases may well represent the investment of the profits of
war.[4] The Black Prince made £20,000 out of the sale of prisoners
captured at Poitiers, and under the rules for the division of the spoils
of war, a magnate who commanded a retinue had the right to receive
one third of the plunder and prisoners taken by those under his command. But though victories might be profitable, defeat and stagnation
were not, and they showed that there could be a two-way traffic in
ransoms. The Earl of Pembroke was captured at La Rochelle and had
to be ransomed from du Guesclin, who bought him from the Castilians.

[1] K. B. McFarlane, 'The Investment of Sir John Fastolf's Profits of War', *TRHS*
5th series, VII (1957) pp. 91–116.
[2] Froissart, *Oeuvres*, Vol. XIV, p. 314.
[3] D. Hay, 'Booty in Border Warfare', *Transactions of the Dumfriesshire and Galloway Natural History and Antiquarian Society* 3rd series XXXI (1954) pp. 145–66.
[4] *Feet of Fines for the County of Sussex* Vol. III, ed. L. F. Salzman (Sussex 1916).

In 1388, after the English defeat at Otterburn, the government had to pay part of Hotspur's ransom.[1] Furthermore, the government's financial difficulties meant that a noble might well have to wait months or years before he received from the exchequer even part of what he was owed. In 1386 the Earl of Northumberland accepted £700 in settlement of all the exchequer owed him, and in 1391 the executors of a seneschal in Aquitaine who had 'long sued before king and council' for the 9000 marks due him for wages for him and his retinue agreed to settle for £1100.[2] If it was at all routine for the exchequer to default on this scale, military service or the holding of military office might well prove a considerable liability rather than a source of profit. The premature abandonment of a campaign, too, might leave its leader out of pocket. In 1375 the Earl of March's expedition to France was halted when Gaunt and the French agreed to a truce, and although March had engaged troops for a year, he received money only for six months' wages.[3]

These, then, were among the reasons for the magnates' criticism of the government's handling of the war in the 1370s. But it was by no means simply the government's fault; in this period few of the earls had the necessary experience to give an effective lead in war. Weak leadership was not merely the result of the incapacity or indifference of the royal family, but also of the death of many of the magnates who had taken a prominent part in the first phase of the war, Edward's own comrades in arms. The Earl of Northampton died in 1363; the Earl of Warwick in 1369; the Earl of Stafford in 1372; the Earl of Hereford in 1373; and the Earl of Arundel in 1376, while the Earl of Pembroke, captured at La Rochelle, died shortly after his release in 1375, probably as a result of ill-treatment in his Castilian gaol.[4] With the exception of the Earl of Hereford, all these men had sons to succeed them, and those of their sons who were of age took part in the expeditions of the last years of Edward's reign. But the sons necessarily lacked their fathers' experience of campaigning and their fathers' association with success in the earlier stages of the war.

---

[1] H. J. Hewitt, *The Black Prince's Expedition* of 1355–57 (Manchester 1958) pp. 152–65; M. H. Keen, *The Laws of War in the Late Middle Ages* (London 1965) pp. 146–7; *Calendar of Documents relating to Scotland* Vol. IV, no. 395, ed. J. Bain (Edinburgh 1888).

[2] PRO Exchequer Accounts, various, E.101/40/30; Warrants for Issues, E.404/14/96 i.

[3] G. A. Holmes, *The Nobility under Edward III*, unpublished Ph.D. thesis (Cambridge University Library 1952) pp. 245ff.

[4] *Walsingham, HA* Vol. I, p. 319.

A new generation of magnates took the political stage in the 1370s, a generation anxious to enjoy the profits and prestige of victory as their fathers had done, but unable to do so.

The first signs of tension appeared in the parliament of 1371, when the Commons and some lords joined to demand the removal of the clerical ministers of state, William of Wykeham Bishop of Winchester (the chancellor) and Thomas Brantingham Bishop of Exeter (the treasurer). The warrior nobility blamed the clerical ministers for the unsatisfactory conduct of the war since its resumption in 1369, and their specific criticisms were reinforced by the more general anti-clericalism of the lay elements in parliament. This anti-clericalism within the political community is one of the complicating cross-currents of politics in the 1370s. There was little hostility within the community to the structure or doctrine of the church; the lay and ecclesiastical hierarchies were seen as complementary, while the lay nobility and gentry and the king himself made great use of the church as a means of advancement for clients and kinsmen and, indirectly, as a means of rewarding and financing administrators and other government servants. Lay society had an obvious interest in maintaining the structure of the church; yet, paradoxically, the church's very involvement with lay society rendered it vulnerable to criticism from the laity. The wealth and ostentation of non-resident pluralist bishops was not condoned because such bishops performed important functions in the administration; indeed it rendered such men more unpopular. Lower down the ecclesiastical hierarchy, similar complaints of pluralism and non-residence were prevalent, together with criticism of the incompetence and corruption of many lesser clerks. Yet the unsatisfactory state of the church at this level was, partly at least, a consequence of the financial burdens placed upon it by the state, and to a lesser extent by the papacy. The church bore perhaps a heavier burden of taxation than did lay society,[1] yet the Commons maintained more and more often in the parliaments of the 1370s that the church was not making as big a contribution as it should to the finance of the war, and on more than one occasion they proposed disendowment. In their attacks upon the church, Gaunt made use of (as the Commons evidently welcomed) John Wycliffe, whose academic work at Oxford appeared to provide a theoretical justification for attacks upon the wealth of the

---

[1] The clergy paid tax at the rate of one tenth on moveable property, whereas rural communities paid at one fifteenth. The clergy also had occasionally (e.g. in 1375) to pay papal taxes.

church.[1] The hostility between lay and ecclesiastical elements within the political community remained strong throughout the decade until, again perhaps paradoxically, Wycliffe's emergence as an open heretic and the growth of a popular movement deriving its doctrine from his heresies, induced church and laity to come together to repress a movement which they regarded as far more potentially dangerous than the anti-clericalism of the 1370s.

The success of anti-clericalism in the 1371 parliament did not, however, lead to the hoped-for success in war. Indeed, the new ministers, behind whom the influence of Gaunt may perhaps be seen,[2] proved as unsatisfactory as their predecessors, and by 1376 the new generation of magnates was in open opposition to the ministers who had come to power in 1371. Leadership of the faction of hostile magnates in 1376 fell to the Earl of March, perhaps the man best qualified by position and inheritance to challenge Gaunt and the king's ministers. March had an enormous inheritance; probably only Gaunt's was larger. He owned land in East Anglia (the former Clare inheritance), in the southwest of England, and in the marches of Wales. Through his mother, the heiress of the last de Burgo Earl of Ulster, he had acquired title to the earldom of Ulster and the lordships of Connacht, Trim, and Leix—enormous territories but mainly in the hands of the native Irish chiefs or hibernicized Anglo-Norman lords. March was also the male representative of the line of Lionel Duke of Clarence, his father-in-law, and according to the strict rules of hereditary succession, only the already failing Black Prince and the young Richard stood between him and the throne. It is scarcely surprising that in a political conflict between March and Lancaster (who would succeed Richard if descent through females were held to debar title), rumours about the succession should be rife.[3]

March, however, also had his own personal reasons for opposition to Gaunt and the ministers who were responsible for the conduct of government and war between 1371 and 1376. After Gaunt's long march from Calais to Bordeaux in 1373, there had been renewed dissension over strategy. Gaunt's experiences in 1373 probably convinced him that the traditional strategy of invading western France and impressing the French by marching with impunity through their country should

[1] J. A. Robson, *Wyclif and the Oxford Schools* (Cambridge 1961) esp. pp. 190–91; K. B. McFarlane, *John Wycliffe and the Beginnings of English Nonconformity* (London 1952) esp. chapter 11.
[2] Tout, *Chapters* Vol. III, pp. 274ff.
[3] *Chronicon Angliae* ed. E. M. Thompson, Rolls Series (London 1874) p. 92.

be abandoned. He favoured negotiating a truce with France, and concentrating instead on an expedition to enforce his claim to the Castilian throne. March and a number of other earls, however, took the view that a traditional campaign, if properly conducted, might still prove worth while. In effect, therefore, two foreign policies were being pursued in 1374 and 1375. Gaunt was negotiating a truce with the French at Bruges, while March and his associates were preparing an expedition to Brittany. Gaunt and the Dukes of Brittany and Anjou agreed to a truce on the 25th of June 1375, just as March's assault of Quimperlé seemed about to succeed. March had to abandon the siege, and this hurt his pride as well as his pocket.[1] The terms of the truce of Bruges also envisaged handing over to the French the Norman fortress of St Sauveur, in the keeping of Lord Latimer. This seemed to opinion in England to be foolishness, if not treason, and Latimer's earlier private arrangement to hand over the Breton fortress of Becherel intensified suspicion of his motives and contributed to the hostility manifested towards him in the Good Parliament of 1376.[2] Other earls had joined the expedition to Brittany and were no doubt equally angry at its abandonment; but March and Cambridge had led it, and in the absence of any initiative from Cambridge, it was for March to lead the attack on the men whom he regarded as responsible for the abandonment of a profitable and fruitful enterprise.

The campaign of 1375 and the truce of Bruges were not, however, the only grounds March had for criticizing the government. He also opposed its handling of Irish affairs. He himself was nominally the largest landowner in the country, but most of his estates were in rebel hands and he could expect little income from them.[3] By inheritance from the Duke of Clarence and the Earls of Ulster and by territorial position he was perhaps the man best fitted to undertake the government of the country and to attempt to end the erosion of the English colony there. In 1369, however, Edward III had appointed William of Windsor, his mistress's husband, as lieutenant there.[4] In all probability Alice Perrers engineered his appointment, for he was a man lacking most of the qualifications for the office. He had no great social standing, and only limited military and administrative experience. He did little except arouse the hostility of the Anglo-Irish magnates and the

[1] G. C. Bayley, 'The Campaign of 1375 and the Good Parliament', *EHR* LV (1940) pp. 370–83; G. A. Holmes, *Nobility under Edward III* pp. 245ff.
[2] *Rot. Parl.* Vol. II, pp. 324–6.
[3] E. Curtis, *A History of Medieval Ireland* (London 1923) pp. 236–42.
[4] M. V. Clarke, *Fourteenth Century Studies* (Oxford 1937) pp. 148–9.

loyal colonists by heavy and continuous taxation. Windsor's misgovernment provoked a demand from Ireland for his dismissal, and
replacement by March himself. Edward gave way, recalled Windsor
in 1371, and March made preparations to leave for Ireland in 1373.
But his expedition was suddenly and inexplicably abandoned, and
Windsor reinstated. He governed Ireland as badly during his second
term of office as he had done during his first, and March was no
doubt only too pleased to support the charges levelled against him in
the Good Parliament.[1] After the Good Parliament, Edward nominated
Sir Nicholas Dagworth as supervisor of the government of Ireland,[2]
but this was only a temporary measure, and in 1378 March himself
set out for Ireland. He died there from pneumonia caught while
crossing a river in County Cork in late December 1381.

As Maude Clarke has pointed out,[3] therefore, two independent currents of criticism merged in the Good Parliament of 1376, and the Earl
of March was the champion of the aggrieved in both England and
Ireland. But the success of the attack on the king's ministers in the
Good Parliament was made possible at least partly by the support of
the Commons, whose place in the politics of the 1370s is important.
It has been argued in the past that the magnates ensured the support
of the Commons by arranging for their own retainers and dependents
to be elected as knights of the shires.[4] This argument rested on the
undoubted fact that many members of the Commons could be shown
to have had formal or informal connections with the great magnates;
upwards of twenty men associated with John of Gaunt, for instance,
sat in the parliament of January 1377 which accepted the reversal of the
acts of the Good Parliament.[5] But this fact need not imply any packing
of parliament. There is no evidence that magnates intervened in
elections in order to ensure the return of their dependents, and no
evidence that boroughs accepted the patronage of outsiders of whatever
social position. The tradition of freely electing the county members at
the county court was still strong, and complaints of unfair practices
tended to be directed against the sheriff rather than the local magnates.

---

[1] *ibid.*   [2] *CPR* 1374-7, p. 117.
[3] M. V. Clarke, *Fourteenth Century Studies* p. 148.
[4] S. Armitage-Smith, *John of Gaunt* (London 1904) pp. 137-8. His view is criticized by J. C. Wedgwood, 'John of Gaunt and the Packing of Parliament',
EHR XLV (1930) pp. 621-5. See also H. G. Richardson, 'John of Gaunt and the
Parliamentary Representation of Lancashire', *BJRL* XXII (1938) pp. 175-222;
and K. B. McFarlane, 'Bastard Feudalism', XX (1947) pp. 161-80.
[5] J. C. Wedgwood, 'John of Gaunt'.

Richard II came up against the strength of this tradition when he attempted to influence the elections to the parliament of February 1388.[1] If the crown was unable to persuade sheriffs to return members favourable to its interests, it is unlikely that a great magnate, even the Duke of Lancaster, would be able to do any better. But perhaps more important is the lack of any evidence that magnates tried to influence the elections. Almost certainly, they did not do so because they had no need to do so. If a magnate, or a group of magnates, wished to make his voice heard in parliament, he did so directly, and took the initiative in making political demands on the king and his ministers. Parliament was the magnates' political stage not because they had influenced the elections to the Commons, but because they judged that they could count on the Commons' sympathy gained by other methods. Support of the Commons, arguably, was won not by influencing elections but by careful management of the House when it assembled and by choosing to fight on issues which were in any case likely to be popular with the Commons, and this applied to the king as much as to the nobility. The Commons, too, might judge that their interests would best be served by support of a dominant faction, and a sense of deference to social superiors may also have played some part. Analysis of these factors, rather than of connections between individual members of the Commons and particular magnates, is more likely to explain the attitude of the Commons in the last thirty years of the fourteenth century.

Little evidence survives for the techniques of parliamentary management in the late fourteenth century. Perhaps the most important method by which the views of the lords and council were conveyed to the Commons, and vice versa, was the practice of intercommuning, whereby a committee of lords and councillors periodically met a committee selected from among the Commons. This device was clearly of great importance from at least mid-century onwards, and the evidence of the *Anonimalle Chronicle*[2] suggests that in the Good Parliament the Commons took the initiative in asking for the appointment of a committee, and that they envisaged the delegates from the lords 'hearing and witnessing' what the Commons' delegates had to say. In this way the Commons might make known the grievances about which they felt most strongly, and a group of critical magnates could obviously use such information for their own advantage—could make much, in

---

[1] See pp. 112–13 below.
[2] *Anon. Chron.* pp. 84–5.

fact of those issues which seemed to matter most to the Commons.[1] The composition of the intercommuning committee set up in the Good Parliament certainly suggests that March and his associates were anxious to understand the critical mood of the Commons. But intercommuning was not the only means of contact between lords and council on the one hand and Commons on the other. In the Good Parliament the Commons appointed, for the first time that we know of, a speaker to represent them and speak on their behalf before the lords for the whole session of parliament.[2] There is no reason to believe that the choice of speaker was imposed or even greatly influenced by the lords or the council. The *Anonimalle Chronicle* makes it clear that in the Good Parliament Sir Peter de la Mare's own persuasiveness earned him his appointment.[3] But in making such an appointment, the Commons would have every reason to choose someone likely to command the respect and attention of the ascendant group of magnates. De la Mare, the steward of the Earl of March, was eminently fitted by his connections as well as his ability in debate to play the part expected of him. The same might be said of the appointment of Sir Thomas Hungerford in the parliament of January 1377.[4]

Management of the Commons in these fairly informal ways suggests a certain community of interest between the knightly element in the Commons and those lords who were critical of the government in 1376. There seems little doubt that in the years preceding the Good Parliament the group in the community from which the knights of the shire were chosen—the smaller landowners—shared the magnates' sense of growing frustration and hostility to government. Their reasons for discontent were similar to those of the titled nobility. They may not have participated in the war as eagerly or profited from it so extensively as the titled nobility, but they shared the growing alarm at England's vulnerability to attack; they criticized inept and divided leadership; and they expected a war which they paid for to be conducted with efficiency and success. By 1362 they had established their exclusive right to consent both to the lay subsidy on moveable property

---

[1] For a discussion of this subject, see J. G. Edwards, 'The Commons in Medieval English Parliaments', *Creighton Lecture* (London 1957).
[2] J. S. Roskell, *The Commons and their Speakers in English Parliaments 1376–1523* (Manchester 1965) pp. 16–17.
[3] *Anon Chron.* p. 83.
[4] He was the Duke of Lancaster's chief steward of south parts, and had also served the Black Prince (K. B. McFarlane, 'Bastard Feudalism' p. 176).

and to the taxes on commodities,[1] and they expected value for money. After Crécy, for instance, the Commons 'thanked God for the great victory he had given the king, and said that all their money had been well-spent'.[2] But by the 1370s they had become convinced that their money was not being well spent. Taxation remained heavy and regular, yet there was little to show for the taxes the Commons granted. Expeditions to France soaked up money, but so far as opinion at home was concerned they made little impact. Indeed, England's position gradually deteriorated, and whereas the Commons were quite prepared to pay for success, they objected to paying for failure. Furthermore, English failure in the 1370s was not sharp or obvious; the war stagnated and her position in France was gradually eroded, and in these circumstances the temptation to blame incompetent administrators and corrupt financiers at home naturally became strong. The king's ministers, not the military leaders, had to bear the blame for failure, and in the Good Parliament the Commons concentrated their attacks on those officials and financiers whom they suspected of maladministration, dishonesty, and private profiteering. The Commons' traditional concern with taxation ensured them a hearing when they chose to fight on this issue.

Judging from the *Anonimalle Chronicle*,[3] leadership of the Commons in the Good Parliament devolved upon the knights of the shire, who though a numerical minority within the House appear to dominate discussion to the exclusion of members representing boroughs and cities. There is no reason to suppose that the position was different in any of the other parliaments of the late fourteenth century, yet this leadership by a minority is not obviously explicable. Merchants had played a very large part in the finance of the war; they were as interested as the knights in value for money, perhaps as exporters even more interested than the knights in the safety of shipping at sea and the protection of the English coasts; and some of the most important merchants had close personal links with the government. Yet the merchants who sat in parliament as members for the great sea ports, as well as the lesser merchants important in their own localities who sat for smaller towns, seem to have left political action to the knights. The burgess element in parliament may have deferred to the knights out of a sense of social inferiority, and the knights for their part may have been the more active and forceful group through the confidence

[1] *Rot. Parl.* Vol. II, p. 271.   [2] *ibid.* p. 159.
[3] *Anon. Chron.* pp. 80–94.

that came from friendship, blood ties, and neighbourly relations with members of the lords. These were strong reasons why the knights should dominate the Commons' discussions and monopolize the office of speaker. Furthermore, there were few major differences of interest between the knights and the burgesses that might induce the burgesses to resent the dominance of the landed element in the Commons. All but the greatest merchants had been as hostile as the knights to Edward III's manipulation of the wool trade for fiscal purposes earlier in the reign[1] and on the issue of taxation of moveable property the knights and burgesses shared a common point of view. The burgesses, indeed, had even more reason than the knights to keep a careful eye on taxation, for towns were taxed at a tenth, whereas rural areas paid only a fifteenth.

The knights, therefore, took the lead in the Commons' discussions and in negotiations with the lords. But in dealing with the lords, the knights were faced not with a large assembly of peers, but with an assembly which can often have been little more than an afforced session of the king's council.[2] Membership of the lords was nominally very large. All the titled lay nobility received writs of summons, as did all the bishops, and upwards of twenty mitred abbots. The number of other laymen summoned by individual writ, who may conveniently but inaccurately be called barons, fluctuated from parliament to parliament, but was generally somewhere about fifty.[3] Seldom if ever, however, did all those summoned attend. Most of the abbots regularly sent proxies;[4] earls and bishops might often be 'in remotis agens', or, in the case of northerners, required to attend to the defence of the border.[5] And many of the barons evidently did not bother to come.[6] Even when they did, the sources suggest they played only a small part in parliamentary business. They were perhaps overshadowed by the great earls, for there was little if any social distinction between many of the barons and many of the knights of the shire. In the parliaments of the 1370s and 1380s men who were styled 'knight' received

---

[1] This is discussed most accessibly in E. Power, *The Wool Trade in English Medieval History* (Oxford 1941) chapter iv.
[2] J. S. Roskell, 'The Problem of the Attendance of the Lords in Medieval English Parliaments', *BIHR* XXIX (1956) p. 199.
[3] This is based on an analysis of the writs of summons from *Reports . . . touching the dignity of a peer* (*RDP*).
[4] J. S. Roskell, 'Problem of the Attendance of the Lords' pp. 164ff.
[5] As in 1388 *RDP* iv p. 732, exempting Lord Dacre from attending the Cambridge parliament.
[6] J. S. Roskell, 'Problem of the Attendance of the Lords' *passim*.

individual writs of summons,[1] and in 1383 a Surrey knight, Sir Thomas Camoys, was elected to sit for the county and at the same time received a writ of individual summons to the lords.[2] From the social point of view, lords and Commons shade into one another: there is no sharp division between the two, and this is clearly important in explaining their ability to work together. But the men who dominated the business of the lords were the titled nobility and the king's ministers, a small body accustomed to working together in council as well as parliament; and it appears that the government tried to secure a wider attendance only when great acts of state requiring the widest possible assent were being played out.[3]

In criticizing the government on many matters, the Commons could count on the sympathy and support of many of the active group among the lords. But lords and Commons did not think identically on every political issue. In the 1370s they were agreed on the most important questions that were raised; but the Commons had other interests and other grievances where their views did not coincide with those of the magnates, and on these issues they were quite capable of taking an independent line. Although, strictly speaking, the only legislative action of the Commons was their vote of a subsidy, the development of the device of the common petition in the second half of the century enabled the Commons to present their wishes and grievances to the lords and council in a form that carried weight because it was a communal document forming the basis for the statutes promulgated by the whole body of parliament.[4] There is no reason to believe that the common petitions were inspired by magnates, and although the Commons' demands were considered and sometimes modified by the council,[5] many of the statutes of Richard's reign show clear signs of Commons' initiative.[6]

Perhaps the most important of the issues on which the Commons took an independent line, and the one with which they were to be

[1] As, for instance, Sir Richard Lescrope, Sir John Devereux, Sir Ralph Cromwell and Sir Philip Darcy. Some of those who were so summoned were bannerets, a group whose position needs fuller investigation.
[2] *CPR* 1381–5, p. 398.
[3] As, for instance, in the Merciless Parliament of 1388: *RDP* iv p. 729.
[4] For this subject, see D. Rayner, 'The Form and Machinery of the "Commune Petition" in the Fourteenth Century', *EHR* LVI (1941) pp. 198–233.
[5] *ibid.*; and B. H. Putnam, 'Chief Justice Shareshull and the Economic and Legal Codes of 1351–52', *Toronto Law Journal* V (1943–4) p. 256.
[6] E.g. the labour legislation of the Cambridge Parliament, 1388: see J. A. Tuck, 'The Cambridge Parliament 1388', *EHR* LXXXIV (1969) pp. 236–7.

increasingly concerned in the second half of Richard's reign, was the maintenance of law and order. This subject is ill-researched, and it is impossible to determine how extensively magnates' retainers interfered in legal proceedings and attempted to make their masters' will prevail by force and threats. Popular literature suggests that the problem was widespread and involved not only violence by lords' retainers, but also corruption and partiality by justices who were retainers of great lords.[1] Corruption and violence of this kind bred its own violent opposition, but those who opposed it, even though violent themselves, clearly acquired popularity; the outlaw or gentleman bandit is favourably regarded in popular literature.[2] At least two accounts of aristocratic banditry in the fourteenth century have been published,[3] and it seems clear that no society whose system of values was military and which was involved in warfare as continuously as was fourteenth-century England could escape such a phenomenon.[4] The Commons had complained about violent interference with the course of justice at intervals throughout the century, and a statute specifically condemning livery and maintenance had been passed as early as 1346.[5] The Commons did not demand the abolition of the whole system of retaining, which was a basic social form. Many members of the Commons were themselves retainers of great magnates; and without retainers, bound by formal or informal contracts, magnates could not hope to run their estates and households. Commons' criticism was directed against liveried servants who were merely paid followers and played no part in the management of an inheritance or household—hired thugs, in effect, whose sole function was to make their lords' will prevail by force. The Commons demanded that lords should no longer be permitted to engage such men, and although parliament passed several statutes against livery and maintenance, they remained ineffective until Richard II (in the second half of his reign) took more vigorous measures to enforce them.[6]

[1] M. H. Keen, *The Outlaws of Medieval Legend* (London 1961) pp. 136–8.
[2] *ibid.*
[3] E. L. G. Stones, 'The Folvilles of Ashby de la Zouch', *TRHS* 5th series VII (1957) pp. 117–36; J. G. Bellamy, 'The Coterel Gang', *EHR* LXXIX (1964) pp. 698–717.
[4] This is suggested by the remarks in E. Hobsbawm, *Bandits* (London 1969) p. 30. Discussion of the Robin Hood ballads is to be found in three articles in *Past & Present* 14, 18, 19 (1958, 1960–61) by Professor Hilton and Professor Holt. Professor Holt argues for a thirteenth-century date for the ballads; but in any case they still have some relevance for the fourteenth century.
[5] *Statutes of the Realm* p. 304.   [6] See pp. 212–18 below.

On such an issue the Commons were prepared to take an independent line, and as the events of 1388–9 were to show, they persevered in the face of opposition from the lords.[1] Neither the government nor any group of hostile magnates could count on the automatic support of the Commons. The knights of the shire came from a social group accustomed to acting independently and to taking the initiative in local affairs, and accustomed too, perhaps, to playing an important part in the management of magnates' inheritances. They were used to dealing directly with the king and his ministers as office-holders in the counties, and many of them had personal experience of military campaigns. They had the experience and the standing to take independent attitudes in political controversies; they were not blindly subservient to whatever group happened momentarily to be in ascendancy.

In the Good Parliament of 1376, then, the Commons and a group of hostile lords launched a successful attack upon the king's ministers and upon John of Gaunt, the representative of the failing king. Peter de la Mare and his Commons demanded the arrest of Lord Latimer and the merchant Lyons, assuming that their conviction would follow because their guilt was obvious; conviction by notoriety was still a potent part of the criminal law.[2] But Latimer demanded a full trial. Neither the king nor Gaunt was likely to undertake his prosecution, and the Commons thereupon offered to act as a collective prosecutor, thus, as Professor Plucknett has pointed out, stumbling almost by accident on the process of impeachment.[3] The procedure thus developed was formalized with great rapidity, and other less prominent members of the government were dealt with in the same way later in the parliament, the Commons now proceeding by written bill rather than by presenting charges orally.[4] The Commons' prosecutions were successful, and so too was their demand for the removal of the king's mistress from court and the reform of the council. The new councillors were nominated and sworn in parliament (the first time this had been done), and it was the intention of parliament that the council should exercise some permanent restraint on king and court.[5] Finally a statute was passed embodying the acts of the parliament. But a reaction by the court swiftly followed. In the autumn at a meeting of the great council at Westminster, de la Mare was arrested and consigned to prison, the acts of the Good Parliament were annulled, Latimer was restored to the

[1] J. A. Tuck, 'The Cambridge Parliament 1388' pp. 234–5.
[2] T. F. Plucknett, 'The Impeachments of 1376', *TRHS* 5th series I (1951) p. 153.
[3] *ibid.*   [4] *ibid.* pp. 161–2.   [5] Tout, *Chapters* Vol. III, pp. 299–300.

council and Alice Perrers to court, and the office of marshal was transferred from March to Henry Percy.[1] In January 1377 parliament met.
The Commons protested against the annulment of statutes without
parliamentary consent and demanded de la Mare's release,[2] but they
lacked the power to do anything to uphold the work of the Good
Parliament. By the exercise of patronage, Gaunt had broken up the
party of lords who had opposed him, and he now presented parliament
with a *fait accompli*. They could do little but acquiesce. The whole
episode illustrates the strength of the court, and the difficulty of imposing any permanent restraint upon the king. The magnates accepted
that the initiative in government lay ultimately with the king. In
normal times, when there was a large measure of *rapport* between king
and nobility, neither magnates nor Commons sought to restrain the
king's initiative and freedom of action in any area other than taxation.
The magnates did not believe that the king should be permanently
or formally controlled, and they had no institutional means of permanently enforcing their will. The monarchy had great reserves of
strength on which to draw, and once the Good Parliament ended,
power flowed back rapidly towards Gaunt and the court. Gaunt dismissed the ministers appointed by the Good Parliament, and by the
time the next parliament met the political initiative lay firmly in his
hands.

However, although Gaunt had successfully countered the attack
upon the royal prerogative, he had drawn upon himself much unpopularity. The chronicler Walsingham, who stood in the St Albans'
tradition of writing history from a baronial point of view,[3] wrote a
ferociously hostile attack on him which may reflect the strength of
popular feeling. The Londoners loathed him, and he had aroused the
hostility of the Church by his use of Wycliffe and his attack upon
William of Wykeham.[4] Although he had worsted the magnates who
had opposed him in the Good Parliament, they still represented a
formidable concentration of political power. The summer of 1377
however, was a most inopportune moment to renew political strife.
The truce with France was due to expire on the 24th of June; the
French and Spanish admirals were making preparations for an invasion of the south coast of England; and Gaunt had impressed a large

[1] M. McKisack, *The Fourteenth Century* (Oxford 1959) p. 394.
[2] *Rot. Parl.* Vol. II, p. 368.
[3] V. H. Galbraith, *Roger Wendover and Matthew Paris* (Glasgow 1944) p. 20.
[4] S. Armitage-Smith, *John of Gaunt* pp. 145–83.

number of ships in preparation for a naval expedition to repel the threatened invasion. In the event, Edward III's death, which occurred at a most unfortunate moment for England, compelled Gaunt to abandon the expedition. The king's last illness, however, and the imminent expiry of the truce served to lower the political temperature from the height it had reached after the abortive trial of Wycliffe at St Paul's in February. The credit for this belongs in part to the Princess Joan, who successfully mediated between Gaunt and the Londoners in February, and partly upon Gaunt's own evident determination to heal the wounds of the past year. His preparations for an expedition to keep the seas were likely to be popular, and on the 18th of June, as a gesture of good will, the king and council ordered William of Wykeham's temporalities to be restored to him. Three days later, the king died.

2

Court and Councils
1377-81

Only once before in England's post-conquest history had a child king succeeded to the throne. In 1216, when John died, his son Henry III had been only nine years old, and William Marshall had been appointed *rector regis et regni*. Armed with formal powers as regent, Marshall, together with a group of politically moderate nobles and prelates, succeeded in restoring domestic harmony after the civil war of John's last year. It is hard to believe that the precedent of 1216 had been entirely forgotten when Edward III died. The parallel between the overt civil war and the presence of a French army on English soil in 1216, and the political tension and invasion scares of 1376-7, though obviously not exact, might not have been entirely overlooked. Certainly the chronicler Walsingham looked for a new era of tranquillity in the accession of the young Richard. The coronation of the eleven-year-old king, he said, was 'a day of pleasure and joy, the long-awaited day when peace and the country's laws, long weakened by the strife and greed of the followers of the aged king, were renewed'.[1] Yet the precedent of 1216 was not followed. No one was appointed regent, and the pretence was made that Richard himself was fully competent to govern. He was allowed his own great seal, privy seal, and signet; the government transacted business in his name, and in the purely formal sense he was as fully responsible for the activities of government as his grandfather had been. A regency might appear a more satisfactory solution to the problem of a minority than the fiction adopted in 1377; it might have ensured strong and consistent leadership, and it might have made the eventual transition to Richard's personal rule more clear-cut and more acceptable than it actually was. But in 1377 there

[1] *Walsingham, HA* Vol. I, p. 331.

was no acceptable candidate for the regency, no noble who, like Marshall, might have commanded the support of the various groups within the political community. Of all the nobles, Gaunt was the most powerful and politically experienced, and stood closest in blood to the new king. Yet as a consequence of the events of the previous year, he above all was likely to prove unacceptable to two groups whose support and confidence were essential: the City of London and the Commons in parliament. Although the government of the country during the king's minority was obviously in the forefront of men's minds in the summer of 1377, the need to raise money and take military action to resist the Franco-Castilian threat was even more urgent and pressing. Whatever constitutional arrangements were made, therefore, had to be acceptable to the London merchants who would lend money, to the Commons who would grant the taxes upon which the loans could be secured, and to the nobility upon whom would fall much of the responsibility for home defence and for naval operations in the Channel. None of these three groups would have been happy with Gaunt as regent, and Gaunt appears to have accepted the situation. From the outset of the reign, he adopted a co-operative attitude. He soon came to terms with London,[1] and there is no firm evidence to support the suggestion that he resented the presence on the first of the continual councils of the reign of several of the Black Prince's former followers.[2] Gaunt's speech to the October parliament of 1377 in all probability expressed his real feelings.[3] His political attitude was one of loyalty to the crown and defence of the royal prerogative. He stood too near to the throne himself to wish to see the monarchy abased in civil war, and his argument that he had too much to lose by treason is, as Professor McKisack has remarked,[4] unanswerable. Furthermore, Gaunt's informal power in the first three years of the reign amply compensated him for his lack of formal power, though it roused the suspicions of his most vehement literary opponent, Thomas Walsingham.

However, if Gaunt were not appointed regent, no other noble could expect to assume the role. Gaunt might not have overtly used his influence to undermine the authority of whoever became regent, but such a person's difficulties would have been enormously increased by

[1] *Chronicon Angliae* ed. E. M. Thompson, Rolls Series (London 1874) pp. 148–9.
[2] A. B. Steel, *Richard II* (Cambridge 1941) p. 44; Tout, *Chapters* Vol. III, p. 329.
[3] *Rot. Parl.* Vol. III, p. 5.
[4] M. McKisack, *The Fourteenth Century* (Oxford 1959) p. 402.

the sheer fact of Gaunt's power and his undeniable right, as the eldest surviving son of Edward III, to informal influence at court. Neither of Gaunt's two younger brothers, Edmund Langley Earl of Cambridge and Thomas of Woodstock Earl of Buckingham, stood much chance of achieving power over Gaunt's head, but there remained the Earl of March, a noble second only to Gaunt in the extent of his territorial power and much more likely than Gaunt to command the support of the Commons. He was also closely connected to the royal family; indeed, arguably he was the heir to the throne. Yet of all the nobles he was likely to be least acceptable to Gaunt because of his activities in 1376, and in any case his extensive Irish interests meant that he would soon be required over there as lieutenant, for he was the one man likely to be acceptable to the Anglo–Irish magnates and ministers. No one could have foreseen, however, that in less than four years March would be dead, and throughout Richard's reign the nullification of the March influence by absence in Ireland, early death, and lengthy minorities was to prove an important, if negative, factor in politics.

The expedient of collective government which was adopted after Richard's coronation was perhaps the most sensible arrangement that could have been devised in the political and personal circumstances of the summer of 1377. In the few weeks that elapsed between Richard's accession and his coronation, a council (about which little is known)[1] was in charge of government and responsible for measures against the threatened invasion; but Gaunt still held the centre of the stage. No sooner was Edward III dead than he and the Londoners publicly and formally reconciled themselves to one another, and Gaunt, according to Walsingham, then asked that 'those who had been imprisoned for any misdemeanour imputed to them should be freed by royal grace'.[2] Presumably it was by virtue of this request that Peter de la Mare was released from Nottingham Castle and compensated for his imprisonment. The order for his release was made on the authority of the council,[3] but there seems no reason to disbelieve Walsingham's statement that Gaunt suggested it in the first place, both as a gesture to please the Londoners (who received de la Mare rapturously) and as a means of ensuring that arguments over his fate would not bedevil the negotiations with the Commons in the next parliament. Once these

[1] The composition of the council is unknown, but its range of activity is revealed by the notes of warranty to letters patent, *CPR* 1377–81, pp. 1–6.

[2] *Chronicon Angliae* p. 149.

[3] *CCR* 1377–81, p. 7; PRO Exchequer Issue Rolls E.403/468/11, quoted in Tout, *Chapters* Vol. III, p. 325, n. 1.

political matters had been settled, Gaunt devoted himself, as steward
of England, to organizing the coronation. Both in the events leading
up to the ceremony and in the ceremony itself he took care to show
that he enjoyed a primacy at least of honour among the nobles.[1]

On the day after the coronation, a great council of magnates took
steps to formalize the system of collective government.[2] A council of
twelve was set up, whose formal duties were to help the chancellor and
treasurer and to raise money to resist the French. The council's terms
of reference were not as all-embracing as those of its successor, drawn
up in the October parliament of 1377, but there is no reason to disagree
with Tout's verdict that this council was 'in fact, and almost in name,
a council of regency'.[3] This council, and the two succeeding it, have
generally been interpreted as attempts to represent in government the
two factions which had opposed one another at the time of the Good
Parliament, together with a number of other men, the former followers
of the Black Prince, who naturally expected a share in power now that
their patron's son was king.[4] Yet the situation was perhaps not so
clear-cut as that. In particular, it is doubtful whether the Earl of March,
who was on both the first and second councils, saw himself in any
sense as a leader of an opposition or popular faction. The issues on
which he had opposed the court in the previous year were dead: the
truce negotiated in 1375 had expired, and the government of Ireland
had been placed in the hands of the Earl of Ormond, after an earlier
decision to send William of Windsor over had been countermanded.[5]
It was the Commons, not the Earl of March, who were likely to press
for a return to the policies of the Good Parliament. The Earl of
Arundel, the other earl on the first council, cannot be identified with
any particular political position. Later in Richard's reign he was to
become a bitter opponent both of Gaunt and of the court, but his
experiences in the 1370s did not play a large part in shaping his political
attitudes after 1384. He had been a member of the council established
in the Good Parliament, but in all probability had been motivated
primarily by dissatisfaction with the conduct of foreign policy in

[1] He presided over the court of claims, which heard petitions from those entitled
by hereditary right to perform the various services at the coronation, and he
arranged the actual ceremony. His son, Henry Earl of Derby, played a part in
the ceremony (*Anon. Chron.* p. 114).
[2] *Foedera* Vol. VII, pp. 161–2.
[3] Tout, *Chapters* Vol. III, p. 326.
[4] *ibid.* p. 327; A. B. Steel, *Richard II* p. 44.
[5] *CPR* 1374–7, pp. 336, 337; *Calendar of Ormond Deeds* 1350–1413 ed. E. Curtis,
Irish Mss Commission (Dublin 1934) nos. 214, 215.

1375–6. Of the two bishops on the council, one, Ralph Erghum of Salisbury, was almost certainly a surrogate for Gaunt, for he was the chancellor of the duchy of Lancaster; but the other, Courtenay of London, though an opponent of Gaunt in the controversies of 1376–7, was perhaps valuable mainly through his knowledge of opinion in the City and his popularity there. William Latimer was of course a friend of Gaunt, but the remaining six members of the council were distinguished primarily by their association with the Black Prince and the Princess Joan. The death of a king, in the fourteenth as much as in the eighteenth century, in itself brought about a sharp change in the political situation and brought new men to the forefront of politics. The continual councils were chosen so that estates rather than factions might be represented, each council having representatives from the ranks of bishop, earl, baron, banneret, and knight; in determining the membership of the councils a high degree of status consciousness is evident. They were also chosen so that due weight might be given to political and administrative experience, but above all, as Tout justly remarked,[1] so that the former followers of the Black Prince should have their share of power.

Gaunt himself, of course, was not a member either of the first or of the two subsequent councils, though the Bishop of Salisbury and William Latimer could be expected to represent his point of view. After the coronation, Gaunt withdrew from court. Walsingham saw this as a means whereby he might avoid responsibility for any disasters that occurred during the summer, such as a French invasion, and Tout interpreted it as an expression of displeasure at the composition of the council.[2] But once again, perhaps, Walsingham has misled historians about Gaunt's motives. The military situation rather than personal pique provoked his departure from court, for the truce with Scotland had expired and he was needed on the northern border. In early August he was ordered to array his retinue and hasten to the marches.[3] In all probability, too, the Scottish threat rather than the supposed eclipse of Gaunt at court explains Northumberland's resignation of the office of marshal. He himself said that the office was so burdensome that it left him insufficient time to attend to his own affairs, and there may have been some truth in the rumour that Segrave (or possibly John Mowbray, the newly created Earl of Nottingham) was pressing

[1] Tout, *Chapters* Vol. III, p. 328.
[2] *Chronicon Angliae* p. 163; Tout, *Chapters* Vol. III, p. 329.
[3] PRO Exchequer Issue Rolls E.403/463 m.4.

his hereditary claim to the office, thus leading Northumberland to the view that it was more dignified to resign than to be dismissed.[1] Perhaps, then, the composition of the first continual council was more acceptable to Gaunt than has sometimes been supposed.

The assembly of parliament on the 13th gave the Commons their first chance to express their views on the arrangements for the government of the country during the king's minority. The government's need for money was so urgent that it was bound to pay attention to the Commons' wishes, yet the Commons did not have everything their own way, and the evidence suggests that the council was well in command. Sensing their power, the Commons again appointed de la Mare as speaker, and he asked the lords and councillors to appoint a new continual council, representing the various estates, with full powers of government in co-operation with the chief officers of state. He also asked for the king's personal attendants to be nominated in parliament, and for the royal household to be financed entirely out of the ordinary revenue of the crown. He concluded with a general and unexceptionable request that the common law should be upheld.[2] Tout suggested that 'the king's advisers dealt favourably with these requests';[3] but it is not clear that the Commons made their will prevail to more than a limited extent. A continual council of nine, rather than the eight suggested by the Commons, was appointed, and its powers were described in terms which resemble the wording used when the powers of the council set up in the Good Parliament of 1376 were defined. It may well be that the decision now firmly made to govern by council during the minority was partly influenced by the precedent of 1376, and Speaker de la Mare was perhaps thinking of that precedent when he asked for the appointment of a council.

The Black Prince's followers were again strongly represented on the council.[4] The Earl of March and Bishop Courtenay retained their places, as did Bishop Erghum, but Latimer was precluded from membership by virtue of a Commons petition asking that all those against whom proceedings had been taken in the Good Parliament should be ineligible.[5] The inclusion on the council of Bishop Appleby of Carlisle may also have been a gesture towards the Commons, for he had taken a strong line both in his diocese and in earlier parliaments against heavy

---

[1] *Chronicon Angliae* pp. 164-5.
[2] *Rot. Parl.* Vol. III, pp. 5-6.
[3] Tout, *Chapters* Vol. III, p. 333.
[4] *Rot. Parl.* Vol. III, p. 6.   [5] *ibid.* p. 16.

and persistent taxation, and had been reprimanded by Edward III for failing to levy taxes in his diocese.[1] In their resistance to what they regarded as excessive taxation, the Commons could count on his sympathy. But the Commons' second request was much less favourably received. The lords took the view that in seeking the nomination in parliament of the king's personal attendants, the Commons asked too much and infringed the royal prerogative.[2] The most the lords would allow was that those around the king should be forbidden, 'while he was of tender age', to sue for lands, wardships, or offices. Even on the question of the expenses of the household, the lords returned a guarded reply. They undertook to consult the chief officers of the household, and if in their opinion, and 'saving the estate and honour of the king', the Commons' proposal was feasible, then it should be implemented.[3] The lords were clearly opposed to any measure that might infringe the prerogative of the young king, and they reacted very cautiously to any suggestion that appeared to involve conciliar control or supervision of the household. After another year had passed, and the power of the household officers had become more obvious, the lords were forced to take a stronger line over the household, but in this parliament the Commons made little real headway on any point except the establishment of another continual council. At some point in the parliament the Commons also requested that the councillors, together with the chancellor, the treasurer, the two chief justices, the chief baron of the exchequer, the steward, treasurer and chamberlain of the household, the keeper of the Privy Seal, and the two keepers of the forests should be nominated in full parliament until the king came of age. This request too was only partially met, for it was agreed that the councillors and four officers, the chancellor, the treasurer, and the steward, and chamberlain of the household, should be 'chosen by the lords in parliament',[4] an important difference of wording, excluding the Commons from any direct say in the choice of councillors or officers. The Commons had succeeded in securing some measures to ensure the financial probity of those round the king, and they made a tax grant of two tenths and fifteenths, but they had not been able to subject the household to control either by parliament or by the council. The lords were not willing, at this stage, to deny the young king the freedom to order his household as he, or rather those who spoke for him, wished. This

---

[1] Carlisle Record Office, *Register of Bishop Appleby* ff. 222–6.
[2] *Rot. Parl.* Vol. III, p. 7.
[3] *ibid.*   [4] *ibid.* p. 16.

lack of control, however, was to prove a crucial weakness in the years that lay ahead.

The Commons in this parliament were also formally reconciled with John of Gaunt. He was nominated a member of the intercommuning committee, and the Commons went so far as to declare that they had chosen him 'to be their principal aid, strength and counsellor in this parliament',[1] an odd wording to choose if his political eclipse had really been as great as is sometimes supposed. He declined to serve on the committee until he had been cleared of accusations of treason, which the Commons readily did, pointing out that they would hardly have chosen him as their principal counsellor unless they had already accepted his innocence.[2] Furthermore, Gaunt and his two royal brothers received a parliamentary commission to investigate any breaches by the continual council of the rules concerning corruption which parliament had imposed upon it.[3]

For the next year, the continual council exercised responsibility for the day-to-day government of the country, and some of its members, especially the Earl of March and the three bishops, were notably assiduous in attendance.[4] The council was responsible for the whole range of governmental activity, but from time to time it was afforced by other nobles. Gaunt, for instance, was summoned to attend a meeting of the king's council at least three times between March and June 1378, and he could thus make his influence felt directly.[5] Gaunt's personal presence at the council from time to time is an important illustration of the general point that the titled nobility could express their views personally and directly when they wished to do so, without the need to ensure representation through underlings. It is perhaps as unreal to see Gaunt exercising influence covertly by manipulating his friends on the council as it is to see him exercising influence in parliament by attempting to pack the Commons. Bishop Erghum, and Latimer on the first council, might put forward Gaunt's point of view if he had one, on the more routine matters that came before the council, but on major issues of policy Gaunt was his own spokesman. Although it is not entirely clear what matters came before these afforced sessions of the council, there is some evidence that they handled the raising of loans and the confirmation of annuities granted by Edward III, a

[1] *Rot. Parl.* Vol. III, p. 5.   [2] *ibid.*   [3] *ibid.* p. 6.
[4] Tout, *Chapters* Vol. III, p. 344; N. B. Lewis, 'The "Continual Council" in the Early Years of Richard II', *EHR* XLI (1926) pp. 246–51.
[5] PRO Exchequer Issue Rolls E.403/465 m.18; E.403/468 mm.1,6.

matter on which the Commons had urged great caution.[1] In all probability, too, they dealt with the planning of military expeditions; it is inconceivable, for instance, that Gaunt was not present when the naval expedition of 1378, which he was to lead, came under discussion. It is clear that the council readily sought the advice of nobles and prelates who were not members, and in practice the collective government of the first three years of the reign was widely based. The rapid narrowing of the range of men involved in government after 1381, and Richard's apparent failure to give due weight to status and experience, provides one reason for the growth of aristocratic hostility to his regime.

To the chroniclers, however, the careful conduct of government by the council during 1378 was of much less interest than the sacrilegious murder in Westminster Abbey of a Spanish esquire by the constable of the Tower, Sir Alan Buxhill, and one of the king's knights, Sir Ralph Ferrers, an old servant of the Black Prince who had been on the first council and whom a contemporary chronicler described as 'old in years and experienced in evil-doing'. Bishop Courtenay excommunicated all those involved in this flagrant violation of the right of sanctuary, but his fulmination served to provoke a collision between the church and anti-clerical elements on the whole question of the ecclesiastical privilege of sanctuary. Walsingham implies that Gaunt was responsible for the outrage, and that it led to a renewal of his feud with the Londoners, who supported their bishop. The autumn parliament of 1378, he adds, had to be held at Gloucester rather than at Westminster because of the tension. There is obviously some truth in this, but parliament was also about to negotiate an agreement with the Hanse which, they suspected, might not be at all popular in London and might be more smoothly dealt with away from the city.[2] The *Anonimalle Chronicle*, however, attributes responsibility for the whole sequence of events to the king's advisers.[3] Ferrers was a king's knight, and he and Buxhill took with them to the Abbey 'several yeomen of the king's household'. After the publication of the sentence of excommunication it was the king and his council, not Gaunt, who proposed the abolition of the liberties of Westminster Abbey, and it was they who summoned Wycliffe to parliament to argue against the right

---

[1] *CPR* 1377-81, pp. 24, 186-8; PRO Chancery Warrants C. 81/1539/1-4, 7, 9A, 9B, 11, 12, 17A, 19, 20; *Rot. Parl.* Vol. III, p. 16.
[2] *Chronicon Angliae* pp. 206-11; Tout, *Chapters* Vol. III, p. 328; H. Palais, 'England's First Attempt to Break the Commercial Monopoly of the Hanseatic League', *American Historical Review* LXIV (1959) p. 862.
[3] *Anon. Chron.* pp. 121-3.

of sanctuary. The *Anonimalle Chronicle* goes on to point out that Wycliffe appeared before the Commons 'at the instigation of Sir Simon Burley, then the king's tutor, and Sir Thomas Percy'.[1] In view of the *Anonimalle Chronicle's* testimony[2] it must remain doubtful whether Gaunt's reputation suffered much as a result of the murder. He was in any case out of the country when it happened, and it is more likely that it intensified the suspicion already being felt about the activities of those round the king.

The Commons in the Gloucester parliament were also concerned about the government's conduct of financial affairs. In reply to the chancellor's request for a tax, they pointed out that the king's landed resources were now very large. He had inherited not only the crown estate of his grandfather, but also the lands of his father, the Black Prince. He also had in his hands the alien priories and the lands of several lords who were under age. With these resources, they argued, the king should have no need of another tax yet, and the chancellor's request seemed to them evidence of profligacy or mismanagement. They went on to air their suspicions about the manner in which the last subsidy had been collected and spent.[3] There was little substance to the Commons' fears. The special treasurers of war appointed, at the Commons' instigation in the first parliament of the reign, appear to have discharged their responsibilities honestly and competently. The truth of the matter was that the Commons were becoming increasingly reluctant to finance overseas campaigns at all, and they insisted that their only responsibility was to provide money for home defence. In the end, they were induced to grant a tax by the argument that English possessions overseas were in fact the kingdom's first line of defence.[4] The Commons' parsimony perhaps explains why the government's strategy over the next two years was confined to the defence of the seas and intervention in Brittany.

The Commons also asked to be told 'who would be the king's councillors and governors of his person'. They were still greatly concerned about the lack of any formal arrangements for the supervision of the king, and they probably suspected that those around the king were enriching themselves at public expense with royal lands and feudal incidents. In order to allay this disquiet and bring courtiers and councillors into closer association, Aubrey de Vere, the acting chamberlain, and Sir Robert Rous, one of the king's knights, were placed on

1 *Anon. Chron.* p. 123.   2 On this point see *ibid.*, introduction p. xli.
3 *Rot. Parl.* Vol. III, p. 35.   4 *ibid.* p. 36.

the third and last continual council, which took office on the 26th of November 1378.[1] But this attempt at co-operation does not seem to have worked, for neither de Vere nor Rous attended at all regularly. In the year and a week during which it held office, de Vere attended for only 113 days and Rous for only 80, less than half as often as the three clerical members and Sir Roger Beauchamp, who must have been responsible for the day-to-day direction of policy.[2] De Vere and Rous, in fact, seem to have used their position to ensure that the court's business was dealt with by the council. From the beginning of the reign, some petitions for favours were addressed to the king himself, and the acting chamberlain, Aubrey de Vere, and the under-chamberlain, Simon Burley, seem to have been responsible for dealing with them. They signed successful petitions, and then transmitted them either to the council for approval or to the chancellor for direct action. Early in 1379, for instance, more than twenty household clerks were presented to benefices, and in procuring the grants Aubrey de Vere acted as intermediary between the king and the officers of state.[3] At about the same time he steered a petition from Sir Thomas Percy through the council.[4] By virtue of their position within the household, Aubrey de Vere and Simon Burley wielded considerable power, and from very early in the reign were able to influence the direction of royal patronage. The appointment of de Vere to the council can only have strengthened household influence at the centre of government, and if anything militated against increased conciliar supervision of the household.

In the parliament which met after Easter 1379 the Commons renewed their pressure on financial matters. They successfully sought the appointment of a committee 'to examine the estate of the king'. This committee was to have power to investigate royal income and expenditure, and survey all wards, marriages, forfeitures and escheats which had fallen to the crown since the beginning of the reign. The commission was to report to the council and make recommendations for the future, but there is no evidence that it ever met.[5] Shortly after

---

[1] *ibid.* p. 35; N. B. Lewis, 'The "Continual Council" ', p. 250.
[2] Tout, *Chapters* Vol. III, p. 344; N. B. Lewis, 'The "Continual Council" ', p. 250.
[3] *CPR* 1377–81, pp. 328–30.
[4] PRO Ancient Petitions SC.8/236/11793; CPR 1377–81, p. 350, warranted 'By K., and by petition endorsed by the Great Council', See also J. A. Tuck, 'Richard II's System of Patronage', in *The Reign of Richard II* ed. F. R. H. du Boulay and Caroline M. Barron (London 1971) pp. 5–6.
[5] *Rot. Parl.* Vol. III, p. 57.

parliament dispersed, the lords appointed Sir John Cobham 'to remain in the household for the safeguard of the king's person',[1] an attempt perhaps to counterbalance the influence of Burley and Aubrey de Vere. But although Cobham received wages for this duty from the 6th of June 1379 until the 18th of February 1380, his supervision seems to have had little effect.[2]

By early 1380, the Commons had developed a consistent view about the government's financial problems. They believed that royal resources were sufficient to pay for the defence of the country, provided they were managed with care and probity;[3] those round the king were partly responsible for the lack of such virtues in royal financial management, and they believed, with good reason, that successive continual councils had been unable to exercise any effective supervision over the household. They also took the view that if taxes had to be imposed, the burden should be spread widely; hence their grant of the graduated poll-tax in the Easter parliament of 1379, described by the *Anonimalle Chronicle* as 'a subsidy so remarkable that such a thing had never been seen or heard of before',[4] and their proposals for other fiscal innovations in these years. The Easter 1379 parliament also authorized the collection of a local tax for local defence in Yorkshire, an expedient which, had it been more widely adopted, might have lessened resistance to the gathering of taxes and their expenditure on measures which seemed ineffective to the Commons.[5]

These considerations lie behind the attack on the administration which the Commons launched in the January parliament of 1380. Through their speaker, Sir John Gildesborough, they demanded that the lords of the continual council should be discharged, and that 'no such councillors should any longer be appointed for the king. in view of his age, which is now almost the same as that of his noble grandfather at the time of his coronation'. They went on to point out that Edward III had had no councillors at the beginning of his reign except the five officers of state, whom the Commons now asked to be nominated in

[1] PRO Exchequer Issue Rolls E.403/475 m.8.
[2] *ibid*. Walsingham states that the earl of Warwick was appointed after Cobham 'ut iugiter cum rege moram traheret' at an annual fee from the exchequer, but there is no other evidence of his appointment or of his ever receiving any wages for such a duty. In all probability Cobham had no successor (*Chronicon Angliae* p. 255).
[3] For a general discussion of the Commons' attitude towards royal resources. see B. P. Wolffe, *The Royal Demesne in English History* (London 1971) pp. 72–5,
[4] *Anon. Chron.* p. 127.
[5] *CPR* 1377–81, p. 355.

parliament.[1] All these requests were agreed to, and the system of formally appointed continual councils came to an end. The lords do not appear to have argued the point nor to have offered any opposition at all to the Commons' demand. The Commons also asked for a thorough inquiry into the crown's finances and the state of the royal household; this was agreed, and a committee was appointed whose terms of reference were wider than those of the previous one, though like its predecessor it seems never to have met. A petition in the November parliament of 1380 requested its assembly for January 1381, but though the king agreed to the petition there is no evidence that it ever began its work.[2]

The Commons' demands arose primarily from concern about the state of the household and the royal finances, but there was another factor in the situation in 1380. The speaker of the Commons, Sir John Gildesborough, was a tenant and a retainer of Thomas of Woodstock Earl of Buckingham, one of the many whom Buckingham had inherited from his father-in-law Humphrey Bohun Earl of Hereford and Essex.[3] Gildesborough had not sat in parliament before, and in all probability his election as speaker is a sign of Buckingham's growing political influence. The one and a half fifteenths and tenths which the Commons granted in this parliament was earmarked for the expedition to Brittany which Buckingham intended to lead in the coming summer, and in June Gildesborough was one of the four men appointed to receive and distribute the money allocated for the Breton expedition.[4] Buckingham, too, may have had an even more personal interest in the financial problems of the early years of the reign. Through his wife, Buckingham could expect to dispose of half the Bohun inheritance; but she was not due to come of age until June 1380, and until then Buckingham derived the greater part of his income from exchequer annuities. When he was created earl at Richard's coronation, he received an annuity of £1000 to maintain his estate; he also had an annuity of £300 to maintain himself and his wife until she came of age, and £666–13–4 worth of Bohun property.[5] Buckingham's income was thus dangerously dependent upon the solvency of the exchequer,

[1] *Rot. Parl.* Vol. III, p. 73.   [2] *ibid.* pp. 73–4, 93.
[3] PRO Duchy of Lancaster Accounts DL.30/67/837; J. S. Roskell, *The Commons and their Speakers in English Parliaments 1376–1523* (Manchester 1965) pp. 124–7, 355.
[4] *Rot. Parl.* Vol. III, p. 75.
[5] CPR 1374–7, p. 337; 1377–81, pp. 66–7; Anthony Goodman, *The Loyal Conspiracy* (London 1971) pp. 88–9.

and the more embarrassed the government's financial position became, the more precarious was his income. He above all the lords must have sympathized with the Commons' criticism of the government's financial management. The appointment of Gildesborough to the committee of inquiry set up in 1380 would have given Buckingham some indirect influence in its deliberations, had it ever met.

The system of continual councils which now came to an end has received much criticism from historians. Tout criticized them for incompetence, and Steel found them guilty of mismanagement 'in all departments, military, naval and financial'.[1] This view goes back in part to Walsingham, who said that the council of 1379 had spent a great deal of money from the royal treasury and achieved nothing, or very little, with it,[2] and in part to the record of the Commons' incessant complaints of financial mismanagement. If carefully examined, however, the Commons' complaints appear to be increasingly directed at the royal household rather than at the councils, and it may be that historians' judgement of the councils has been unduly harsh. On the military and naval side, the expeditions mounted were on a larger scale than at any previous time in the war, and it is thus hardly surprising that they cost more. The barbican policy which the government had adopted by 1378, and which was sold to the Commons in the parliament of that year as a means of home defence as well as a means of establishing bases from which to attack the French, was extremely expensive, but it was effective and the councils deserve credit for pursuing it. The Commons, however, were quite unwilling to meet the real costs either of the barbican policy or of the huge expedition mounted in 1378. There is no good evidence for corruption or systematic mismanagement of finances by the council, nor is there any evidence that the royal household was unreasonably costly. The blame for the recurrent financial crises must lie mainly with the Commons. Indeed, the councils appear to have been honest and prudent in their administration of the crown's financial resources. The annuities granted by Edward III were confirmed only after investigation by the council afforced by other lords, and they were careful not to grant out other assets and windfalls indiscriminately. The Despenser inheritance came to the king's hands during the minority of the heir, and was farmed to the dowager lady Despenser for £700 p.a. The inheritance was valued at £956–1–3¾, but £700 appears a reasonable sum when it is

[1] Tout, *Chapters* Vol. III, p. 339; A. B. Steel, *Richard II* p. 47.
[2] *Chronicon Angliae* p. 255.

borne in mind that the valuation includes charges on several of the manors.[1] The inheritance of the Earl of Pembroke, also in the king's hands during the heir's minority, was farmed for its value as found by inquisition.[2] Two financial officials made surveys of the alien priories in 1378 to serve as a basis for the farms agreed upon with their priors and some lay farmers.[3] Here there seems to have been some slight favour shown to certain lay farmers, but nothing on the scale of the preferential terms offered to the lay farmers who took the lands of the priories in the early 1380s, when Richard and his courtiers were responsible for the control and direction of patronage. Furthermore, when the Bedford inheritance fell to the crown after Ingelram de Coucy renounced his allegiance in August 1377, the bulk of it was assigned to the use of his wife, Edward III's daughter, who remained in the English allegiance; but that part of it on the Isle of Wight, including the strategically important Carisbrooke Castle, was retained in royal hands to ensure its proper defence under the threat of French invasion.[4] In short, therefore, there is little sign of extravagance or mismanagement in the council's control of patronage. In an extremely difficult situation they appear to have acted prudently and honestly.

Nor should the council be held responsible for the unsatisfactory outcome to the military expeditions of 1378 and 1379. The expeditions were financed out of the proceeds of taxation, and obviously the council was limited by the amount of money the Commons were prepared to grant. Arguably, shortage of money and the incompetence of some of the nobility in charge of the expeditions prevented England taking full advantage of the diplomatic and strategic opportunities negotiated by the councils. In pursuance of the barbican policy, the English had leased Brest from the Duke of Brittany in April 1378 and Cherbourg from the King of Navarre in July, while Gaunt's attempt in the early summer of 1378 to take St Malo should perhaps be seen as an aspect of the same policy. Furthermore, in the summer of 1379 the Duke of Brittany returned to his duchy, and by the 15th of March 1380 he had negotiated a formal treaty with Richard II.[5] The council had thus carefully arranged a series of bases which might not only help the defence of England, but would also provide useful

[1] *CFR* 1377–83, pp. 46, 252–3.
[2] PRO Chancery Inquisitions Post Mortem C.135/246, 247.
[3] *CPR* 1377–81, p. 253.
[4] *CPR* 1377–81, p. 174.
[5] J. J. N. Palmer, *England, France and Christendom* (London 1972) pp. 7–8; M. C. E. Jones, *Ducal Brittany 1364–1399* (Oxford 1970) pp. 76–92.

points of entry into France. Yet England failed to exploit these opportunities; her failure was partly a consequence of the parsimony of the Commons, and partly a reflection on the military competence of the various commanders. The 1379 expedition to Brittany had to be reduced in size from 4000 men to 1300 because of the lack of money, and although Walsingham held Gaunt responsible for the failure of the attack on St Malo in the previous year, Froissart's account gives the impression that the blame lay primarily with the Earl of Arundel for failing to mount a proper guard over a mine.[1] It may be that once again Walsingham's criticism of Gaunt is baseless, and in any case the main purpose of Gaunt's expedition was to 'keep the seas', that is to defend England against naval raids; the attack on St Malo was something of an afterthought. The attempt to seize Nantes in the winter of 1379–80 also failed, partly because Sir John Arundel turned the expedition into a drunken and licentious debauch, and according to Walsingham got his just deserts when he and most of his companions were drowned in a storm off the Irish coast.[2] Hoping to do better, Buckingham led a march through northwest France in the summer of 1380, and then spent the autumn and winter besieging Nantes. But meanwhile behind his back the Duke of Brittany came to terms with the French and then in effect bought Buckingham off.[3]

The ending of the system of continual councils left governmental power in England in the hands of the chief officers of state and the king's informal councillors. There is very little information about who these men were, but there is reason to believe that household influence over government increased still further during 1380 and the early months of 1381. A document dating from the spring of 1381 names the members of the king's council as the Archbishop of Canterbury, now chancellor; the treasurer; the keeper of the Privy Seal; the acting chamberlain, Aubrey de Vere; the Chief Justice of Common Pleas, and others.[4] Throughout these early years of the reign, whenever we can catch a glimpse of the informal processes of government, Aubrey de Vere occupies a key position, and must have been primarily responsible for the assertion of the power of the royal household. Furthermore, at this time close links were forged between the household and the exchequer. In 1380 the king appointed the two chamberlains of the

[1] J. J. N. Palmer, *England, France and Christendom* p. 9; *Chronicon Angliae* p. 205; Froissart, *Oeuvres* Vol. IX, pp. 91–2.
[2] *Chronicon Angliae* pp. 247–54; *Anon. Chron.* p. 131.
[3] *Chronicon Angliae* pp. 266–7; M. C. E. Jones, *Ducal Brittany* pp. 90–92.
[4] PRO Exchequer Bill E.207/6/10.

exchequer to positions within the household, John Bacon becoming receiver of the chamber and John Hermesthorpe keeper of the privy wardrobe; while on the 6th of January 1381 William Packington, keeper of the wardrobe of the household, was appointed chancellor of the exchequer.[1] At the same time, however, ministerial leadership became weaker. Sir Richard Lescrope, who had handled the Commons with some skill in the parliaments of 1379 and 1380, resigned as chancellor after the ending of the system of continual councils, and was replaced on the 30th of January 1380 by Simon of Sudbury Archbishop of Canterbury. Sudbury had not served the king before, and his main concern in the previous two years had been the raising of funds to pay for the new nave of his cathedral.[2] His inexperience in the service of the state, and the burden of bearing high office in church and government simultaneously, probably account for the impression of lack of drive and initiative which he has left. Walsingham criticized the appointment as unsuitable, and insinuated that he may have been drafted.[3] His modern historian admits that he was 'easy-going, to the point of complaisance'.[4] His main value to the government was his mastery of Convocation which ensured the grant of clerical subsidies to the crown. A year later, Thomas Brantingham, Bishop of Exeter, who had held office as treasurer since the beginning of the reign was replaced by Robert Hales, Prior of the Hospital of St John of Jerusalem. Hales had sat on the last of the continual councils, but otherwise had no experience in government, though he had held office as admiral in the west in 1376. The keeper of the Privy Seal, John Fordham, retained office until after the Peasants' Revolt, but if his later career is any guide to his attitude he is unlikely to have stood up to the king and his advisers.

If ministerial leadership was weak in 1380–81, magnate leadership was seriously lacking. In May 1380 the Earl of March set off for Ireland, never to return to England; in July Buckingham left for France, and did not come back until the following spring; and in August, Gaunt went north prepared for a campaign against the Scots. At a meeting with Scottish representatives, however, the truce was prolonged until the 30th of November 1381, but Gaunt did not return

[1] Tout, *Chapters* Vol. III, p. 462; *CPR* 1377–81, pp. 588, 599.
[2] *Eulogium Historiarum sive Temporis* Vol. III, ed. F. S. Haydon, Rolls Series (London 1863) p. 350.
[3] *Chronicon Angliae* p. 255.
[4] W. L. Warren, 'A Reappraisal of Simon Sudbury', *Journal of Ecclesiastical History* X (1959) pp. 141–2.

to the south until after the opening of parliament at Northampton on the 5th of November.[1] The Archbishop of Canterbury, as chancellor, explained to the Commons that money was needed for the expeditions of March, Buckingham, and Lancaster, for home defence, and for the wages of the garrisons of Calais, Cherbourg, and Brest, which were already in arrears. In response to Speaker Gildesborough's request for an estimate of how much was needed, he gave a figure of £160,000. The Commons, after deliberating among themselves, concluded that they did not know how such a sum could be found, and went back to the lords for advice. The lords put forward three alternatives: a poll-tax, a sales tax, and a subsidy of the usual kind. They made it clear that of the three they favoured a poll-tax, and the Commons agreed to raise 100,000 marks by that means. It seems clear, however, that it was the lords and bishops present in the Northampton parliament who were really responsible for the tax which sparked off the Peasants' Revolt.[2] Had more than a 'moelt petite nombre'[3] of lords been present at parliament, wiser counsels might have prevailed, for the risks involved in levying a third poll-tax must have been known to at least some of the lords and prelates who were there. A little over four months previously, the Bishop of St. Davids had been reprimanded by the king for failing to collect the two previous poll-taxes in his diocese;[4] a month before parliament opened the Bishop of London had had to order his archdeacon in Essex to collect the 1378 subsidy;[5] the Bishop of Bangor had complained to the king that some of his clergy had refused to collect the same subsidy;[6] and the Bishop of Carlisle had associated himself with a movement against taxation in his diocese in the 1370s. His clerk made his own view of the 1379 tax quite clear, describing it in the Register as 'malum subsidium' and noting that it was not levied.[7] There was, in fact, a growing climate of resistance to taxation: the Commons expressed their resentment in parliament, and had, or thought they had, means of reducing the burden or spreading it more widely; but the clergy, in the more highly disciplined convocation, had no such power and neither, of course, had the peasantry upon whom the burden of a third poll-tax now fell. The author of the *Anonimalle Chronicle* realized that the Northampton parliament had not discussed the problem of taxation

[1] *Rot. Parl.* Vol. III, p. 88; *Foedera* Vol. VII, pp. 277–9.
[2] *Rot. Parl.* Vol. III, pp. 88–90.
[3] *ibid.* p. 88.   [4] *CFR* 1377–83, pp. 208–9.
[5] *ibid.* p. 217.   [6] *ibid.*
[7] Carlisle Record Office, *Register of Bishop Appleby*, ff. 222-6, 314.

with sufficient thoroughness, recording that 'les subsides furount legerment grauntez'.[1] The Commons did not lay down the principles according to which the tax was to be collected with anything like the care they had devoted to the task in 1379, and they contented themselves with the vague exhortation that the rich should help the poor. Furthermore the actual collection of the tax was marked by corruption, incompetence, and oppression. The whole exercise from its inception was a blunder, and the blame for it must rest squarely upon the Northampton parliament and the men who occupied the chief offices of state in the winter and spring of 1381.

The revolt which the poll-tax sparked has normally been interpreted as a crucial event in the development of Richard II's personality, giving him a taste of authority and a demonstration of loyalty which made a deep impression on him and made him acutely conscious of his position as king.[2] There must be some truth in this; the events at Mile End in particular could not have but induced in him a vivid awareness of the response which his presence evoked among his subjects and the beginnings of an awareness that men outside the circle of nobles and ministers had a direct and simple concept of loyalty to the king. But the revolt was important also in the development of Richard's own rule and his relations with the nobles who had participated in government since the beginning of the reign. Indeed, the part played by the nobility during the revolt has seldom been analysed, but it throws light both on the course of events during the revolt and on the tensions within the political community which arose after the revolt.

Although there was rioting early in the revolt in Dartford, Rochester and Canterbury, the main body of rebels in both Essex and Kent made straight for London, and it fell to the officers of state to attempt to parley with them. In East Anglia, however, the revolt was much more diffuse, with major risings in Cambridgeshire, the Bury and Norwich areas, southwest Norfolk, and the Stour Valley. The widespread nature of the revolt in this region suggests that the nobility, the natural leaders of society in so grave an emergency, allowed the situation to get out of control. Lordship in East Anglia was perhaps at its least effective point in the summer of 1381. The Earl of March, who held the Clare inheritance in southwest Suffolk, had died in Ireland earlier in the year leaving as his heir a child of seven; the inheritance of Thomas of Brotherton Earl of Norfolk, situated mainly in northeast

[1] *Anon. Chron.* p. 134.
[2] See for example A. B. Steel, *Richard II* pp. 81–2, 91.

Suffolk, was in the hands of his aged widow, Margaret Marshall; Gaunt, who had interests in north Norfolk, was away in Scotland, and the other landowner of consequence in East Anglia, William Ufford Earl of Suffolk, simply ran away when he heard of the risings, fleeing first to St Albans and then to London.[1] Only Bishop Despenser of Norwich showed any fight, and as soon as it was clear that he was prepared to make a stand against the rebels, many of the lesser landowners of East Anglia rallied to him.[2] But the local gentry, accustomed to aristocratic leadership in war, lacked the necessary standing, experience, and perhaps even knowledge of each other to organize resistance effectively. Without a clear lead from the nobility, most of the gentry remained passive until the storm had passed, and a few actually joined the rebels,[3] some intending to pay off old scores, some perhaps hoping to gain the approval of the peasants by identifying with them and perhaps thereby obtaining the loyalty and service which they could not hope to command through their wealth or their social position.

The outcome of the revolt, however, was to be decided in London, and on the 13th, 14th, and 15th June those around the king worked out the policy which led to the Mile End and Smithfield confrontations. It is important therefore to establish who was with the king in the Tower during the revolt. There is general agreement, and it is obvious from the course of events, that the chancellor and treasurer were there. The *Anonimalle Chronicle*, the best source for the events in London,[4] says that the Earls of Buckingham, Kent, Warwick, and Oxford, with Sir Thomas Percy, Sir Robert Knolles, Aubrey de Vere, the Mayor of London, and many other knights and esquires went to Mile End with the king. Froissart says that Buckingham was on his estates in Wales,[5] but his testimony cannot stand against that of the *Anonimalle Chronicle*: in all probability he was with the king when he was ordered on the 18th of June to go to Essex and put down the insurgents there.[6] Froissart names Salisbury, Kent, Suffolk, and Sir John Holland as among those present, while Knighton adds the name of Henry Earl of Derby.[7] In view of the fact that the Earl of Arundel became chancellor for two days after Sudbury's murder, he too was in

---

[1] *Chronicon Angliae* pp. 301–5.   [2] *ibid.* pp. 306–8.
[3] E. Powell, *The Rising in East Anglia in 1381* (Cambridge 1896); A. Réville, *Le Soulèvement des Travailleurs d'Angleterre en 1381* (Paris 1898); *Chronicon Angliae* p. 305.
[4] *Anon. Chron.* pp. 139–50.   [5] Froissart, *Oeuvres* Vol. IX, p. 397.
[6] *Anon. Chron.* p. 144; *Walsingham, HA* Vol. II, p. 18.
[7] Froissart, *Oeuvres* Vol. IX, p. 395; *Knighton* Vol. II, p. 132.

all probability in the Tower with the king.[1] It is far from clear why so many members of the nobility should have been in London in mid-June; there had been no parliament or council recently, and no social occasion of any consequence since St George's Day. There were two notable absentees: Gaunt was in Scotland, and Simon Burley was abroad, preparing to escort Queen Anne to England. Gaunt would have liked it to be thought that he stayed in Scotland to ensure that the Scots did not take advantage of the turmoil in England to invade, but it was widely believed, perhaps with some justification, that in fact he was too frightened to leave the shelter of the Scottish court.[2] The *Anonimalle Chronicle* makes Burley guilty of sparking off the revolt in north Kent by arresting a man whom he claimed as his serf and refusing to accept less than £300 as the price of his release. The serf was thereupon imprisoned in Rochester Castle, only to be released when the rebels sacked it on the 9th of June.[3] Although Burley himself was abroad, and one of his officials was probably responsible for the episode, the action was bitterly resented, and probably helped to promote the popular animosity against Burley which was to play a part in deciding his fate in 1388.[4]

By the 14th of June, a policy of negotiation and concession had been agreed upon among those with the king. The sincerity with which they pursued it will always be disputed, and it will never be possible to establish who played the major part in the formulation of the policy. According to both Froissart and Walsingham, Sudbury and Hales advocated a hard line, while Froissart adds that the Earl of Salisbury proposed negotiations with the rebels because the nobles lacked the force to carry through a successful policy of repression, and failure would mean the end of aristocratic authority.[5] If this argument was used, no matter by whom, it was likely to be persuasive in the circumstances of the 14th of June. The *Anonimalle Chronicle* gives the impression that the king himself advocated a policy of conciliation, though both this source and the chronicle of the Monk of Evesham describe Richard's feelings as tense, uncertain, and apprehensive, as well they might have been.[6] However, the proclamation offering the rebels pardon and asking them to return home was sealed with his signet, his

---

[1] *Anon. Chron.* p. 146.　　　　[2] *Walsingham, HA* Vol. II, p. 42.

[3] *Anon. Chron.* p. 136.

[4] Burley left England for Bohemia on the 15th of May 1381 and did not return until the 12th of January 1382 (Tout, *Chapters* Vol. IV, p. 340).

[5] Froissart, *Oeuvres* Vol. IX, p. 402; *Walsingham HA* Vol. I, p. 456.

[6] *Anon. Chron.* pp. 138, 143-4; *Evesham* pp. 26-7.

own personal seal,[1] and it may well be that he and his immediate household servants were responsible for proposing the policy and getting it accepted. Once accepted, however, there is strong evidence that the king at least genuinely believed in it. He apparently continued to manumit serfs even after the collapse of the revolt,[2] and in the November parliament of 1381 he offered to free the serfs if parliament would authorize him to do so.[3] His motives for this must remain obscure. He may have been hazily aware of the freer position enjoyed by the peasants on the royal demesne; but he probably had little understanding of the real implications of conceding their demands. There is no sign that he anticipated the immediate and vigorous reaction in favour of property rights which his proposal induced among the landowning class. Richard could carry his nobles with him as long as they saw his policy as a short-term expedient designed to give them a chance to recover their nerve, assemble their forces, and crush the rebels. But should they suspect that the policy was more than a subterfuge, their mistrust of the king would inevitably increase.

The king's assertion of a personal initiative in dealing with the peasants is paralleled in other aspects of government. During and immediately after the revolt there is a striking increase in the king's general administrative activity. The administrative chaos caused by the murder of the chancellor and treasurer encouraged suitors to go straight to the king. Those around the king, taking advantage of an unforeseen situation, moved into the vacuum created by the sudden removal of the two chief officers of state and, temporarily at least, took over the reins of government. After the collapse of the revolt the king himself was required to authorize the appointment of the commissions of oyer and terminer to deal with the rebels, and at the same time (more perhaps to his taste) he authorized a large number of grants to members of his household.[4]

The administrative incompetence which had provoked the revolt, and the activity of the king and his household were bound to give rise to criticism when parliament next assembled. Parliament opened on the 4th of November in an atmosphere of tension created by the quarrel between Gaunt and the Earl of Northumberland, a quarrel which had its immediate origin in Northumberland's treatment of

[1] *Walsingham HA* Vol. I, p. 473; *Anon. Chron.* p. 143.
[2] B. Harvey, 'Draft Letters Patent of Manumission and Pardon for the Men of Somerset in 1381', *EHR LXXX* (1965) pp. 89–91.
[3] *Rot. Parl.* Vol. III, p. 99.
[4] *CPR* 1381–5, pp. 18, 20, 24, 34, 41, 72–8.

Gaunt during the Peasants' Revolt but which really arose out of Northumberland's anxiety to keep Gaunt out of his sphere of influence on the northern border. Both Gaunt and Northumberland brought their retinues to London, and the Londoners, as might be expected, strongly favoured Northumberland.[1] The dispute held up the proceedings of parliament for a full week and deflected attention from the really important issues which had to be dealt with; but after Northumberland had formally apologized to Gaunt, parliament turned its attention to the events of the summer. The treasurer, Segrave, explained to the assembled estates that the king had issued the charters of manumission to the serfs against his will, 'pur estopper et cesse lour clamour et malice', that such action disinherited the lords and prelates of the kingdom and was therefore unlawful and *ultra vires*. However, Segrave went on to say, if it was parliament's will that the serfs should be freed, then the king 'assentera ovesque vous a vostre priere'. The Commons were clearly in some doubt about what Segrave really meant. Perhaps they could not believe that the king was really prepared to free the serfs and thus, in their eyes, diminish the property rights of the landowning class, so they went back to the lords two days later (the 18th of November) and asked for clarification from the new chancellor, Sir Richard Lescrope. Lescrope made it plain to the Commons that they were being asked whether they wanted the charters of manumission to stand repealed or not, and presented squarely with the issue they had no hesitation in joining with the lords to approve the repeal.[2]

The Commons then launched an attack upon the household. They complained of the 'outrageouses nombre des Familiers esteantz en l'hostiel' and the ruinous purveyance to which so large a household gave rise. They complained too about the maladministration of the law, the inadequacy of the country's defences, and the evil officers and counsellors around the king. But it is clear that the household was their main target, and the king agreed to appoint yet another commission 'pur survere et examiner en Prive Conseil si bien l'Estat et Governaill de la Persone nostre dit Seigneur come de son dit Hostiel, et de lour adviser des remedes suffisantz'. The membership of the Commission was more prestigious than that of any of its predecessors: it was headed by Gaunt and the two archbishops, together with the Bishops

---

[1] *Anon. Chron.* pp. 154–6; *Walsingham, HA* Vol. II, pp. 4–5; *Rot. Parl.* Vol. III, p. 98.
[2] *Rot. Parl.* Vol. III, pp. 99–100.

of Winchester, Ely (the Earl of Arundel's brother), Exeter, and Rochester, the Earls of Arundel, Warwick, Suffolk, Stafford, and Salisbury, the chancellor, five bannerets, 'and others'. Its composition does not suggest the supremacy of any particular faction, though it is highly significant that none of the household officials were members; once again, the committee's composition reflected status and experience rather than faction. The Commons asked the committee to appoint good and worthy men to be around the king, to take particular note of 'la grande Repaire des gentz si bien a chival come a pee qi sont repairantz au dit Hostell', and to ensure that the household was such a size that the king could 'vivre honestement de son propre'; in other words that the king should finance his household out of the sources of revenue customarily available to him and not get into debt or engage in extensive purveyance.[1] It may have been with this in mind that the income from the March inheritance during the minority of the heir was assigned for the expenses of the household.[2] The Commons also took the unusual step of requesting the removal from the household of one particular individual, the king's confessor, Thomas Rushook, presumably because he was an undesirable influence on the king.[3] He was a Dominican friar and had been prior provincial of his order in England in 1378.[4] He had been the king's confessor since at least 1379,[5] and seems to have been generally unpopular, though it is not clear why. Gower, in his Tripartite Chronicle,[6] described him as:

> Mollis confessor, blandus scelerisque professor . . .
> Cuius nigredo foedat loca regia credo.
> Hic fuit obliquus procerum latitans inimicus.
> Semper in augendo magis iram quam minuendo.

Parliament decreed that he should be banished from the household except at the four principal festivals of the year. His eclipse, however, was brief: in June 1382 he became Archdeacon of St Asaph, and in January the following year the pope provided him to the See of Llandaff.

Perhaps bearing in mind how ineffective earlier commissions of inquiry into the household had been, parliament also ordained that the

---

[1] *Rot. Parl.* Vol. III, p. 101.
[2] *CPR* 1381–5, p. 184.   [3] *Rot. Parl.* Vol. III, p. 101.
[4] *CPR* 1377–81, p. 310.   [5] *ibid.* p. 342.
[6] *Political Poems and Songs* Vol. I, ed. T. Wright, Rolls Series (London 1859) p. 421.

Earl of Arundel and Michael de la Pole should be placed in the household 'pur conseiller et governer' the person of the king.[1] This measure must have limited the king's freedom of action for a time, because the king's personal administrative activity diminished in the winter of 1381 and the spring of 1382.[2] The committee of inquiry, too, began its work promptly. Before parliament was dissolved it had heard reports of some of the committee's investigations,[3] and in all probability some of the reforms in Exchequer routine embodied in the statute of this parliament arose out of the commission's work.[4] The Commons implied that the commission had drafted an ordinance for the conduct of the household, for they asked the king to require the household officers to swear to uphold it,[5] but no text of the ordinance has survived, nor is there any other evidence of any reform in the organization of the household. After an adjournment for Christmas, parliament was dissolved on the 25th of February 1382, and there is no evidence that the commission continued its inquiries after the dissolution. It produced nothing of any value, and the inadequacy of traditional methods of investigating and controlling the royal household had been thoroughly exposed. It is not clear when the two guardians' term of office came to an end, but by the summer of 1382 the king was once again beginning to take a more active part in government.[6] The king was now restrained neither by a continual council nor by specially appointed committees or guardians; such means of government were discredited and ineffective. The first four and a half years of the reign had demonstrated once again the strength and resilience of the royal household and the virtual impossibility of permanently controlling it from outside. Richard and his closest followers were now in a position to exploit the power latent in the king and his household.

[1] *Rot. Parl.* Vol. III, p. 104.
[2] See notes of warranty to *CPR* and *CCR* 1381–5 *passim*.
[3] *Rot. Parl.* Vol. III, p. 102.
[4] *Statutes of the Realm* Vol. II, pp. 21–3.
[5] *Rot. Parl.* Vol. III, pp. 101, 115.
[6] This is based upon an analysis of notes of warranty in *CPR* and *CCR* 1381–5.

c

3

The Retreat of Aristocratic Influence 1382-6

The principal characteristics of Richard II's personal government between 1382 and 1386 were the development of the machinery of household government to a degree unparalleled since the reign of Edward II, and his reliance for counsel upon the officers of the household and a few other close associates, who, to the virtual exclusion of such lords as Woodstock, Arundel, and perhaps even Gaunt, monopolized access to the king and enjoyed the pleasures and profits of royal favour and patronage. Once again, as in Edward II's reign, men who thought themselves the natural counsellors of the king found their place usurped by others, and their natural disposition to co-operate with the king gradually changed into an attitude of opposition.

The king's household was both a domestic organization and a part of the administrative machinery of the country, and the same individuals were concerned with the domestic life of the king and his court and with general administrative matters. In normal times in the late fourteenth century, the household offices played only a minor part in government; the financial department of the household (the wardrobe) depended for its income upon the exchequer, and the chamber organization dealt with little more than the immediate domestic and financial needs of the king. The circumstances of the early years of Richard's reign, however, were particularly conducive to the development of the household, and in particular of the chamber organization. Subjected to repeated pressure from committees of inquiry which concentrated particularly on scrutinizing household expenditure, and with the major administrative departments of the government liable to parliamentary investigation, criticism and, ideally, reform, the king found in his household offices machinery which, because of its flexibility and its personal connection with him, could be used to meet his needs and give effect to his wishes more directly and more adequately than the bureaucratic departments of state. Furthermore, the freedom from permanent formal control which the young king enjoyed in the early years of his reign naturally tended to increase the power and influence of those officers responsible for the domestic organization of the household, the chamberlain and the under-chamberlain. It was in the chamber, and in the chapel royal, where apart from the king only the chamberlain could exercise authority, that the centre of Richard's power lay in these years.

In the Angevin period, the chamber had been concerned with the king's financial business and with a certain amount of general administrative and secretarial work, but by the end of the thirteenth century it had declined to a subordinate, purely domestic position. Edward II, however, developed it as the special instrument of his personal policy. He made substantial sources of revenue available to it, and endowed it with a permanent income from the revenues of certain manors. It had its own seal, the secret seal, which was used not only for chamber business but also as the king's personal seal for many other purposes. But after Edward's deposition, the chamber reverted to its purely domestic functions, and in 1356 its estate was abolished and its income reduced to an annual allowance of 10,000 marks known as the *certum*, paid into it by the exchequer: in effect, the chamber was now no more than the king's privy purse.[1] In the early part of Richard's reign the chamber officials came to play an important part in government, and to act as links between the council and the royal household. The under-chamberlain, Simon Burley, and Aubrey de Vere, acting for his nephew Robert Earl of Oxford, to whom the office of chamberlain belonged by hereditary right but who was under age, appear to have been the most influential of Richard's courtiers.

It is not surprising, therefore, that the chamber organization shows clear signs of growth and development in the 1380s. It increased sharply in size: in 1376 there had been only three chamber knights (though they were among Edward III's most trusted advisers), but by 1385 the

[1] Tout, *Chapters* Vol. IV, pp. 227–348; J. F. Willard and W. A. Morris, eds., *The English Government at Work 1327–1336* Vol. I (Cambridge, Mass. 1940) section v.

numbers had risen to eleven, and to seventeen by 1388. There were parallel increases in the number of esquires and yeomen of the chamber, and the growth in the size of this section of the household gave some substance to the Commons' repeated complaints in parliament.[1]

The purpose of building up the chamber staff in this way was almost certainly political. The king's intention was to ensure that trusted servants occupied important positions up and down the country, replacing or counterbalancing the influence of nobles whom Richard did not feel he could trust. A chamber knight expected at least the custody of a castle to maintain his estate, and Richard saw to it that they held several of the principal royal castles. Sir William Morers was granted the office of constable of Northampton Castle in October 1378 and held it until he was replaced by Nicholas Exton in 1387.[2] Sir William Neville was entrusted with the custody of Nottingham Castle for life in November 1381,[3] and in 1385 Sir John Clanvowe received the town, castle, and lordship of Haverford for life.[4] More significantly, the keeping of Portchester Castle was in the hands throughout this period of another chamber knight, Sir Robert Bardolf.[5] Portchester was on the edge of the Earl of Arundel's sphere of influence in Sussex and East Hampshire, and the earl's father had been keeper for life in Edward III's reign.[6] This is one of several instances of a position formerly held by the Arundel family falling into the hands of a member of the royal household. In 1387, furthermore, another chamber knight, Sir James Berners, was granted the marriage of Robert, son and heir of Lord Ponynges.[7] Ponynges was a tenant of the Earl of Arundel, holding extensive lands in the Barony of Lewes, and although the law on the matter was vague, Arundel had a good claim to the wardship, which was granted to him as soon as Berners was executed in 1388.[8]

Richard also extended the influence of his chamber into the shires. In 1385 Robert de Vere, now chamberlain, was appointed sheriff of Rutland for life.[9] This office had at one time belonged to William Bohun Earl of Northampton, younger brother of the last Bohun Earl of Hereford. The Earl of Buckingham, who had married the elder of the Hereford co-heiresses, may well have felt he had a claim to it;

---

[1] These figures are based upon an analysis of the wardrobe books for 1376–7 and 1384–5 (PRO Wardrobe and household accounts E.101/398/9, 400/26).
[2] *CPR* 1377–81, p. 277; 1385–9, p. 276.
[3] *ibid.* 1381–5, p. 60.   [4] *ibid.* 1385–9, p. 8.
[5] He received the keeping on the 4th of February 1381 (*ibid.* 1377–81, p. 594).
[6] *ibid.* 1354–8, p. 629.   [7] *ibid.*, 1385–9, p. 371.
[8] *ibid.* p. 501.   [9] *ibid.* p. 14.

he received the reversion of it two years after the Merciless Parliament.[1] Furthermore, in 1383 Richard had granted the office of sheriff of Wiltshire for life to Sir John Lancaster,[2] who was de Vere's chamberlain,[3] and although Lancaster lost the office in September 1385 his successor was Sir John Salesbury, one of the chamber knights. He too was to hold office for life, 'any statute to the contrary notwithstanding'.[4]

The chamber staff also played an important part in Richard's diplomacy. Simon Burley was one of the small group of officials and prelates who handled the negotiations for the Anglo-Luxemburg alliance, and he was in charge of the arrangements for bringing Anne of Bohemia to England as Richard's queen in 1382.[5] This marriage alliance was not well received in England. It was widely believed that the financial arrangements it entailed were too generous to the Emperor Wenceslas, Anne's brother; popular comment had it that Richard had bought his queen from an impoverished emperor.[6] Few imagined that the alliance would bring England any military benefits, and indeed in 1383 and 1384, when Wenceslas's interest in the Low Countries provided an opportunity to breathe some life into the alliance, the English government did nothing.[7] The alliance produced little for England beyond some minor diplomatic friction with the northern countries.[8] Lack of enthusiasm for the imperial alliance, however, fades almost into insignificance beside the unpopularity aroused by the king's negotiations with Charles VI in 1387. Sir John Golafre, a chamber knight, was commissioned to arrange a meeting between Richard and Charles VI, and the three men who were to accompany Richard to the meeting were Robert de Vere himself, his chamberlain Lancaster, and the chamber knight Sir John Salesbury. De Vere and Lancaster succeeded in escaping when Richard's baronial opponents came to power in 1388; Golafre took care not to return to England, where his arrest had been ordered; but Salesbury was

---

[1] *ibid.* 1388–92, p. 255; VCH Rutland Vol. I p. 177.

[2] *CFR* 1383–91, p. 6; de Vere was one of Lancaster's mainpernors.

[3] PRO Ancient Correspondence SC.1/43 no. 80.

[4] PRO Chancery Warrants C.81/1346/43; *CFR* 1383-91, p. 101.

[5] *Foedera* Vol. VII, pp. 280–81, 304–5.

[6] *Chronicon Angliae* ed. E. M. Thompson, Rolls Series (London 1874) p. 283; *Knighton* Vol. II, pp. 150–51; Westminster p. 12; E. Perroy, *L'Angleterre et le Grand Schisme d'Occident* (Paris 1933) pp. 136–56.

[7] J. J. N. Palmer, *England, France and Christendom* (London 1971) p. 57.

[8] J. A. Tuck, 'Some Evidence for Anglo-Scandinavian Relations in the Fourteenth Century', *Medieval Scandinavia* V (1972).

executed with the full barbarity of the law, as guilty of treason both within and without the kingdom. He was the only chamber knight to suffer the full penalty of treason.[1]

The political influence of the chamber was felt not only within the kingdom and in negotiations abroad, but also in North Wales and Cheshire, regions to which Richard looked for military support. His interest in these areas as a possible source of power is evident throughout his reign, and it may have been originally encouraged by the former servants of the Black Prince (many of whom probably appreciated the potential of his Welsh and Cheshire lands), who surrounded Richard in his early years. In 1382 Richard accepted a petition from John Beauchamp of Holt, a chamber knight, for the keeping of Conway Castle in place of Edward St John (a connection of the Earl of Arundel), and in December 1385 he was appointed Justice of North Wales for life.[2] Simon Burley was appointed Justice of South Wales for life in 1382, and received at the same time the lordship of Newcastle Emlyn.[3] He found his Welsh responsibilities too much for him, however, and petitioned for release in 1385, pleading that the king required him to stay at court and that therefore he could not discharge his duties in person.[4] He was allowed to nominate his successor, and it was agreed that when his successor died the office should revert to him.[5] Two years later, in September 1387, as part of his preparations for raising a military force in Cheshire, Richard appointed de Vere Justice of Chester,[6] and the following month he replaced Beauchamp as Justice of North Wales.[7] The office of Justice of North Wales had been held for life by the Earl of Arundel's father, but in the 1380s chamber officials came to hold overwhelming administrative power in an area close to the Arundel sphere of influence and to monopolize offices which had been a source of profit and prestige to the Earl of Arundel's father in Edward III's reign.

[1] Westminster p. 178; *Knighton* Vol. II, p. 243; *CCR* 1385–9, p. 394; J. J. N. Palmer, *England, France and Christendom* pp. 107–8, 118–19.
[2] Conway: PRO Chancery Warrants C.81/1394/86; *CPR* 1381–5, p. 183. N. Wales: *CPR* 1385–9, p. 92.
[3] *CPR* 1381–5, pp. 107, 160.
[4] PRO Ancient Petitions SC.8/249/12443.
[5] *CPR* 1381–5, pp. 534, 536.
[6] PRO Chester Recognizance Rolls, Chester 2/59 m.7. The grant was never enrolled in the English chancery, and in 1388 the Appellants alleged that de Vere had had himself made justice 'sanz commission du Roi ou autre garant suffisant usuele', and that he had used the power he had irregularly acquired to raise an army (*Rot. Parl.* Vol. III, p. 232).
[7] *CPR* 1385–9, p. 357.

In the 1380s, therefore, Richard built up the chamber into the centre of a network of royal power and influence. Like all political organizations, however the more money it had at its disposal, the more effective it was likely to be. Although neither Richard nor Burley intended the chamber to be a financial department rivalling the Exchequer, there is some evidence that they tried to make the chamber financially independent of the exchequer and even to give it a permanent income from landed property. Such a policy, of course, required several years to come to fruition, and the activities of the chamber were halted by the Appellants in 1388. Evidence shows little more than tentative moves towards asserting the independence of the chamber, and it is possible only to guess at what the outcome might have been if Richard had had a longer period in which to develop this aspect of household government.

Between 1377 and 1380 the chamber had only had a small income, and it was of little importance politically. But in 1380, as the king approached adulthood, an allowance of £1500 a year was restored to it, payable from the customs in London, Hull, and Boston[1] where it would compete, it is worth noting, with the Earl of Buckingham for the available money. The income was not, however, to be paid by the exchequer, but was to go directly into the chamber; Burley's receipts were to be sufficient warrant for the collectors when they accounted at the exchequer.[2] This was a departure from previous practice. In Edward III's reign the allowance had been paid into the chamber by the exchequer, and the receivers had accounted there, whereas now they were exempted. Perhaps Burley was trying to free the chamber from its financial subordination to the exchequer, but the exchequer seems to have resisted his efforts. By the Michaelmas term of 1382-3, the chamber's income was once again paid through the exchequer and the receivers accounted there, though at the same time the allowance was increased to £2000 a year.[3]

An allowance of £2000 a year, however, was less than half the annual sum which Edward III's chamber had had at its disposal, and by 1384 it had clearly become insufficient. The king therefore sought to augment its income from other sources. On the 20th of December 1384, Nicholas Brembre, the Mayor of London, paid £993-4-2 into the chamber 'for the king's secret business'.[4] and on the 1st of January

---

[1] *ibid.* 1377-81, p. 490.   [2] *CFR* 1377-83, p. 203.
[3] PRO Exchequer Issue Rolls E.403/493 m.9.
[4] *ibid.* E.403/505 m.16.

1385, £1000 was paid in at the king's order from the wool custom of London 'for certain secret and necessary expenses incurred by the chamber for the honour and benefit of the king and his kingdom'.[1] Next April the king ordered Brembre and others to pay 1000 marks which they owed at the exchequer into the chamber instead.[2] At the same time, the king earmarked the issues of certain lands for the chamber, the first time this had been done since the abolition of the chamber estate more than thirty years earlier. When he confiscated Sir John Holland's lands in 1385 to punish him for the murder of Sir Ralph Stafford, he ordered their issues to be assigned for the expenses of the chamber. The escheators were instructed by signet letter to seize the lands into the king's hands and to answer in the chamber for their issues and profits.[3] Richard soon changed his mind and gave Holland his lands back, but it is the intention which is important. The following September, when the See of Bath and Wells fell vacant, the king (again by signet letter) ordered the keepers of the temporalities to pay their render into the chamber instead of into the exchequer.[4]

Even this additional income, however, did not suffice to meet the king's needs, and it is probable that the 'ancient debts' amounting to £3171–0–3 which the chamber discharged with the aid of exchequer grants in the less stringent financial circumstances of 1392–3 were incurred at this time.[5] So to increase the chamber's regular income, and perhaps to check its increasing indebtedness, the king arranged in the Easter term of 1386 for the allowance to be increased to £4000 a year, to be paid by the exchequer from the customs and subsidy in London, Hull, Boston, and elsewhere.[6] But this arrangement was never carried out in full. Several small sums were paid into the chamber from October 1386 onwards, all described as part of a greater sum to be paid from the customs and subsidy, but the full amount was never paid.[7] This is no doubt explained by the change of treasurer which took place in the Wonderful Parliament of October 1386. John Fordham, who had held office for ten months, was required to resign,[8] and it became the policy of the new treasurer (the Bishop of Hereford) and his colleagues on the newly established commission to cut the allowance down to its old figure of £2000 at most, and to

[1] PRO Exchequer Issue Rolls E.403/505 m.19.
[2] *ibid.* E.403/508 m.2.   [3] *CFR* 1383–91, p. 123.
[4] *CCR* 1385–9, p. 189.
[5] PRO Exchequer Issue Rolls E. 403/538 m.4.
[6] *ibid.* E.403/512 m.7.   [7] *ibid.* E.403/512, 515, 517 *passim*.
[8] See p. 105 below.

restrict the king's freedom of action by paying it over in small instal-ments.[1] From 1384 to 1386 it had been common for as much as £1000 or 1000 marks to be paid in at one time, but after the Wonderful Parliament no more than 500 marks was ever paid in at any one time, and many of the instalments were no more than £200.

On the financial side, the history of the chamber in this period is one of tentative development rather than achievement. Its real im-portance lies in the political influence of its knights and chief officials, the king's most trusted servants and the recipients of extensive favour and patronage. On the secretarial side, however, the development of the household was firmer and more effective. The growth in the importance and independence of the Privy Seal in the fourteenth century had made it necessary to find another means for the direct exercise of the king's personal authority and to evolve another seal to authenticate his private correspondence. A secret seal which is clearly different from the Privy Seal and which fulfilled this need first appears in the reign of Edward II, and it was used especially in business relating to the chamber. Indeed, from at least the time of the Walton Ordin-ances of 1338, it seems likely that the receiver of the chamber had custody of the secret seal.[2] Early in Richard's reign, when the chamber organization was of little political or financial importance, the con-nection between the chamber and the king's personal seal (generally known as the signet) was broken, and its keeper (now regularly called secretary), was simply one of the king's clerks, Robert Braybrook, a kinsman of Princess Joan and subsequently chancellor and Bishop of London. Braybrook was in office as secretary by August 1377, and he held his post until the 16th of May 1381, when he became chan-cellor.[3] In these years the scope of royal administrative activity was very limited, and under Braybrook the signet was restricted to its traditional function of authenticating the king's private correspondence.

In the autumn of 1382, however, the connection between the signet and the chamber was revived when John Bacon, who had been appointed secretary in the spring, took office as receiver of the chamber in succession to Sir Richard Abberbury.[4] Under Bacon's secretaryship the scope of the signet gradually widened. From time to time signet

---

[1] PRO Exchequer Issue Rolls E.403/517.
[2] Tout, *Chapters* Vol. V, p. 179; J. Otway-Ruthven, *The King's Secretary and the Signet Office in the Fifteenth Century* (Cambridge 1939) pp. 19–20.
[3] Tout, *Chapters* Vol. V, p. 211; J. Otway-Ruthven, *The King's Secretary* p. 61.
[4] Tout, *Chapters* Vol. IV, pp. 334–5. There is no record of his appointment, but very little doubt that he acted in this capacity.

letters were sent directly to the chancellor, an abridgement of the normal routine whereby the signet moved the Privy Seal and the chancellor then acted on instructions from the Privy Seal office.[1] The signet was used, too, to authorize public as well as personal business of the king; the writs for the parliament of May 1382 had been issued under its authority, and it was occasionally used to authorize grants to members of the household.[2] But the signet was still a long way from rivalling the Privy Seal as the mainspring of the administration, and there is no sign yet of an organized signet office.

In January 1385, however, Bacon was replaced as secretary by Richard Medford,[3] and under him the clerks of the king's chapel were built up into an organized secretariat which became the special instrument of Richard's personal power, and which could be used to penetrate every branch of government. The personal connection between the signet and the chamber was broken, and the chapel royal became the centre of the secretarial side of the royal household. The clerks of the chapel royal had been organized as a society, under a dean, by the reign of Henry III,[4] and the dean was subject only to the king or the chamberlain. The functions of the chapel royal in the thirteenth and early fourteenth centuries appear to have been 'wholly ecclesiastical and liturgical in character . . . the institution was seemingly geared solely to serving the religious needs of the king, queen, and their immediate entourage'.[5] In this they contrasted with chapels royal on the continent, which early on developed some political and administrative importance. In or about 1317, however, Edward II established at Cambridge a society of king's scholars which later developed into King's Hall, and the purpose of the foundation was to provide for the education of clerks of the chapel royal. Seen in the context of Edward II's development of the household agencies of government, it seems clear that the king's object was to increase the number of educated household clerks at his disposal and thus to reinforce the power of the crown.[6] The connection between the chapel royal and King's Hall remained close throughout Edward III's

---

[1] *CPR* 1381–5 *passim*.
[2] PRO Chancery Warrants C.81/1339/42, 43, 46.
[3] Tout, *Chapters* Vol. V, p. 216.
[4] W. Ullmann, ed., *Liber Regie Capelle* (London, for the Henry Bradshaw Society, 1961) p. 3.
[5] A. B. Cobban, *The King's Hall in the University of Cambridge in the Later Middle Ages* (Cambridge 1969) p. 19.
[6] *ibid.* pp. 22–4.

reign, but it was Richard who appreciated the potential of the supply of trained clerks in his household and organized a group of them as clerks of the signet office.[1]

Richard Medford, who became secretary in 1385, had been a fellow of King's Hall from 1352 to 1378, and had become a king's clerk while still a fellow in 1375.[2] Nicholas Slake, the dean of the chapel royal, was also a clerk in the signet office, as were two other clerks of the chapel, Richard Clifford and Robert Brandon. Brandon had probably been educated at King's Hall, but nothing is known of the background of Slake or Clifford.[3] Another clerk in the signet office, John Lincoln of Grimsby, may have been a clerk of the chapel as well, but apart from the fact that he had taken a degree in canon law by 1390 little is known of his background.[4] During Medford's secretaryship, the signet became the most potent instrument of Richard's personal power. From January 1385 to January 1386 there survive nearly three hundred signet letters sent direct to the chancellor; by the autumn of 1385 as many grants are warranted by the signet as by all other authorities combined; and by the summer of 1386 the signet had become the most common means of moving the great seal. Between January and October 1386 more than two hundred and fifty letters patent were warranted by signet letter.[5] Orders which affected the chamber and its knights and officials were, as might be expected, an important area of signet business. In April 1385 the king sent a signet letter to the treasurer ordering him to pay 1000 marks into the chamber, despite the provision of the Ordinances of Walton that the great and Privy Seals were the only instruments competent to warrant issues from the exchequer. The treasurer did not demur.[6] Several grants to Burley, the under-chamberlain, were authorized under the signet,[7] and in September 1385 it was used to authorize the appointment of a chamber knight, Sir John Salesbury, as sheriff of Wiltshire for life.[8] The signet was also used, however, to authorize grants to many individuals who

[1] The first reference to a signet office is in June 1385 (PRO Exchequer Issue Rolls E.403/508 m.14).

[2] A. B. Emden, *A Biographical Register of the University of Cambridge* (Cambridge 1963) pp. 398–9.   [3] Favent p. 13; A.B. Emden, *Biographical Register* p. 88.

[4] PRO Exchequer KR Memoranda Rolls E.159/163 brevia baronibus 10 RII m. 20d.

[5] These figures are based on an analysis of the Close, Fine, Gascon, Patent and Treaty Rolls.

[6] PRO Exchequer Warrants for Issues E.404/14/91 no. 21.

[7] E.g. *CPR* 1381–5, pp. 366–7; PRO Chancery Warrants C.81/1350/23.

[8] *CFR* 1383–91, p. 101.

had no connection whatever with the chamber; it became, in fact, the administrative means whereby Richard's lavish patronage was dispensed. The secretary also acted personally as an intermediary between the king and the chancellor. In June 1386 a bill containing the names of certain persons to be arrested was 'submitted to the chancellor at Westminster in full council on the king's behalf on the 5th of June by Mr Medford, secretary, and John Beauchamp, keeper of the king's jewels', and Beauchamp and Medford had the king's authority to order the chancellor to give effect to the bill.[1] On other occasions Simon Burley was the intermediary between the king and the officers of state, and on several occasions in these years Burley was responsible for considering petitions that were sent to the king.[2] In all probability, the chamber officials and the staff of the signet office worked closely together in handling the administrative business that came before the household and in communicating with the council and the chief officers of state.

Medford received due reward for his service to the king. Only a month or two after he became secretary, Richard wrote to the seneschal of Aquitaine inquiring how many vacant benefices there were in the duchy, and especially in Bordeaux Cathedral, for he wished to confer the best of them on Medford and the three next best on Slake, Lincoln, and Brandon. The seneschal replied that no benefices were vacant at the moment, so Richard ordered that Medford should be collated to the best of them as soon as it became available.[3] In November the same year the king appointed him Dean of St Martin's le Grand by signet letter, and he later obtained the archdeaconry of Norfolk and numerous prebends.[4] Richard finally tried to procure a bishopric for him. When Bishop Harewell of Bath died in July 1386 Richard sent a signet letter to the chapter, recommending Medford's election, and assuring them of his favour if they agreed to accept his nominee;[5] he wrote to the pope signifying his consent to Medford's election,[6] and he sent one of his clerks, Richard Ronhale, to Rome to sue for confirmation of Medford's election.[7] But Richard was un-

---

[1] PRO Chancery Warrants C.81/1394/88; *CPR* 1385-9, p. 179.
[2] PRO Ancient Petitions SC.8/236/11787A, 11788.
[3] PRO Gascon Rolls C.61/98 m.1.
[4] *CPR* 1381-5, p. 365; Edinburgh University Library Ms. 183 f. 89ᵛ.
[5] *Historical Manuscripts Commission Reports* Dean and Chapter of Wells, I, p. 298.
[6] *CPR* 1385-9, p. 207.
[7] PRO Exchequer KR Memoranda Rolls E.159/165 brevia baronibus Michaelmas 12 RII m. 55d.

successful; royal nomination and diplomacy at the curia were of no avail against the canonical election and papal provision of the keeper of the Privy Seal, Walter Skirlaw, who was consecrated in October 1386. Medford had to wait until 1390, and take part in another struggle, before he obtained a bishopric, that of Chichester.

The development of the signet office depended partly on the co-operation, or at least the acquiescence, of the chancellor and the keeper of the Privy Seal. In December 1381 Sir Richard Lescrope took office as chancellor, and his period in office coincides with a curtailment of royal administrative activity generally. In July 1382, however, Richard dismissed him as the result of a dispute over patronage,[1] and replaced him with the secretary, Robert Braybrook, who was unlikely to raise any objection to the use of the signet to move the great seal. Braybrook, however, found the burden of office too great, and petitioned for release, which was granted on the 10th of March 1383. His place was taken by Michael de la Pole, who remained in office until the Wonderful Parliament of 1386. Pole came from a family of wealthy Hull merchants, but he had little experience of the departments of government and, in the eyes of at least one hostile chronicler, he had no great social standing either,[2] even though he had reached the rank of banneret and the next stage in his promotion would be an earldom. He had served the Black Prince in France in 1359 and again in 1370; when the Prince's health failed, he sought service with Gaunt in 1371 and 1372, an attachment which determined his political stance in the Good Parliament. By 1379 he had become one of Gaunt's retainers.[3] In 1381 he had been placed in the household to supervise the king, and he took part in the negotiations for Richard's marriage. Both duties gave him an excellent opportunity to renew his contacts with men such as Burley who had also served the Black Prince. After 1381, Pole's ties with Gaunt loosened. The suggestion that he was a 'Lancastrian' has been decisively rebutted, and it has been rightly pointed out that he had a longer tradition of service to the Black Prince than to Gaunt.[4] Once at court, he naturally found a place alongside the other followers of the Black Prince who surrounded Richard, and sympathized with their political and administrative activities. It is most unlikely that he raised any objection to the use of the signet letter as a warrant

[1] See pp. 132–3 below.
[2] *Walsingham, HA* Vol. II, p. 141.
[3] *John of Gaunt's Register 1379–1383* ed. E. C. Lodge and R. Somerville (London, Camden Third Series LVI, 1937) I, p. 7.
[4] R. H. Jones, *The Royal Policy of Richard II* (Oxford 1968) p. 188.

for the great seal. Nor did the keeper of the Privy Seal, Walter Skirlaw, offer any opposition. He was often abroad on diplomatic missions, an added reason perhaps for the development of the signet in these years, but until a certain coolness developed between him and the court over Richard's attempt to procure the bishopric of Bath for Medford in 1386, he appears to have been a compliant official.

The new administration which came to power in the October parliament of 1386, however, refused to countenance Richard's administrative methods. The new treasurer, as has already been seen, refused to implement the increase in the chamber allowance ordered by Richard some months earlier. The new chancellor, Thomas Arundel Bishop of Ely, refused to accept the signet as sufficient warrant for the great seal. The sending of signet letters direct to the chancellor stopped abruptly on the 18th of October, six days before Pole was dismissed from the chancery, and during the whole time that Bishop Arundel held office no letters patent were warranted by signet letter.[1] The king was not deprived of the use of the signet, however, and he continued to use it throughout 1387 to authenticate his private correspondence and to send instructions to officials such as the chamberlain of Chester and the chief justices of both benches who still recognized its authority.[2] Nevertheless, the secretary and his clerks could not hope to escape trouble when the Appellants came to power at the beginning of 1388. Medford, Slake, Clifford, and John Lincoln of Grimsby were all arrested,[3] but they were not treated with the savagery shown towards the chamber knights. No formal charges were brought against them, and they were released after the conclusion of the Merciless Parliament.[4] All of them continued their careers in royal service in the second half of the reign.

Thus Richard's methods of government were suppressed by his opponents in 1386 and the most important agents and beneficiaries of his household government were dealt with by the Lords Appellant

---

[1] The last signet letter which moved the great seal directly in 1386 is to be found in PRO Chancery Warrants C.81/1353.
[2] Edinburgh University Library Ms. 183 f.97ᵛ; PRO Exchequer Issue Rolls E.403/517 mm.2, 4; PRO Chester Recognizance Rolls, Chester 2/59 *passim*; PRO Common Law Writs and Returns KB 145/10/1, 2, listed in *Select Cases in the Court of King's Bench* Vol. VII, ed. G. O. Sayles, Selden Society LXXXVIII (London 1971) pp. xxv–xxvi.
[3] Favent p. 13; *Knighton* Vol. II, pp. 256–7.
[4] *CCR* 1385–9, p. 414.

in 1388. The king's approach to government in the 1380s, and especially in 1385 and 1386, is notable for its resemblance to the methods adopted by Edward II in the last decade of his reign. The resemblance was in all probability intentional. Both Richard and his baronial opponents were well versed in and highly conscious of the English political past, and political arguments were frequently conducted with reference to past political events. Richard's attitude to kingship in its governmental aspect bears many marks of reflection upon the reign of Edward II—his use of the chamber, its close connection with the secret seal, and his realization of the ability and administrative potential of the clerks of the chapel royal. Like his great-grandfather, in fact, he appreciated the strength inherent in the royal household and the governmental power that could be wielded through its offices. The self-consciousness of Richard's return to some of the methods of Edward II is complemented by his efforts to ensure that the abbey of Gloucester, where Edward lay buried, properly observed his anniversaries, and in the 1390s, by his efforts to get him canonized.[1] Richard was not alone in his awareness of the precedents of his great-grandfather's reign; a number of the Commons' petitions in the parliament of October 1377 bear a remarkable resemblance to the Ordinances of 1311,[2] and in the Wonderful Parliament of 1386 Gloucester and Bishop Arundel brought Richard to heel by reminding him of Edward's deposition.[3] In both the methods of government and the rhetoric of political argument the first half of Richard's reign was characterized by a recalling of the events of Edward II's reign. Far from being innovatory or influenced by continental ideas or political practice,[4] the methods and arguments both of the king and of his baronial opponents had their roots in the English political past.

As in Edward II's reign, however, aristocratic hostility was provoked not only by the methods, which denied some nobles the place in government they thought rightfully theirs, but also by the consequences, domestic and foreign, of the king's government. For Richard, like Edward, rewarded his closest friends and supporters with lavish grants of lands, offices, and titles. In effect, Richard attempted to create a group of nobles bound to the crown by common interests, by the

[1] *CPR* 1381-5, p. 273; F. Devon, *Issues of the Exchequer* (London 1837) pp. 248, 264.
[2] J. G. Edwards, 'Some Common Petitions in Richard II's First Parliament', *BIHR* XXVI (1953) pp. 200–13.
[3] *Knighton* Vol. II, p. 219.
[4] Cf. R. H. Jones, *Royal Policy* pp. 61–3.

loyalty created by extensive endowments, and by the grant of titles according to principles which differed sharply from those which had hitherto determined a noble's place in the *cursus honorum*. Such men as Gloucester and Arundel opposed Richard's policies partly because they considered that they, rather than the household officials, should have the ear of the king; partly because they directly conflicted with their own interests as landowners and office holders; partly because the policies represented an affront to their sense of social status; and partly because they threatened their influence with their clients and dependants. A good lord was expected to obtain favours at court for his clients, to sponsor petitions, and to 'provide connections with the institutional order'.[1] He had to act as a link between the client and the central institutions which could provide what the client wanted, and to fulfil such a function it was vital for the lord to have personal access to the king or influence with the great officers of state. The possibility that disappointed clients might look to another lord provided a strong incentive for a magnate to oppose men who appeared to be monopolizing the king too completely. He had to safeguard not only his own interests but also the interests of all those who looked to him to provide good lordship.

Lords opposed the king in part, therefore, because of the problems which his patronage created for them. The Commons in parliament also opposed the direction of royal patronage in the 1380s, but their concern was financial rather than personal. The crown's financial difficulties led to pressure from the Commons to retain in the king's hand or farm for the greatest possible amount property that came to the crown from various incidental sources—not only feudal escheats and wardships, but also such windfalls as the alien priories, lands held by tenants with a life interest only, or the lands of outlaws, felons, and lunatics. It was, however, extremely difficult for the crown to draw the line between the legitimate use of resources to endow and to reward, and the profligate distribution of lands to courtiers and favourites; the distinction was a rhetorical one, and depended upon the point of view of the persons making it. In 1382, for example, an estate valued at £4500 had to be settled upon the queen;[2] provision had to be made for the king's younger half-brother, John Holland; and it was almost unimaginable, in any reign except perhaps that of Edward I, that an

---

[1] J. A. Tuck, 'Richard II's System of Patronage', in *The Reign of Richard II* ed. F. R. H. du Boulay and Caroline M. Barron (London 1971) pp. 15–16.
[2] *CPR* 1381–5, pp. 125–7.

inheritance as large as the Ufford earldom of Suffolk, which escheated
to the crown in 1382, could remain permanently annexed to the
crown. On the other hand, there is some evidence that the king did
not conserve his resources as carefully as he might. The alien priories
were granted out in the 1380s to lay farmers, many of whom were
members of the royal household, and recently attention has been drawn
to the dismemberment of the estates of the Duchy of Cornwall, in
contravention of the great charter of the duchy granted by Edward III
in 1337.[1] In 1382 two manors, Climsland and Liskeard, were granted
to the queen, and in 1385, when Princess Joan died, the duchy manors
which she had held in dower were granted to members of the household and the royal family. Furthermore, the duchy estate was not
managed with any great efficiency during Richard's reign,[2] and
Richard seems to have been more interested in the duchy's military
potential than in its profitability. Indeed, in general it seems possible
that Richard valued his private estates as military recruiting grounds
and as lands where taxes could be levied without the need to secure
parliamentary grants rather than as property from which a steady
income could be obtained. It is not surprising that the Commons resented paying taxes while the king appeared to waste his own resources,
and both in 1386 and 1388 the nobility found little difficulty in enlisting
the Commons' sympathy by attacking the king for profligacy and
over-generosity towards his favourites.

The four greatest beneficiaries of Richard's favour in the 1380s
were the chancellor, Michael de la Pole; the chamberlain, Robert de
Vere; the under-chamberlain, Simon Burley; and John Beauchamp of
Holt, the receiver of the chamber from 1385 to 1387. Of the four, only
de Vere, Earl of Oxford, possessed a substantial inheritance before he
rose in favour at court. Burley was virtually landless when he entered
the Black Prince's service; Beauchamp had some property in Worcestershire, and Pole land in Yorkshire. Yet by 1386 Pole and de Vere
had become two of the greatest landowners in the country, and Burley
and Beauchamp had substantially increased their possessions and
influence. All four received grants in areas which the great magnates
considered their spheres of influence, and this must have contributed
substantially to the growth of hostility to the king.

The possessions of the family of Beauchamp of Holt (a cadet branch

---

[1] J. Hatcher, *Rural Economy and Society in the Duchy of Cornwall 1300–1500* (Cambridge 1970) pp. 6–7, 137–8.
[2] *ibid.* pp. 138, 145.

of the Earl of Warwick's family) lay chiefly in Worcestershire, and most of the property the king granted him was in that county. In 1384 he received the custody of the lands of the heir of Sir John Talbot of Richard's Castle, with the special concession that he and the chaplain with whom he was associated should not be deprived of the custody, 'even though another person shall be willing to give more for the same'.[1] Later in the same year he secured the reversion of the manor of Kidderminster, and the lands of the alien priories of Astley and Deerhurst:[2] a new power was beginning to rise within the sphere of influence of the Earl of Warwick. He also received certain lands outside Worcestershire. In 1383 the king granted him the manor of Whitfield in the Isle of Wight, which had reverted to the crown in 1332 and remained crown property, subject to various leases, until the seventeenth century[3]—an instance of that alienation of royal property which, the Appellants claimed in 1388, was impoverishing the kingdom. The king also granted Beauchamp land in Middlesex which had been forfeited by John Northampton and the commotes of Dynllaen and Cwmwdmaer in Caernarvonshire with all the revenues from them.[4] These grants too could be held to represent the alienation of resources which the king ought to have kept in his own hands. In North Wales Beauchamp was entrusted with important offices, and his tenure from 1370 to 1387 of the post of constable of Bridgnorth Castle gave him a footing within the sphere of influence of the Earl of Arundel.[5]

Simon Burley was even more lavishly endowed than John Beauchamp of Holt. Burley had begun accumulating possessions before the death of Edward III, and in 1377 already held the castle and lordship of Llanstephan and the castle of Carmarthen.[6] In the 1380s he rapidly added to his property. In 1382 he acquired Newcastle Emlyn, and sometime before 1384 Robert de Vere granted him the castle and lordship of Lyonshall in Herefordshire.[7] In 1385 the king granted him the manor of Castlefrome, also in Herefordshire, which had been forfeited by Elizabeth Clodeshale because she 'covined with others to murder Thomas Yeduyn, king's esquire, and absconded'.[8] From 1382 to 1385,

[1] *CFR* 1383–91, p. 41.
[2] *CPR* 1381–5, p. 461; 1385–9, pp. 153, 348.
[3] *CPR* 1381–5, p. 318; *Rot. Parl.* Vol. III, p. 230; *VCH* Hampshire Vol. V, p. 159.
[4] *CPR* 1381–5, p. 493; 1385–9, p. 25.
[5] *CPR* 1367–70, p. 341; 1385–9, p. 292.
[6] *CPR* 1377–81, pp. 223, 262.
[7] *CPR* 1381–5, pp. 107, 447.
[8] *CPR* 1285–9, p. 45.

as Justice of South Wales, he possessed the administrative complement to his territorial power, but in 1385 he surrendered the office. Nearer London, however, he went on increasing his possessions and influence. In 1378 he became constable of Windsor Castle; in 1382 Robert Goshalm of Essex granted him lands and rents in Gravesend, Milton, Northfleet, and Swanscombe.[1] In 1383, however, it became clear that there was some policy behind his acquisition of property in Kent. In that year the king granted him a group of manors in the northwest of the country which had been the property of Juliana de Leybourne, a substantial heiress in her own right and widow of William de Clinton Earl of Huntingdon who had died in 1354. Edward III had acquired these manors from the Countess Juliana, intending to use them as the endowment for three religious houses, the house of Friars Preachers at King's Langley, the abbey of St Mary Graces in London, and the college of St Stephen at Westminster. In fulfilment of Edward's intentions, his executors, chief among whom was John of Gaunt, had granted the lands in mortmain to the religious houses, but Richard countermanded the grant. The following year the king granted Burley the castle and lordship of Leybourne, which Edward III had also acquired from Julian de Leybourne and which his executors had alienated for the same purpose.[2] Richard's excuse was that the alienation greatly weakened the defences of Kent, but his intention appears to have been to recreate the Leybourne inheritance for Burley's benefit, and perhaps eventually to confer upon him the earldom of Huntingdon, a title which had been borne by Guichard d'Angle, Burley's predecessor as tutor to the king.

Such interference with the actions of Edward III's executors could not but make the nobility fearful of Richard's intentions towards landed property, for it amounted to the use of royal power to defeat the plain intentions of the late king and his executors. The security of landed property was a fundamental interest of the nobility, but lack of trust between Richard and his nobles on this vital issue was to grow during the reign until it proved fatal for Richard in 1399. Richard's interference with property in the 1380s was trivial by comparison with the heights it reached after 1397, but already one aspect

[1] *CPR* 1377–81, p. 257; 1381–5, p. 204.
[2] *CPR* 1381–5, pp. 305, 343, 367–8; 1385–9, p. 37; *Knighton* Vol. II, p. 205; *Royal Wills* ed. J. Nichols (London 1780) pp. 59–64; N. B. Lewis, 'Simon Burley and Baldwin of Raddington', *EHR* LII (1937) pp. 662–9; J. J. N. Palmer, 'The Parliament of 1385 and the Constitutional Crisis of 1386', *Speculum* XLVI (1971) p. 490.

of the attitude which was to precipitate his downfall had come into
sight. After the Merciless Parliament of 1388, the religious houses who
felt themselves wronged by Richard's actions, received the land that
had been earmarked for them.[1] Burley, however, was given office
as well as land in Kent. In 1384 he became constable of Dover Castle
and Warden of the Cinque Ports,[2] a position to which the nobility
had begun to aspire in the fourteenth century. In Edward III's reign
the Earls of Kent and March had at various times held it,[3] and Burley's
appointment probably made the nobility more than ever suspicious
of Richard's policy towards France. The growth of Burley's territorial
and administrative power in Kent perhaps also explains why Sir John
Cobham, a prominent Kentish landowner, sided with the Appellants
in the Merciless Parliament.[4] Burley's rise was remarkably rapid; the
chronicler Henry Knighton said that in the space of a few years he
increased his income from 20 marks a year to 2000 and the Kirkstall
chronicler said that 'no equal of his rank was more glorious in outward
apparel; he excelled all lords in the equipment of his horses and his
worldly show'.[5] Burley's ostentatious style of life probably aroused
the hostility of the Appellants only a little less readily than his accumu-
lation of property and office.

Michael de la Pole's unpopularity, however, arose as much from his
conduct of foreign policy and his disregard of another commission of
inquiry into royal finances (appointed in the October parliament of
1385)[6] as from the range and variety of gifts he received from his royal
master. Pole's most important acquisition was the title and much of
the inheritance of the last Ufford Earl of Suffolk. William Ufford,
second and last Earl of Suffolk of that line, died suddenly in September
1382 while leaving the chapter house of Westminster Abbey after a
meeting with the Commons. He was widely mourned, for he was a
well-liked and respected figure and, said Walsingham, 'throughout
his life he exuded amiability'.[7] He held his title and much of his inheritance in tail male, and since he died without issue of either sex,
his title and lands escheated to the crown. In his will, however, he

---

[1] *Rot. Parl.* Vol. III, p. 180; *CCR* 1385-9, pp. 530-1.
[2] *CPR* 1381-5, p. 366.
[3] K. M. E. Murray, *Constitutional History of the Cinque Ports* (Manchester 1935) p. 89.
[4] *Rot. Parl.* Vol. III, pp. 381-2. He was a member of the 1386 commission.
[5] *Knighton* Vol. II, p. 294; *Kirkstall Chronicle* p. 128.
[6] See pp. 99-100 below.
[7] *Walsingham, HA* Vol. II, pp. 48-9; Westminster p. 11.

named his nephew Robert de Willoughby as his heir, and he instructed his feoffees to enfeoff Willoughby with that part of his inheritance which was not held in tail male.[1] Pole seems to have had his eye on the escheated portion of the inheritance at once, for although the bulk of it was granted to the queen, he received the manors of Benhale and Dedham in fee simple in 1382.[2] The grant of Benhale was the subject of a suit in chancery by two of the Ufford feoffees, who claimed that Ufford had granted it to them, but, not surprisingly, their suit was dismissed and the property was confirmed to Pole.[3] Then, on the Scottish campaign in 1385, he was created Earl of Suffolk. To maintain his estate he received the bulk of the Ufford inheritance, and the reversion of the portion which Ufford's widow the Countess Isabella held in dower.[4] There was nothing at all irregular about Pole's acquisition of the Ufford lands; the grant of earldoms in tail male had been a regular practice in Edward III's reign, and the crown clearly had the right to dispose in whatever way it wished of lands and titles which reverted to it through the failure of lineal male heirs. Nor had Pole been chancellor when the dispute over one part of the inheritance was heard; but nevertheless some of the other nobles regarded Pole as a creature of the king, unworthy of the dignity of an earldom. When he was impeached in 1386, Sir Richard Lescrope, defending him, felt it necessary to rebut the suggestion that he had been 'raised from low estate to this honour of earl,' and to point out that he had possessed sufficient means to maintain his estate as banneret, the rank immediately below that of earl. He had been worthy of an earldom, Lescrope argued, and when he received it the king had endowed him with lands and rents sufficient to maintain that estate.[5] The nobles' objection was grounded in social and political prejudice, not fact, for Pole had been so well endowed that he was now a powerful neighbour of the Duke of Gloucester.

Gloucester, however, was probably even more unhappy about the rise of Robert de Vere, for of all the king's favourites he was the most lavishly rewarded. De Vere came of ancient lineage, for the first Earl of Oxford had received his title, and the hereditary chamberlainship, from the Empress Matilda. But by the beginning of the fourteenth

---

[1] G. A. Holmes, *The Estates of the Higher Nobility in Fourteenth Century England* (Cambridge 1957) p. 42; *CCR* 1377–81, p. 136; *CFR* 1377–83, pp. 287, 302.
[2] *CPR* 1381–5, pp. 123, 125–6, 156; *Rot. Parl.* Vol. III, pp. 216–17.
[3] *CPR* 1381–5, p. 317.
[4] *CPR* 1385–9, pp. 18, 24.
[5] *Rot. Parl.* Vol. III, pp. 216, 17.

century they had become 'the most insignificant of English earls. . . . Their only considerable estate was in north Essex. Castle Hedingham was their chief seat, and round it their chief manors were grouped.[1] During the fourteenth century the inheritance had grown a little, mainly as a consequence of the marriage of John, seventh earl, to Maud, daughter and co-heiress of Giles de Badlesmere. She brought with her a number of manors in Kent, Sussex, and the east midlands, but that so small an acquisition could be so important is a measure of the family's insignificance.[2] In 1377 the de Vere inheritance was smaller than that of any other titled family, and smaller than the inheritances of several families, mainly in the north, who had not attained the rank of earl. It cannot have been easy for the de Veres to maintain the style of life appropriate to their rank out of the revenues of so small an inheritance. Letters patent issued to Robert de Vere in 1383 acknowledged that he could not maintain his estate,[3] and it must have been with an eye to the possibilities of profit and advancement that his uncle, Aubrey de Vere, who eventually inherited the title himself, introduced Robert at court in the early years of the reign, when he was still under age.

Robert de Vere made a marriage which promised well: his bride was Philippa, daughter and heiress of Ingelram de Coucy Earl of Bedford and Isabella, Edward III's favourite daughter. But de Coucy renounced his allegiance in August 1377, and most of his inheritance was granted to a group of feoffees who were to make the revenues available to the Countess Isabella.[4] De Vere and his wife were granted the reversions of parts of the inheritance which had been granted out, but the future of the whole inheritance was uncertain, and de Vere can have had no clear territorial expectations from his marriage; from the point of view of his own advancement it was probably a mistake. This may have been one reason why he had no inhibitions about divorcing his wife in 1387 and marrying a Bohemian woman, Agnes Lancecrona, who had come over in the queen's retinue. The divorce gave great offence to the nobility, especially the Duke of Gloucester, who felt very strongly that his niece had been slighted and the royal family insulted.[5] The affair is a very powerful reason for the bitter animosity towards de Vere in 1387 and 1388.

[1] T. F. Tout, 'The Earldoms under Edward I', *TRHS* new series VIII (1894) p. 154.
[2] G. A. Holmes, *Estates of the Higher Nobility* pp. 29–32.
[3] *CPR 1381–5*, p. 177.   [4] *CPR 1377–81*, p. 174.
[5] *Walsingham, HA* Vol. II, pp. 160–61; Westminster p. 95.

De Vere did not have to wait long after his coming of age in 1382 for the king to bestow lavish endowments upon him. In July 1384 Richard removed George Felbrigg, one of the esquires of the chamber, from the keeping of the castle and town of Colchester and the hundred of Tendring, and granted them both to de Vere.[1] In the same month de Vere received one of the most important wardships to come on the market that year, that of the heir of Sir Thomas Roos of Helmsley,[2] and early in the following year he obtained the castle and lordship of Queenborough. The terms of this grant are extraordinary: de Vere was to hold the castle and lordship for the term of the lives of the king and himself. If he died first, it was to revert to the king, and if the king died first de Vere was to have it in tail male. The grant concluded: 'The curse of God and St Edward and the king on any who do or attempt aught against this grant!'[3] There could hardly be a better illustration of the closeness of the king's relationship with his favourite, a relationship which must have recalled that of Edward II and Gaveston. Furthermore, the implications for the defence of the kingdom of granting Queenborough, newly constructed in Edward III's reign and the key to the defence of the Thames,[4] to a favourite totally unversed in military matters could not have been lost on the nobility. Indeed, the concluding clause of the grant suggests that Richard himself was aware of this, and felt rather insecure in making it.

De Vere even profited at the expense of the king's half-brother, Sir John Holland. On the Scottish expedition in 1385, Holland murdered the heir of the Earl of Stafford in a brawl. His mother, Princess Joan, died shortly afterwards, and these two events led to his withdrawal from court. Enraged at the murder, Richard ordered his lands to be confiscated. His own property was soon returned to him, but the reversion of the lands of James Lord Audley, granted to him in 1384, had meanwhile been granted to de Vere, and there could be no question of persuading de Vere to give up so lucrative an acquisition. After de Vere's disgrace and exile, Holland successfully petitioned for the recovery of the reversion, alleging that the king, 'at the instigation of various persons ill-disposed to the said John who were about the king', had ordered him to surrender his patent.[5] His allegation was

---

[1] *CPR* 1381–5, pp. 440, 442.
[2] *ibid.* p. 442.   [3] *ibid.* p. 542.
[4] R. A. Brown, H. M. Colvin and A. J. Taylor, *The History of the King's Works* Vol. II (London 1963) pp. 793–804.
[5] *CPR* 1381–5, p. 515; 1385–9, p. 115; PRO Ancient Petitions SC.8/129/6431, the reply to which stresses that the matter is 'notorious'.

probably quite true, and Holland may well have sympathized with the Duke of Gloucester and his associates in 1387 and 1388. He received the earldom of Huntingdon during the Appellants' period of power, a title he may well have been reluctant to accept had he been at all close to Burley or the other courtiers. Although it has been suggested that the Appellants gave him the title in order to placate John of Gaunt,[1] with whom he was serving in Castile, the explanation may simply be that they wished to honour a member of the royal family who shared their view of the court.

De Vere's influence at court ensured benefits for his clients and dependants. His chamberlain, Sir John Lancaster, became sheriff of Wiltshire for life, and de Vere's own position as sheriff of Rutland meant that the post of deputy was open to another of his associates. In January 1385, John Routhe, one of his esquires, received the wardship of the lands in Sussex of William Lylle at the supplication of de Vere, and in the following year another of his connections, John Ripon, became Archdeacon of Wells, and subsequently acted as his emissary to the Curia when he petitioned the pope for a divorce. In July 1386, Martin Medritz, described as a servant of the Marquis of Dublin, was granted the farm of Ilchester, and such opportunities for advancement perhaps encouraged some to claim fraudulently that they were de Vere's servants. In April 1387 a pardon for murder was granted to John Malweden of Walden, described as 'servant, so he says, of our most dear cousin the Duke of Ireland'.[2] The king intervened on behalf of Aubrey de Vere in a dispute between his tenants and the tenants of the Earl of Derby, and since the king intervened in other legal cases involving members of his household, it is possible that de Vere and his followers benefited substantially in this way as well.[3] The favour and the ready access to the king which de Vere enjoyed had repercussions throughout society, and men would naturally seek to enter the following of a lord who enjoyed such a position at court. Equally, the threat to a lord's social position if he lacked access to the king was sufficient in itself to create hostility to the king and the court.

De Vere's own future, however, was to be determined not only by the king's affection for him but also by events in Ireland. Sir Philip Courtenay, the uncle of the Earl of Devon, had been appointed

---

[1] A. B. Steel, *Richard II* (Cambridge 1941) p. 163; Tout, *Chapters* Vol. III, p. 437.
[2] *CFR* 1383–91, p. 6; *CPR* 1381–5, p. 516; *ibid.* 1385–9 pp. 201, 246, 291; PRO Chancery Warrants C.81/494/4149, C.81/495/4250.
[3] PRO Duchy of Lancaster Accounts DL.28/1/1; *Select Cases in King's Bench* pp. xxv–xxvi.

lieutenant in Ireland in July 1383 after a distinguished military career, but his term of office was marred by ill-health and by deteriorating relations with the Dublin administration.[1] At a great council held at Dublin in October it was agreed to petition the king to come over in person 'for the rescue and salvation of his lordship of Ireland', or at least to send 'the greatest and most trustworthy English lord'. The Archbishop of Dublin and the Bishop of Ossory were chosen to go over to England and deliver the petition to the king.[2] At the same time in England, parliament was in session and on the 1st of December 1385, Richard conferred on de Vere the title of Marquis of Dublin, granting him the land and lordship of Ireland with all that pertained to it to hold for life, saving only liege homage and superior lordship.[3] In bestowing this title upon de Vere it is most unlikely that Richard knew nothing of the movement of opinion in Ireland.[4] Ministers in the Dublin government were constantly travelling to and fro between England and Ireland, and feeling against Courtenay had been growing for at least six months. The proposal to ask the king to send over one of his great magnates had been made unofficially in July,[5] and no doubt originated in the feeling that a member of one of the less prominent comital families with no interests in Ireland was an unsuitable choice as lieutenant. But the Irish can hardly have expected Richard to choose as his successor the young Earl of Oxford, whose family was if anything less distinguished than the Courtenays and whose rise was due entirely to royal favour. The family had liquidated its few Irish interests almost twenty years previously,[6] and Robert de Vere had no experience of administration and campaigning there, or indeed anywhere else.

De Vere's powers in Ireland were wider than those of any previous lieutenant there: writs ran in his name, and he was licensed to bear the arms of Ireland.[7] The proceeds from the Audley lands were to be used to pay for his campaign,[8] and so too was the ransom of John of Blois, claimant to the Duchy of Brittany.[9] His acquisition of the

---

[1] J. A. Tuck, 'Anglo-Irish Relations 1382–1393', *Proceedings of the Royal Irish Academy* LXIX (1970) pp. 20–23.
[2] *Early Statutes of Ireland*, ed. H. F. Berry (Dublin 1907) pp. 484–6.
[3] *Rot. Parl.* Vol. III, pp. 209–10; *RDP* Vol. V, pp. 78–9.
[4] The Archbishop of Dublin did not arrive in England until January 1387, but other envoys may have preceded him (PRO (Dublin) Ferguson Collectanea II, p. 85). [5] *CCPRI* p. 123.
[6] *Calendar of Ormond Deeds* II 1350–1413 ed. E. Curtis, Irish Manuscripts Commission (Dublin 1934) pp. 101, 102.
[7] *CCPRI* p. 130; *CPR* 1385–9, p. 78.
[8] *CPR* 1385–9, p. 115. [9] *ibid.* p. 123.

ransom was to be one of the charges against him in the Appeal of Treason in 1388, partly no doubt because England gained no political advantage from setting him at liberty; it was simply a money-making exercise.[1] Walsingham stated that the grant of the ransom was conditional upon de Vere's leaving for Ireland by Easter 1387, but although some preparations were made for his departure he never went and probably never intended to go.[2] He preferred to stay in England and enjoy the profits of the lands granted to him to finance his Irish campaigns. His council in England concerned itself with Irish affairs, however, and made at least one appointment, that of Richard White as justiciar.[3] On the 20th of March 1386 de Vere appointed Sir John Stanley his lieutenant in Ireland, and it was Stanley who led the expedition which eventually set out in August 1387.[4]

Meanwhile, however, in October 1386, Richard enlarged his favourite's power in Ireland still further by creating him Duke of Ireland and granting him full palatine powers.[5] He also, realistically, dropped the obligation imposed on de Vere in his previous patent to contribute the surplus revenues of Ireland to the English exchequer after the reconquest of the colony.[6] The title can have made little difference in practice to de Vere's authority in Ireland, and its purpose was almost certainly to give him equality in status and palatine powers with John of Gaunt. There is evidence that de Vere was seeking to undermine Gaunt's influence at court in 1385[7], and with Gaunt now out of the country the moment was right to elevate de Vere. The palatine duchy of Ireland could never provide de Vere with a really effective power base, for the task of subduing the country was beyond him, and the grant of the title was a shrewd means of conferring on de Vere the shadow and trappings of power without its substance. But the king's intentions in Ireland alarmed the nobility. They seem to have been genuinely apprehensive of the growth of his power there and in North Wales and Cheshire.[8] The Appellants alleged in 1388 that Richard had written to the pope to obtain his consent to the conferring of the crown of Ireland upon de Vere,[9] but this is almost

---

[1] M. C. E. Jones, 'The Ransom of Jean de Bretagne, Count of Penthievre', *BIHR* XLV (1972) pp. 7-26; J. J. N. Palmer, *England, France and Christendom* pp. 63-4; *Rot Parl.* Vol. III, p. 232.
[2] *Walsingham, HA* Vol. II, pp. 150-1.
[3] NLI, Harris Mss. Vol. IV, f. 31.
[4] PRO Chancery Miscellanea C.47/10/24; *CPR* 1385-9, p. 131.
[5] *RDP* Vol. V, pp. 79-80.
[6] *ibid.*
[7] See pp. 142-3 below.
[8] *Rot. Parl.* Vol. III, p. 231.
[9] *ibid.*

certainly untrue. De Vere's position was king-like, and his diplomatic style had an arrogant vice-regal ring to it,[1] but there is no evidence whatsoever that Richard intended to make him king. Almost sixty years earlier, in the 1320s, the Earl of Desmond, who was then in revolt against Edward II, was accused of trying to gain control of Ireland and make himself king, but in both cases the charges appear to have been baseless.[2] The reasons for the magnates' fears are difficult to establish. They may have over-estimated the ease with which English authority could be re-established in Ireland, and they may have heard of the formidable military reputation of the gallowglasses, the mercenary soldiers from the western highlands and islands of Scotland who served the native Irish chiefs. But in reality there was no possibility either that de Vere would subdue the country and turn it into a military recruiting ground, or that he would persuade the chiefs to put their military resources at his disposal. Nonetheless, these fears, however irrational, of a royalist army recruited from outside the realm remained strong, and were given justification in 1397 when Richard recruited his Cheshire army.

Richard's liberality towards his favourites extended not only to grants of lands and offices, but also to the bestowal of titles of nobility, and these too were important in influencing political attitudes in the first ten years of Richard's reign. Status was treated realistically in the fourteenth century. It was supposed to correspond to wealth and power, and a magnate was not usually elevated to an earldom or a dukedom unless he possessed or was being granted an inheritance sufficient to maintain his rank. By the reign of Edward III it was generally accepted that titles should have a territorial basis, and it was commonly assumed that an income in land of £1000 a year was necessary to maintain the estate of earl.[3] The rank of duke was even more jealously guarded, and before 1337 only the king as Duke of Aquitaine had borne the title. In that year Edward III conferred on the Black Prince the dukedom of Cornwall, and later in the reign Henry of Grosmont was created Duke of Lancaster. Apart from this, dukedoms in Edward's reign were

[1] PRO Exchequer LTR Memoranda Rolls E.368/159 presentationes etc. Michaelmas 10 RII m. 2: two letters which end with the date 'le vint et primer iour doctobre lan du regne nostre seigneur le Roy . . . disme et de nostre duchee primer'.
[2] G. O. Sayles, 'The Rebellious First Earl of Desmond', in *Medieval Studies Presented to Aubrey Gwynn* (Dublin 1961) pp. 203–27.
[3] L. O. Pike, *Constitutional History of the House of Lords* (London 1894) pp. 62–75; K. B. McFarlane, 'The English Nobility in the Later Middle Ages', *12th International Congress of Historical Sciences* (1965) pp. 337–45.

confined to members of the royal family; on receiving the Lancastrian inheritance, John of Gaunt became Duke of Lancaster, and his brother Lionel was created Duke of Clarence.

Richard's attitude towards nobility, however, contrasted sharply with that of Edward III. His exclusion of them from power in the 1380s is a sufficiently clear indication that he rejected Edward III's belief that the nobility had a natural right to participate in government. In the patents of creation of the Earl of Suffolk and the Dukes of York and Gloucester in 1385, Richard described the nobility as gems in the royal diadem, as luminaries casting their light upon the king. In Pole's patent, the image was expressed more precisely. 'We believe,' Richard stated, 'that the more we bestow honours on wise and honourable men, the more our crown is adorned with gems and precious stones.'[1] The aristocracy, in Richard's view, existed to shed lustre on the crown, and the practical implication of this view is that the titled nobility do not need any independent territorial standing or any great wealth or military reputation to justify their ennoblement: title depended upon royal favour, and upon the particular noble's relationship with the crown.

Richard's views can be seen in practice in the 1380s. When the Earl of Buckingham was created Duke of Gloucester in 1385, he was granted £1000 a year to maintain his estate. In significant contrast to the custom of Edward III's reign, this income was not given in the form of landed property but as an annuity assigned upon the customs.[2] Gloucester thus lacked the independent landed base to which as a duke he thought he was entitled, and instead had a much more precariously based income, over which the king had extensive control. Gloucester's lack of a proper endowment probably ranks high amongst his motives for opposition to the king in 1386 and 1388,[3] and Richard's treatment of him seemed to undermine the relationship between land and status which had become so firmly established in Edward III's reign.

Richard's ennoblement of John Beauchamp of Holt, one of his chamber knights, in 1387 must have seemed an even more decisive blow against the traditional view of status, for Beauchamp had a small inheritance in the west midlands, augmented in small ways by royal grant. Yet in 1387 the king conferred on him by letters patent the title

[1] *RDP* Vol. V, pp. 62, 64-5.
[2] *ibid.* pp. 65-6; *CPR* 1385-9, pp. 55, 209.
[3] A. Goodman, *The Loyal Conspiracy* (London 1971) pp. 91-2.

of Baron Kidderminster.[1] This was the first time a barony had been conferred in such a way, and has been rightly described as 'the first undoubted instance of a barony conferred as a dignity apart from any considerations relating to the tenure of land'.[2] His title was conferred as a personal honour, and was wholly inconsistent with the idea that the peers of the realm were distinguished from other groups by the possession of great estates. The Lords Appellant appear never to have recognized his title. He was summoned by personal writ to the Merciless Parliament in 1388 as John Beauchamp of Kidderminster, but throughout its proceedings he was referred to simply as John Beauchamp, knight.[3]

In other ways too Richard broke with precedent. In 1385, by conferring a marquisate (a hitherto unknown title) on de Vere, he elaborated the *cursus honorum* for the benefit of one who had, in the eyes of the other magnates at least, little enough claim to be an earl, let alone to take precedence over all the earls by virtue of his new title. When he took his place publicly in parliament between the dukes and earls, the chronicler Walsingham notes that the other magnates were furious, for they saw one who was in no way their superior in valour or wisdom rising above them in the social scale merely by virtue of royal favour.[4] But to Richard, de Vere was perhaps the brightest of the jewels in the royal diadem. Even greater hostility was aroused a year later when de Vere exchanged his outlandish marquisate for a dukedom. De Vere had no royal blood in his veins, and had married only a king's grand-daughter, yet he had received the highest honour of all, an honour which had hitherto been bestowed upon only one man who was not of royal blood, and he the greatest of the magnates at Edward III's court. De Vere was now, by virtue of royal favour, the equal in status of the Duke of Lancaster. He even had a palatinate in Ireland, yet in no other way, in no way acceptable to the established nobility, could de Vere rank as Lancaster's equal. Feeling against de Vere still ran high in 1395, when the magnates pointedly stayed away from his reburial at Colne Priory, 'because they had not yet forgotten the ill-will they had borne him'.[5] Even Pole's title was resented, because although he had sufficient lands to maintain his estate, some of the nobility did not believe that he had, and they despised him for his

---

[1] *CPR* 1385–9, p. 363; *RDP* Vol. V, p. 81.
[2] L. O. Pike, *Constitutional History* p. 111.
[3] *Rot. Parl.* Vol. III, pp. 241–3; *RDP* Vol. IV, p. 725.
[4] *Walsingham, HA* Vol. II, p. 140; *Westminster* pp. 72–3.
[5] Walsingham, *Annales* p. 185.

mercantile origins. A new courtier nobility was coming into existence which took precedence over the established aristocracy in access to the king, in patronage, and even to some degree in influence in the localities. Behind Richard's creations there lay a view of the nature and function of nobility at variance with that which had developed during Edward III's reign.

4

The Growth of Aristocratic Hostility 1382-8

In the first four years of Richard's reign, criticism of the court had come mainly from the Commons. As long as the system of continual councils lasted, the nobility had little reason to revive the ancient cry of evil counsellors, and for two and a half years after the system came to an end, aristocratic criticism was occasional and indirect. But from the autumn parliament of 1383 onwards, aristocratic hostility towards the king and his courtiers became more open and intense, culminating in the Wonderful Parliament of October 1386. The principal ground of complaint was the king's unwise choice of advisers, and implicit in the criticism offered by certain nobles is resentment at the favour and patronage shown to the men with whom the king surrounded himself. The Commons for their part continued their attacks on the king's financial mismanagement, but the two currents of criticism did not merge until October 1386. When they did, a political crisis parallel in some ways to that of 1376 quickly developed. Richard's response to the restraints placed upon his power in October 1386 made his opponents move from constitutional methods to violence. At the battle of Radcot Bridge on the 20th of December 1387, five lords (the Duke of Gloucester and the Earls of Arundel, Warwick, Derby, and Nottingham) defeated a force raised by Robert de Vere, the king's arch-favourite, and in the subsequent parliament, named 'Merciless', they condemned to death or exile many of those most closely associated with royal policy in the 1380s.

The first hint of friction between the court and the nobility occurred in 1382, when the king dismissed the chancellor, Sir Richard Lescrope, in a dispute over the custody of the March inheritance. Edmund Mortimer Earl of March and lieutenant in Ireland, died suddenly at Cork in December 1381 after a successful campaign against the Irish of Connacht and Munster. His son and heir Roger was a minor, and the king therefore received custody of the inheritance. On the 10th of June 1382 the king's clerk, William de Forde, was appointed to survey all the March land in England and Wales which were in the king's hands. He was given full power to put them up for farm.[1] In the following months the keeping of the manors and lordships of the inheritance was granted piecemeal to more than a dozen individuals, many of whom were members of the royal household or close associates of the court, and none of whom was of greater rank than knight.[2] There appears, however, to have been some uncertainty even at this stage surrounding the disposal of the inheritance, for Henry Englissh, an associate of de Vere, who had been appointed steward of the honour of Clare, complained to the council that he could not find anyone willing to take the lands of the honour at farm 'unless he could have them until the heir came of age'.[3] The fears of prospective farmers proved justified, for on the 16th of December 1383 the keeping of the whole inheritance was committed, by the advice of the council, to Roger Mortimer, the Earls of Arundel, Warwick and Northumberland, and John Lord Neville of Raby, 'notwithstanding any grant or gift made by the king to any person after Edmund's death of any lordships, manors, lands, tenements, annuities, rents, or other charges and profits out of any of the lands (etc.) of the said inheritance'.[4] Richard had evidently given way to pressure from the nobility to ensure that the custody of the inheritance should go to a group of fellow-nobles who could be trusted to discharge their obligation to Mortimer honestly and competently. The three earls and Lord Neville proved trustworthy: the Wigmore chronicler praised their administration of the inheritances. 'Castles, houses and other dwelling-places,' he said, were 'well maintained', and a sum of 40,000 marks was accumulated for the young earl.[5] But Richard evidently gave way only after a struggle.

[1] *CFR* 1377–83, p. 296.
[2] *ibid.* pp. 320, 323, 331, 333, 358; *CPR* 1381–5, p. 104.
[3] PRO Exchequer Bille E.207/6/14.
[4] *CFR* 1383–91, pp. 22–3. For an example of one of the original farmers refunding the issues he had received, see PRO Privy Seal Office, warrants, PSO.1/1/4.
[5] *Monasticon Anglicanum* by Sir William Dugdale, Vol. VI, pt. 1, ed. Caley *et al.* (London 1830) p. 354.

According to Walsingham, on the 11th of July 1382 the king called upon the chancellor, Sir Richard Lescrope, to surrender the great seal. He was apparently dismissed for refusing to seal certain grants. When Mortimer and certain other lords died, Walsingham states, a group of 'ambitious men', knights and esquires from families of low degree, came to the king and asked him to grant them the lands and lordships of the magnates while they were in the king's hands. The king agreed, and ordered Lescrope to draw up charters for them. He refused, and Richard dismissed him.[1] The nobility forbore from making a political issue out of Lescrope's dismissal, preferring to put it down to the king's youth and inexperience, but the episode had raised for the first time in the reign the question of the control and direction of patronage.

The Lescrope episode indicated that the king's choice of friends and advisers was already giving rise to concern, but questions of finance and foreign policy arose in 1383 which provoked hostility between lords and Commons and prevented any unity in opposition to king and court: only when the two could combine was effective opposition likely. In the parliament of February 1383, the Commons, acting very much in the tradition of the early years of the reign, asked the king to surround himself with honourable, wise, and discreet men, and also so to arrange the conduct of the household that he could live within his income. The king merely replied that he would do what seemed best to him.[2] He made no specific promise at all, and the Commons thus made less headway on the issues most dear to them than at any time since the reign began. At least part of the reason for this may lie in the strained relations between lords and Commons which arose out of the discussions about foreign policy in this parliament. The lords strongly opposed the proposal of the Bishop of Norwich, Henry Despenser, to send help to Ghent in the guise of a crusade against the schismatics of Flanders and France. The proposal reminded the lords too closely of Henry III's plan in 1258 to wrest the throne of Naples from the pope's enemies, and they also thought it unwise to organize a crusade against people who were in theory (in their view) the king's own subjects of France. The king's, not the church's rights should be upheld in Flanders.[3] The Monk of Evesham adds the information that the lords would have preferred Gaunt to lead an expedition to Flanders, but in

---

[1] *Walsingham, HA* Vol. II, pp. 69–70.
[2] *Rot. Parl.* Vol. III, p. 147.
[3] Westminster pp. 17–18.

D

view of Gaunt's known preference for an expedition to the Iberian peninsula, it is doubtful whether he would have been prepared to do so.[1] The Commons on the other hand, understandably taking a poor view of aristocratic leadership of previous expeditions, favoured the bishop.[2] No doubt too they remembered that he had been the only lord in East Anglia to stand up to the peasants eighteen months earlier. Perhaps in order to mollify the royal uncles the Commons added that none of them could be spared to go abroad at the moment because of the need to defend the northern border against the Scots.[3] The Westminster chronicler suggests that the bishop's most insistent supporters were the two sons of the Earl of Devon, Philip and Peter Courtenay. Philip sat in this parliament as knight of the shire for Devon, but Peter is not known to have been present.[4] Their partisanship stirred the smouldering embers of the feud between Gaunt and the Courtenay family, and Gaunt was apparently so annoyed by the Commons' advocacy of the bishop's expedition that he withdrew from parliament.[5] The Commons, however, stood firm and carried the day, but in the circumstances it was hardly likely that the lords would actively support the Commons' complaints about the household.

The effect of the Bishop of Norwich's failure in Flanders, however, seems to have been to transfer the lords' hostility from the Commons to the king, and in the parliament which opened on the 26th of October 1383 they launched their first overt attack upon the court. It is not clear whether the king and those round him had favoured the bishop's expedition in the previous parliament, but once the expedition began to run into trouble the new chancellor, Pole, lost little time in authorizing the Duke of Lancaster to treat for peace.[6] Furthermore, although the king put up an impression of vigorous activity to save the bishop from military disaster in mid-September,[7] he moved too late, for the French were already on the Channel coast. Gaunt and Buckingham had written to the king as long ago as late August warning him of the danger the bishop was in, and although (according to Froissart) Gaunt was not unduly upset about the outcome of the crusade, both he and Buckingham were bound to take the view that the king himself was to blame for failing to take swift and resolute

---

[1] *Evesham* p. 44.   [2] Westminster p. 18.
[3] *Rot. Parl.* Vol. III, p. 145.
[4] Westminster p. 18.   [5] *ibid.*
[6] *Foedera* Vol. VII, pp. 407–8, 410; J. J. N. Palmer, *England, France and Christendom* (London 1971) p. 50.
[7] *Walsingham, HA* Vol. II, p. 103; Westminster p. 23.

action to rescue the bishop.[1] The king's dilatoriness and eventual irresoluteness over Flanders, together with Pole's peace policy and the disquiet felt since the Lescrope episode over the control and direction of royal patronage (which the king's actions over the past year had done nothing to diminish) therefore explain the outburst of hostility in the October parliament of 1383.

The lords complained that the king was listening to foolish advice, and told him that he ought to assume full personal responsibility for government.[2] Their complaint is an important indication that the lords thought that policy was still being made by those round the king rather than the king himself, a belief borne out both by Pole's new foreign policy and by the activities of the chamberlain and under-chamberlain. The lords further pointed out, inaccurately and inconsistently, that in the past the kingdom had flourished when the king had accepted aristocratic guidance in government. The king, however, replied that he would be guided by whomsoever he wished.[3] For the first time in the reign the complaint of evil counsel had been made; the lines of division between king and nobles had been established, and were to become sharper and more insistently expressed over the next three years. In this parliament, however, the king fended off criticism without much difficulty. The Commons were less critical than they had been in earlier parliaments, even though the nobles had given them an opportunity which they could have exploited had they wished to do so. But there is no evidence that they opposed Pole's foreign policy, which may have seemed to them to promise an end to incessant heavy taxation. Furthermore, Gaunt himself, though critical of the manner in which the king had acted over the rescue of the Bishop of Norwich, was most unlikely to take an openly hostile line against the king and the court.

In the parliament which opened at Salisbury on the 29th of April 1384, however, political tension became even more explicit. The year had begun with a disaster in Scotland when Lochmaben Castle (the last English outpost in the western borders) fell, leaving the Cumberland frontier more vulnerable than it had been for the past fifty years.[4] Gaunt and Buckingham retaliated by leading a *chevauchée* through the central borders which penetrated to Edinburgh;[5] but although the

---

[1] Froissart, *Oeuvres* Vol. X, pp. 247–8; M. Aston, 'The Impeachment of Bishop Despenser', *BIHR* XXXVIII (1965) pp. 141–7.
[2] Westminster p. 26.   [3] *ibid.*
[4] *ibid.* p. 28.   [5] *ibid.* pp. 28–9.

march may have satisfied English pride, it did little to offset the strategic disadvantage which the English suffered with the fall of Lochmaben. The government meanwhile had succeeded in negotiating a provisional peace treaty with France, and it asked both lords and Commons to approve its terms in the Salisbury Parliament.[1] But neither lords nor Commons would commit themselves firmly either for or against the treaty, and foreign policy appears to have played little part in the disputes which punctuated the parliament. The parliament began with the lords spiritual and the lords temporal both quarrelling amongst themselves, until Gaunt at last brought them to order. The Earl of Arundel thereupon launched a characteristically violent and tactless attack upon the king. He said that the kingdom lacked good govern-ance, that it was falling into grave danger, and that unless something was done quickly the kingdom would suffer great harm.[2] Arundel's outburst was so generalized that it is hard to tell whether he was objecting to the government's handling of foreign affairs, to the influence and expense of the household, or to the company the king chose to keep. But Richard exploded with anger at Arundel's speech, and turning on the earl, told him to go to the devil, saying that if the earl was blaming him for the misgovernment of the realm he lied in his teeth. Not surprisingly, Richard's retort reduced everyone to silence, and it was left to Gaunt, once again, to act as mediator and to mollify the king by explaining to him what Arundel had really meant.[3] Arundel's outburst, however, was followed by an episode even more crudely violent and equally fraught with political danger. A Carmelite friar, who was believed (not without reason) to be insane, came to the king and told him that Gaunt was plotting to put the king to death. According to the Monk of Westminster, the king's reaction was violent and impetuous: 'he ordered the Duke to be put to death without trial'.[4] Walsingham, however, states that the king, having heard the charges, took advice not from the lords, but from his accustomed counsellors, two clerks of his chapel (Nicholas Slake and another)[5]: a statement which has a ring of truth about it in view of Richard's reliance on his chapel clerks in administration. The duke denied the charge, and the friar was immediately taken into custody. The Monk of Evesham gives an even more moderate account, and

[1] *Rot. Parl.* Vol. III, p. 170; J. J. N. Palmer, *England, France and Christendom* p. 50.
[2] Westminster p. 33.
[3] *ibid.*   [4] *ibid.* pp. 33–4.
[5] *Walsingham, HA* Vol. II, pp. 112–13.

reports the name of the friar as John Latimer.[1] The king apparently confronted Gaunt with the charge, while the friar listened behind a curtain. Gaunt denied the accusation, and the friar first replied that Lord Zouche would prove its truth, and then, when he too flatly denied it, the friar declared that there was 'a worthy esquire of the Earl of Oxford' who would witness the accusation's truth. But de Vere too rejected any suggestion that he was involved in the affair, and the friar was imprisoned and subsequently tortured to death. On balance, therefore, the evidence is against Westminster on the question of Richard's reaction. He accepted Gaunt's word, and indeed probably realized as clearly as anyone else that the friar was mad. The most violent reaction of all came from Buckingham, who apparently burst into the king's chamber and threatened to put to death anyone who impugned his brother's honour.[2] There remains, however, the question of who, if anyone, was behind the friar. The chroniclers all agree that the friar tried to implicate William Lord Zouche of Harringworth,[3] and having failed to do so, Evesham says he tried to implicate de Vere.[4] Furthermore, the friar made his accusation after celebrating mass before the king in de Vere's chamber.[5] There is just a possibility that de Vere used the friar in an attempt to undermine Gaunt's standing with the king, and to make Gaunt feel uncomfortable at court; but it is more likely that the episode represents the last open sign of hostility between Gaunt and the friars, a hostility generated by Gaunt's support of Wycliffe and going back to at least 1374–5, when a group of Cambridge friars were said to have been plotting Gaunt's death.[6]

This unsavoury episode perhaps served to deflect attention from Arundel's criticism of the court, and once again there is no sign that the Commons were willing to support the lords in their complaints of misgovernment. Indeed, the Commons raised an issue which was to become of increasing importance from 1388 onwards and which was to divide lords from Commons—the issue of law and order. The extent of lawlessness in the 1380s still awaits investigation, but it is unlikely to have been less than in earlier decades, and in this parliament

---

[1] *Evesham* p. 50; for confirmation of the name, see *CPR* 1381–5, p. 428.
[2] *Walsingham, HA* Vol. II, pp. 114–15.
[3] *Westminster* p. 34; *Walsingham, HA* Vol. II, p. 114; *Evesham* p. 50.
[4] *Evesham* p. 50.
[5] *Westminster* p. 33.
[6] *John of Gaunt's Register 1372–1376* Vol. II, ed. S. Armitage-Smith, Camden Third Series XXI (London 1911) p. 355; J. R. H. Moorman, *The Grey Friars in Cambridge* (Cambridge 1952) p. 115.

the Commons asked for a statute to curb violence and intimidation by the liveried retainers of the magnates. Gaunt, however, speaking for his two brothers as well, took the line that the lords were to take again in the Cambridge Parliament of 1388. Gratuitously remarking that he ranked first among the lords of the kingdom after the king, he argued that the lords were capable of maintaining discipline amongst their retainers, and that that in itself was a sufficient remedy. The Commons thereupon dropped the matter.[1] But this was potentially a most serious issue, one which was likely to give rise to bitter dissension between lords and Commons, and one which the king sought to exploit for his own advantage later in the reign.

The outcome of the parliament left Gaunt with a sense of insecurity: hence, perhaps, his insistence to the Commons on his standing as first lord of the kingdom. But he had still been able to play a role as mediator between the king and the more extreme nobles. This position, however, was to be decisively undermined in the next eighteen months, and there is good reason to believe that de Vere took at least some part in the moves against Gaunt. The precise sequence of events is difficult to establish. The Monk of Evesham says that after Christmas 1384 the king held a council at Waltham, from which Gaunt asked to be excused because he had been warned that some of those around the king were plotting his death. Richard ordered Gaunt to attend upon his allegiance, which he did, with an armed retinue. Richard told Gaunt that he had no knowledge of any plot against him, an assurance which Gaunt was not disposed to believe, and so 'subsequently he trusted him less'.[2] The monk of Westminster mentions the holding of the council, but suggests that the plot against Gaunt happened as a result of the council meeting, not before it.[3] Westminster's account is fuller, more circumstantial, and perhaps more reliable. At the council, Gaunt and his brothers advocated a royal expedition to France, but the majority of the council members took the view that an expedition to Scotland would be more advisable. Gaunt, however, refused to co-operate with any other plan, and the others on the council were afraid openly to press their proposal to a decision. The council broke up without reaching agreement, and Gaunt's opponents hatched a plot against his life at a tournament at Westminster on the 14th of February 1385. Gaunt, forewarned, fled, perhaps to Pontefract. By the 24th of February, however, Gaunt was back in the south and went to confront

[1] Westminster pp. 40–41. [2] *Evesham* p. 57.
[3] Westminster pp. 55–6.

the king at Sheen.[1] He now took up the cry of evil counsellors, warning Richard that he ought to remove them and listen to the advice of wiser men. His role as mediator had now collapsed. He insisted that it was disgraceful for the king to countenance murder by conspiracy when he was the embodiment of the law, where the power to take life and limb alone should lie. The king was in no mood to treat his uncle as he had Arundel the previous year. He replied with 'soft and sweet words', and promised to act more justly in future. Gaunt thereupon withdrew from the king's presence, and it was left to the Princess Joan to complete the reconciliation. Gaunt had, however, drawn attention to a trait in Richard's character which was to become of considerable political importance—a tendency towards secretive and arbitrary action which created insecurity and called in question the whole basis of the relationship between the king and the law.

There is general agreement among the chroniclers about who was responsible for the plot against Gaunt: Walsingham accuses the young men round the king; Evesham points to the young men 'who were brought up with the king'; and Westminster singles out the Earls of Oxford, Salisbury, and Nottingham as men against whom Gaunt bore a particular grudge for their part in the plot.[2] It is hard to believe that Salisbury could have been involved; he was neither a young man nor particularly close to the king. As the divorced husband of Richard's mother he was unlikely to have been one of the king's more intimate companions or counsellors, and earlier in the reign he had sat on a commission of inquiry into the household. The chronicler may mean the earl's nephew and heir, John Montagu, who had become one of the king's knights by 1383, but he did not inherit the earldom until 1397, after the Westminster chronicler was dead. It is much more probable that Oxford and Nottingham were involved. Thomas Mowbray Earl of Nottingham inherited his title unexpectedly in February 1383 when his elder brother died. Before this chance took him into the ranks of the nobility he had been retained at court, hoping, as a younger son might, to make his way by favour and service. Even after he became an earl, his inheritance was small: the Isle of Axholme, the honour of Bramber in Sussex, and scattered manors in the east midlands and Yorkshire. He had great expectations: his mother was Elizabeth, only daughter and heiress of John Lord Segrave and Margaret Marshall, elder daughter of Thomas of Brotherton Earl of Norfolk and Earl Marshal: when Margaret Marshall died,

---

[1] *ibid.* p. 56.
[2] *Walsingham, HA* Vol. II, p. 126; Westminster p. 58; *Evesham* p. 60.

Mowbray would inherit the entire Segrave and Norfolk inheritances. But because his present estate was small, he remained at court hoping for preferment, and was not disappointed. The king bought for him the marriage of Elizabeth, daughter of John Lord Lestrange of Blakemere and thus the prospect of acquiring her inheritance in Shropshire.[1] However, Elizabeth died only a few months after being married, and under the terms of the agreement whereby Mowbray had been granted his own marriage while under age, his marriage should then have reverted to the king. But in 1385, he married without licence the daughter of the Earl of Arundel, in open contempt of the king's wishes, and Richard thereupon ordered his lands to be distrained until he had recovered the full value of the marriage.[2] Such action can have served only to strengthen Mowbray's connection with Arundel, and it is clear that by the summer of 1385 Mowbray rightly felt himself out of favour at court. In all probability he resented Richard's obvious preference for de Vere, and if both were involved in the plot against Gaunt, it may be evidence of competition for the king's favour rather than co-operation between them.

The sequel to the plot was yet another violent episode. At a council at Westminster in late February or early March 1385, the Archbishop of Canterbury led other lords of the council, lay and ecclesiastical, in complaining about the encouragement the king had received from those around him to murder Gaunt, and in pointing out that such plots undermined the laws and customs of the kingdom.[3] The archbishop undertook to convey the lords' opinion to the king, but the king made a threatening reply, and later the same day, while returning by barge from dinner with the Lord Mayor of London, he met the archbishop, also travelling on the river. Buckingham, who was apparently with the king, guaranteed the archbishop's safety, and king and prelate had an interview at which the archbishop repeated his earlier complaints. The king thereupon drew his sword, and (the Westminster annalist reports) would have run the archbishop through had not Buckingham, Sir John Devereux, and Sir Thomas Trivet intervened. The meeting then broke up abruptly, but the whole episode reveals not only a streak of violence in Richard's character, not unusual by the standards of the time, but also a growing concern on the part of the lords that the king should not appear by his own

[1] *CPR* 1381–5, pp. 229, 236.
[2] PRO Exchequer LTR Memoranda Roll E.368/159 **brevia** retornabilia Easter 10 RII m.2.   [3] Westminster p. 58.

impatient reactions to ignore or undermine the law of which he was the embodiment.

Another dispute between the king and Gaunt flared up on the Scottish expedition in the summer of 1385. The expedition marks the attainment, in military terms, of the king's independence, and he celebrated the raising of his standard at his first entry into Scotland by conferring dukedoms on Cambridge and Buckingham and an earldom on Michael de la Pole.[1] Behind the symbolic grandeur of the king's first expedition, however, lay problems of finance and strategy. The Commons had granted a generous subsidy in the previous parliament of two fifteenths and tenths, with the condition that if the king failed to lead an army to the continent in the summer of 1385, half the subsidy was to be cancelled.[2] When it was agreed that the king should go against Scotland rather than France, the government decided not to take the politically risky course of contravening the terms of the parliamentary grant, and resorted instead to the archaic measure of proposing to levy scutage for the expedition.[3] But the proposed levy was abandoned in the face of strong opposition, mainly from the knights in parliament. The king's financial embarrassment was thus brought home sharply to the knights, and not unnaturally led to renewed criticism in the October parliament of 1385.[4] It may also have had some bearing on the dispute over strategy which broke out between the king and Gaunt. The expedition had been planned as a retaliation for the invasion of England the previous year at the instigation of Jean de Vienne, somewhat against the wishes of Robert II.[5] As a punitive raid, Richard's expedition was successful. It destroyed Melrose, Newbattle, and Holyrood Abbeys, laid waste much of Lothian, and entered Edinburgh. But once at Edinburgh, disagreement broke out between the king and Gaunt about what to do next.[6] Gaunt advised the king to go on over the Forth and devastate Fife and Strathmore; but the king argued that this was unwise, that his army's supply lines could not sustain such a march, and that although the king and the lords might have enough to eat, the rank and file of the army

[1] *RDP* Vol. V, pp. 67, 69.
[2] *Rot. Parl.* Vol. III, p. 185; J. J. N. Palmer, 'The Last Summons of the Feudal Army in England', *EHR* LXXXIII (1968) pp. 771–5.
[3] J. J. N. Palmer, 'The Last Summons'; N. B. Lewis, 'The Last Summons of the English Feudal Levy, 13 June 1385', *EHR* LXXIII (1958) pp. 1–26.
[4] *Rot. Parl.* Vol. III, pp. 213–14.
[5] *Chronique du Religieux de Saint Denys* Vol. I, ed. M. Bellaguet (Paris 1839) pp. 364–6.
[6] *Westminster* p. 65; *Walsingham, HA* Vol. II, p. 131.

would run the risk of perishing from hunger and thirst. The argument throws remarkable light on Richard as a strategist. He had achieved a limited but important objective—retaliation for a Scottish raid into England—and had convincingly demonstrated that an English army could ravage southeast Scotland at will. But even as the army reached Edinburgh, supplies were beginning to fail, and Richard clearly appreciated the folly of sending an army beyond the Forth where experience proved it could not be properly supplied and where it would suffer from the guerilla strikes of the Scots as they retreated before the invaders into the valleys of the central highlands and the Mounth. It is hard to understand what advantage Gaunt thought might come from a display of English might in Fife and Strathmore. There was a great difference between a march through the fertile lowlands of northwestern France and a march into the highlands of Scotland with autumn approaching. Gaunt, who had some experience of Scotland, must have appreciated this point. Richard's attitude also reveals an unusual sensitivity towards the hardship the ordinary soldiers would suffer through marching and fighting in such inhospitable country, an attitude consistent with his sensitivity towards the peasants' grievances in 1381. Both Westminster and Walsingham suggest that the dispute with Gaunt was bitter, and according to Walsingham, Richard ended by telling Gaunt that he could go on over the Forth if he wanted to, but 'I and my men are going home'.

Gaunt, however, gave way and returned to England with the king. Relations between the two were now worse than ever, for no one had attempted to mediate in this dispute, and both Westminster and Walsingham make it clear that Richard thought Gaunt's motives in suggesting an advance over the Forth were treacherous.[1] But the news of the Portuguese victory over the Castilians at Aljubarrotta, which reached England during the parliament which opened at Westminster on the 20th of October 1385, gave him the opportunity to press, this time successfully, for the launching of an expedition to Castile, and he left England the following July.[2] It is sometimes argued that he left with a sense of relief, realizing that his political position at home had become impossible, but despite his quarrels with Richard and the evidence of plots against him, it is doubtful whether this was more than a marginal consideration. Had it not been for Aljubarrotta, which seemed to open the way for a settlement either by force or diplomacy

[1] Westminster p. 65; *Walsingham, HA* Vol. II, p. 131.
[2] Westminster p. 71.

of Gaunt's claim to Castile,[1] it is improbable that he would have embarked upon the venture at this point. His departure, however, left the way open for more extreme members of the nobility to take the lead in opposition to the king.

Although the parliament of October 1385 granted a subsidy which was to be used in part for Gaunt's expedition, it showed itself much more concerned with domestic than with foreign affairs. The Monk of Westminster gives a hint of what happened, saying that 'many things were proposed by the community for the safeguarding of the kingdom',[2] and a fragmentary petition on the parliament roll implies that another commission was set up to inquire into the royal finances.[3] The recent publication of the original bill proposing such an inquiry, however, makes possible a fuller understanding of parliament's demands.[4] The essence of their complaint, which in all probability came first from the Commons but which was then supported by the lords, was the king's extravagance, and specifically the misuse of his powers of patronage so that the crown was impoverished. The bill pointed out that the revenues of the exchequer could be increased if the king were better advised about his gifts; that the profits from wards and marriages could be increased if the king took his council's advice about their value instead of granting them out 'hastily', and that he should take advice before granting escheats. This attack on the king's use of his powers of patronage is understandable in view of his lavish flow of grants towards his favourites and household officials over the previous three years. Criticism of his extravagance came into the open in this parliament because of the financial embarrassment caused by the Scottish expedition. The Commons wanted financial rather than political or personal criteria to determine the use the king made of the feudal incidents that fell to the crown. They also wanted the council to exercise some control over the appointment of revenue officers. They asked that no sheriffs, escheators, or other ministers accountable for royal revenue should be appointed 'by petition or individual request' but rather by the council on the advice of the great officers of state. They also asked that the same principle

---

[1] P. E. Russell, *The English Intervention in Spain and Portugal in the Time of Edward III and Richard II* (Oxford 1955) pp. 400–6; J. J. N. Palmer, *England, France and Christendom* p. 69.

[2] Westminster p. 69.

[3] *Rot. Parl.* Vol. III, pp. 213–14.

[4] J. J. N. Palmer, 'The Impeachment of Michael de la Pole in 1386', *BIHR* XLIII (1970) pp. 100–1.

should apply to the appointment of customs officials. There is some
evidence that sheriffs had been appointed by the personal instructions
of the king rather than by the council in 1383, 1384, and 1385. The
sheriffs of Wiltshire, Gloucestershire, and Warwickshire were appointed by the king directly in 1383; in 1384 Thomas de Berkeley was
appointed sheriff of Gloucestershire by signet letter, and his successor
in the following year was similarly appointed. The office of sheriff of
Wiltshire was granted to Sir John Salesbury, a chamber knight, for
life by signet letter.[1] The number of sheriffs directly appointed by the
king was small, but his intervention in favour of his friends in the
routine of their appointment was sufficient to make the Commons fear
that favour with the king was a more important consideration in their
appointment than probity or standing in the shire.

The king gave way before parliamentary pressure, and agreed to the
appointment of a committee of nine 'to survey his estate, and inquire
into his revenues, and diminish his expenses'.[2] The committee appears
to have been chosen with an eye to administrative experience, and is
remarkable for the absence from it of any of the royal uncles, or indeed
any of the nobles who had earlier criticized the king's conduct of
government. The Bishops of Winchester and Exeter, Wykeham and
Brantingham, had served as chancellor and treasurer respectively in
Edward III's reign, and Brantingham had held office again from July
1377 to February 1381. The Bishop of Durham, John Fordham, had
been keeper of the Privy Seal for the first four and a half years of
Richard's reign; Sir John Cobham had been placed in the royal household, and Sir Richard Lescrope was a former chancellor whose resistance to Richard's use of patronage had led to his dismissal. Stafford
and Devereux had both served on the continual councils of the early
years, and Salisbury had been a member of an earlier committee of
inquiry into royal finances. Only the Earl of Northumberland had no
experience of this kind. The composition of the committee could hardly
have been to Richard's taste, and must have seemed to him almost
deliberately designed to bring together men who had watched over
him in the first years of the reign, and to revive the financial measures
of the period of the continual councils, measures which (in parliament's
mind) contrasted so sharply with the king's own manner of conducting
his finances.

A committee composed of such people, and set up specifically to

[1] *CFR* 1383–91, pp. 6–7, 76–7, 101. See p. 67 above.
[2] J. J. N. Palmer, 'Impeachment' p. 101.

restrain the king from using his powers of patronage in the way he wished, was bound to intensify Richard's sense of insecurity and to justify in his mind his retreat into his household, where he could find men and institutions which were not readily amenable to outside pressure. It was bound also to make Richard even more hostile to the whole idea of supervision by committee. But circumstances had changed since the early years of the reign, and the power of the king and the court had increased sufficiently to enable him to resist outside pressure. It is clear from the articles of impeachment brought against the chancellor in the Wonderful Parliament that Pole simply ignored the parliamentary ordinance establishing the committee, and thus it never met.[1] Pole's failure to allow the committee to operate was bound to intensify political opposition to the court. The flouting of a parliamentary ordinance ensured the hostility of the Commons; the continuation of the flow of grants towards the king's friends, made magnate opposition more vigorous; and in the following year lords and Commons were able to unite and for the first time to bring effective pressure to bear upon the king.

By that time, the Duke of Gloucester had emerged as Richard's main opponent among the nobility. The departure for Spain of Gaunt in July 1386 perhaps gave Gloucester the opportunity to take the lead, but his reasons for doing so are to be found in his own political and financial experiences in the previous ten years. Even as a duke he was still heavily dependent upon annuities instead of land for his income. In November 1385 he had been granted £1000 a year to maintain his estate: £60 from the fee farm of Gloucester and the remainder from the customs of London, Boston, Hull, Lynn, Ipswich, and Yarmouth. But he had difficulty in obtaining full payment from the ports,[2] and he received little else from the king, much less than a man of his standing might normally expect to obtain. In June 1385 the king granted him the Castle of St Briavel's and the forest of Dean, subject to Sir Guy de Brienne the elder having their custody during his lifetime (he died in 1390).[3] At about the same time, in anticipation of the Duke of Brittany's going over to the king of France, he was granted the castle and honour of Rising in Norfolk, to hold in tail male 'from the time when they shall first come into the king's hands'.[4] But he received little else, and was engaged at the same time in a long dispute with his

---

[1] *Rot. Parl.* Vol. III, p. 216.
[2] *CPR* 1385–9, pp. 55, 209; *RDP* Vol. V, pp. 65–6.
[3] *CPR* 1381–5, p. 579.   [4] *ibid.* 1385–9, p. 147.

brother-in-law, the Earl of Derby, over the division of the Bohun inheritance.[1] Gloucester was short of money and insecure in some of his territorial possessions, and it seems to have been the king's policy to keep him so.[2] He above all the nobility must have resented the favour and preference shown to the king's favourites and the financial policies which might jeopardize the regular payment of his annuities. In all probability too, Gloucester had little time for the court's foreign policy, preferring war to negotiation and eventual settlement. He and his brothers had apparently advocated an expedition to the continent in 1385 but had seen the court ignore their advice and decide eventually upon an invasion of Scotland.

Gloucester had come late to the honours he might expect of right as a prince of the royal blood; he was poorly endowed compared with his elder brothers of Lancaster and York; and he suffered first the thwarting of his plan to obtain the entire Bohun inheritance and then the problems of an income largely dependent upon annuities from an over-committed royal exchequer. Furthermore, the effect of royal patronage in the 1380s had been to raise up two of the king's favourites, de Vere and Pole, as territorial powers in the region where his favourite residence and much of his inheritance lay. Pole and de Vere could command ready access to the king and were the recipients of his favour. They were thus likely to prove more attractive patrons to lesser men than was the duke, and so Gloucester's social position, his ability to command a following in Essex, was endangered by Richard's policies. Political activity to end these policies which so threatened his interests and his security, and which might make possible the more vigorous prosecution of the war, was thus an attractive prospect. Yet his ambition seems to have transcended these objectives. His vengeful attitude towards Burley in 1388[3] brought upon him the bitter and unforgiving hostility of the king. There were no compensating political gains, except perhaps a temporary popularity with the Commons which he may have enjoyed for its own sake as much as for the political advantages it gave him. His actions in the last days of December 1387, when the king may have been deposed for a few days, gave rise to the suspicion that he had designs upon the crown itself.[4] So perhaps his

[1] For the partition of the Bohun inheritance, see *CCR* 1377–81, pp. 390–95; *ibid.* 1381–5, pp. 511–16; *ibid.* 1385–9, pp 56–7; for the dispute between Derby and Gloucester, PRO Duchy of Lancaster Miscellanea DL 41/2/3, DL.41/5/1.
[2] For details see A. Goodman, *The Loyal Conspiracy* (London 1971) pp. 90–91.
[3] See pp. 125–6 below.
[4] See p. 119 below.

earlier disappointments made him more ambitious than his two brothers; yet he was also, like many of his peers, a man of piety and cultivation, and he was sufficiently interested in his duties as constable of England to write a treatise on the working of the Court of Chivalry.[1]

Gloucester's political attitudes were formed not only by considerations of prestige and self interest, however, but also by a view of government and of the relationship between the king and the law which was common and traditional among men of his class. In the interview with the king at Eltham in October 1386, he and Bishop Arundel, presenting an address from the whole parliament, insisted upon the king's obligation to rule in accordance with the laws of the kingdom and the advice of the magnates, contrasting this ideal with the king's stubborn adherence to unwise council and to his own will in government. The final and most telling point of their speech was their assertion that the community had the right to depose a king if he refused to be governed and ruled by the laws of the kingdom and the advice of the lords,[2] an oblique but unmistakeable reference to the deposition of Edward II. In January 1388 he had a search made for all 'records and memoranda touching the governance of the king's estate and realm', and it is possible that in the 1386 parliament a statute of 1310 was produced as a precedent for giving a commission of government statutory authority.[3] The events of the reign of Edward II were brought to mind by Richard's rule in the 1380s, and in such an atmosphere it is hardly surprising that in 1390 Walsingham recorded, incorrectly, that 'St Thomas of Lancaster was canonized'.[4] Richard attempted to have Edward II canonized in 1395;[5] and Walsingham describes Arundel's execution and immediate veneration in 1397 in a way which was surely intended to remind his readers of Thomas of Lancaster.[6] To this extent, therefore, both king and nobles were

---

[1] 'The Ordenaunce and Fourme of Fightyng within Listes', in *The Black Book of the Admiralty* Vol. I, ed. Sir Travers Twiss, Rolls Series (London 1871) pp. 300–28. The date of composition is unknown. Gloucester clearly thought the court was competent to try cases of treason, and that those found guilty of treason by the court should suffer the common law penalty. This may have some bearing on his approach to the problem of dealing with the favourites in 1388.
[2] *Knighton* Vol. II, pp. 216–20.
[3] PRO Chancery Warrants C.81/1539/44; D. Clementi, 'Richard II's Ninth Question to the Judges', *EHR* LXXXVI (1971) pp. 96–113.
[4] *Walsingham, HA* Vol. II, p. 195.
[5] See p. 71 above.
[6] Walsingham, *Annales* pp. 216–18.

acting in self-conscious awareness of the events of Edward II's reign: the English political past influenced their actions and informed their rhetoric. In Walsingham, too, the nobility who opposed Richard found a supporter and propagandist. He wrote his *Chronica* in the tradition of Roger of Wendover and Matthew Paris, and his anti-curialist attitude is similar to theirs. The scriptorium of St Albans Abbey showed a clear political commitment in its work, and since Gloucester's godfather was the Abbot of St Albans, it is just possible that he derived some of his knowledge of the political past from that source.[1] Perhaps, then, Gloucester saw himself as acting not just to safeguard his own political and social interests, but also to impose upon the king a particular view of government, requiring him to abide by the advice of his natural counsellors (the nobility) and to accept that he was bound by the laws made with the consent of the community. The practical effects of Richard's personal government gave rise to these issues of principle. Gloucester's stand won him the hostility of the king, but popularity with the Commons and the applause of the St Albans chronicler, who saw him, at the time of his death, as having been the nation's one hope of salvation.[2]

The financial problems which had given rise to parliamentary criticism in October 1385 did not abate during the following year, and the concentration at Sluys during the summer of 1386 of a French force bent on invading England meant that another parliament would eventually have to be summoned to grant money for the defence of the south and east coasts. There is some evidence that the king and his ministers hoped to postpone parliament for as long as possible, for they required the maritime counties to pay the costs of half the defence force, and they imposed a forced loan to raise the rest of the money.[3] A large army was effectively deployed in southeast England,[4] but in fact the French never set out from Sluys. The threat of invasion had lifted when parliament assembled on the 1st of October, but the bills still had to be paid. The chancellor asked the Commons for four tenths and fifteenths, to be collected within the year[5]—the largest grant which had hitherto been asked of parliament. The Commons'

[1] V. H. Galbraith, *Roger Wendover and Matthew Paris* (Glasgow 1944) p. 20; Traison p. 3.
[2] Walsingham, *Annales* p. 206.
[3] PRO Exchequer Receipt Roll E.401/566; *CCR* 1385-9, p. 344; J. J. N. Palmer, *England, France and Christendom* p. 83.
[4] Tout, *Chapters* Vol. III, p. 411.
[5] *Knighton* Vol. II, p. 215.

reply, in which they were supported by the lords, was to demand the dismissal of the chancellor and treasurer, and they added that they had business with Pole that could not be dealt with so long as he remained chancellor,[1] a barely veiled hint that the Commons intended to impeach him, on the precedent of 1376. But Richard refused to meet parliament, and stayed at Eltham palace, whither a deputation went to seek the dismissal of the chancellor and treasurer. Richard scornfully dismissed the deputation with the famous reply that he would not dismiss so much as a scullion from his kitchen at their behest. Amidst rumours of a plot by the king and his friends to murder their leading parliamentary opponents, parliament sent Gloucester and Bishop Arundel to the king to bring greater pressure to bear upon him. Richard eventually gave way under threat of deposition, and agreed to meet parliament. The chancellor and treasurer resigned office on the 23rd of October 1386. Parliament permitted the treasurer to retire from the political scene, but Pole had to face impeachment.[2] It seems clear that the main complaint against him was his failure to implement the ordinance of 1385 setting up the commission of inquiry into royal finances. He was also accused of misusing his powers of patronage for his own benefit and of neglecting to support the garrison of Ghent, so that it fell to the French. Pole's punishment was a sentence of imprisonment; Richard's was the imposition upon him of yet another commission, with even more wide-ranging powers than the abortive one of the previous year. The commission's terms of reference were an implicit indictment of Richard's government over the previous four years, and they show how important parliament considered the financial consequences of Richard's patronage.[3] The commission was to examine all royal revenue, from whatever source it originated, to inquire how that revenue had been spent, and to investigate all grants of land that had been made in the ten years since the coronation. It was empowered once it had carried out the inquiry to make what reforms it thought fit, and in order to perform its duties as thoroughly as possible it was given wide powers of supervision over the administration and the royal household. The eleven commissioners and the three great officers of state were to be allowed to enter the royal household as often as they wished, to compel evidence to be produced, and to

[1] *ibid.*   [2] *ibid.* pp. 215–23.
[3] *Statute of the Realm* Vol. II, pp. 39–43; N. B. Lewis, 'Article VII of the Impeachment of Michael de la Pole in 1386', *EHR* XLII (1927) pp. 402–7; J. J. N. Palmer, 'The Parliament of 1385 and the Constitutional Crisis of 1386', *Speculum* XLVI (1971) pp. 477–90.

reform whatever deficiencies they found within the household. The household officers were to come under scrutiny for their 'defaults and offences . . . whereby the profit of the crown has been diminished or the law disturbed', and all revenue assigned for the household was to be examined. In other words, Richard had to agree to a thorough investigation of his household, and his only gesture of retaliation was his appointment in January 1387 of John Beauchamp of Holt as steward of the household, in defiance of the Commons' request for a parliamentary appointment.[1]

The commission was to remain in power for a year from the 20th of November 1386. It was to be permanently resident at Westminster, where it would have full control of the exchequer and the great and Privy Seals; and Richard was required to take an oath to abide by any ordinance made by a bare majority of the commissioners. He won a small concession on the length of the commission's life. The original petition for its establishment had envisaged that it would run for a year and then have its mandate renewed until a parliament met, but the lords finally agreed that it should last only for the year and expire on the 19th of November 1387.[2] But Richard was now subject to a more stringent and far-reaching measure of control than at any time since the period of the continual councils, and on the dissolution of the parliament he had to content himself for the moment with protesting 'with his own mouth' that he did not regard anything that he had done in the parliament as prejudicial to himself, and that the liberties and prerogatives of his crown were to be safeguarded.[3]

It has sometimes been suggested that the membership of the commission was deliberately moderate, chosen so as to make its imposition less bitter to the king.[4] But such a view is hard to maintain. The bishops of Winchester and Exeter had an anti-curial aura around them as a result of their activities in the last years of Edward III's reign and their membership of the 1385 commission; Archbishop Courtenay, though formally reconciled to the king in October 1385, was unlikely to have very warm feelings towards the man who had tried to assassinate him eighteen months previously; the Archbishop of York had not yet thrown in his lot with the court, and the remaining clerical member, the Abbot of Waltham, was an unknown quantity. The lay members

[1] *Statutes of the Realm* Vol. II, pp. 39–43; *Rot. Parl.* Vol. III, p. 221.
[2] *Rot. Parl.* Vol. III, p. 221.
[3] *ibid.* p. 224.
[4] A. B. Steel, *Richard II* (Cambridge 1941) pp. 124–5.

were likely to prove tougher still. Gloucester had taken the lead in opposing the king at Eltham; Arundel's views were well known and had been stridently voiced in earlier years, while York was unlikely to take a strongly independent line, though he may have been more sympathetic to the king than is sometimes supposed. John Cobham of Kent had been on the 1385 committee, as had Lescrope and Devereux, and Richard could expect no sympathy from any of them. The three officers of state, who were to work with the commissioners, were no friends to the king either: Bishop Arundel succeeded Pole at the chancery; John Gilbert Bishop of Hereford, became treasurer; and John Waltham, formerly keeper of the rolls of chancery, was appointed keeper of the Privy Seal. None of these officers were likely to impede the commission's work in the way Pole had done in the previous year. It was parliament's clear intention that this commission should have the chance to work effectively without obstruction from those around the king.

Richard was fully aware of the seriousness of the attack upon his powers of personal government which parliament had carried through; yet almost at once he began to reassert the powers which the crown still possessed and take action which the new commission could not or would not gainsay. Even before parliament was dismissed the exercise of the royal will began, and the king showed how much initiative he still had in government. He placed one of his signet clerks, John Lincoln of Grimsby, in the exchequer as king's chamberlain on the 20th of November in succession to Thomas Orgrave,[1] and around the end of the month, perhaps as parliament was dissolved, he dismissed the chief baron of the exchequer, Sir Robert Plessington, and replaced him with a royalist knight, Sir John Cary,[2] After his dismissal, the king had an elaborate schedule of charges against him drawn up, in what was perhaps intended as an imitation of, and retaliation for, the impeachment of Pole.[3] Despite evidence for his earlier misconduct while he was Gaunt's chief baron in the Lancaster exchequer,[4] the charges against him are unconvincing and the indictment reads like a hasty and ill-considered document. He was accused of concealing a marriage, thereby depriving the king of the profit from it, a common enough offence. He was accused of allowing

[1] PRO Exchequer KR Memoranda Roll E.159/163 brevia baronibus Michaelmas 10 RII m. 20d.
[2] *CPR* 1385–9, p. 245.
[3] PRO Exchequer KR Miscellanea E.163/6/18.
[4] R. Somerville, *History of the Duchy of Lancaster* Vol. I (London 1953) pp. 372–3.

two debtors to go free, of remitting part of the farm of Northampton-shire, of refusing to hear a case concerning the concealment of the subsidy in Warwickshire and Shropshire, of taking a bribe from the Archdeacon of Richmond, and of keeping the exchequer court open for two weeks longer than he should, so that the king had to pay the officials extra wages. It was finally alleged that he would not listen to apprentices and others who pleaded in his court, but by 'ordes et vileynes paroles' suggested that they were incompetent and doing more harm than good; thus suitors were prevented from pleading that the king lost revenue from fines and amercements. There is not much to be said for any of these charges, and even if they are true, none of them suggest that Plessington went much beyond the normal laxity in accept-ing bribes and douceurs and in showing favour to friends. The charges were probably intended to show that Pole had not been the only official guilty of financial misdemeanours. Plessington was summoned before the council to answer the charges against him,[1] and this in itself is evidence of the extent to which the king could still make his will prevail in government, but nothing is known of the council's decision in the matter. Nor is anything known of Plessington's political attitudes or why Richard chose to dismiss him and proceed against him. He may have been a scapegoat who had made his position vulnerable by one or two unwise transactions. He held lands in York-shire, and may have formed some kind of connection with Mowbray, for in July 1384 the king granted him the office of steward of Rich-mondshire for life at the supplication of the Earl of Nottingham.[2] Whether he was sympathetic to Richard's opponents before 1386 is an open question, but Richard's treatment of him served merely to intensify any sympathies that existed, and he acted as the Appellants' chief spokesman in the Merciless Parliament.[3]

Richard's next act of defiance was the appointment of Beauchamp of Holt as steward of the household, but these events were merely the foretaste of a year of activity which was to demonstrate the resilience of king and court in the face of aristocratic pressure, a resilience which did as much as Richard's widening of the conflict by raising the cry of treason to make Gloucester and his friends move from constitutional methods of opposition to violence. Faced with the commission's plan to enter the royal household to investigate its finances and impose whatever reforms it thought necessary, Richard, like Edward II before

[1] PRO Exchequer TR Council and Privy Seal Records E.28/2/63.
[2] *CPR* 1381–5, p. 434.   [3] Favent p. 14.

him, baulked the commission by withdrawing from London and embarking on a 'gyration' which lasted until nine days before the commission's authority was due to expire.[1] The king left London on the 9th of February 1387 after hearing solemn mass in Westminster Abbey.[2] His progress took him first northwards to York, thence south again to Windsor for St George's Day. In early summer he moved through the midlands to Chester, then to Shrewsbury, Worcester, across to Nottingham, and then by way of Woodstock and Windsor to London. The progress was coherent, if prolonged. There was none of the aimless wandering and rapid moves suggested by the chroniclers.[3]

While on progress, Richard kept in touch with the commission and the officers of state. Messengers went to and fro between London and the king with considerable frequency until late August.[4] The commission periodically sought the king's advice, particularly on diplomatic matters, and it passed on some government business and correspondence to him.[5] For his part, he regularly transmitted his instructions to the chancellor, the keeper of the Privy Seal, and the courts of law, using his signet to authenticate his correspondence, though not to move the great seal directly, for Chancellor Arundel was not prepared to recognize its authority.[6] However, it is clear that Richard was not deprived of his signet,[7] and since the secretary and the clerks of the chapel were of course with the household on progress, the signet probably reverted to its normal role in administration. Furthermore, on at least two occasions, at Easthampstead on the 14th of May and at Worcester about the 10th of August, the king met officers of state in person.[8] It is clear that the commission did not try to govern entirely

---

[1] For Richard's itinerary, see appendix.   [2] Westminster p. 90.

[3] *ibid.* p. 94; *Walsingham, HA* Vol. II, p. 161. Knighton, who gives the most reliable account of Richard's movements during this period, simply says that he went north and returned in August, having visited many places (Vol. II, p. 236).

[4] PRO Exchequer Issue Rolls E. 403/515 m.1; E.403/517 mm.1, 4, 13, 16.

[5] *ibid.* E.403/517 mm. 1, 4, 16.

[6] Signet letters from the king to the keeper of the Privy Seal are to be found in Edinburgh University Library Ms. 183 ff. 81–108; to his Chester officials, PRO Chester Recognizance Rolls, Chester 2/59 *passim*; to the court of King's Bench, PRO Common Law Writs and Returns KB 145/10/1, 2 (as listed in *Select Cases in the Court of King's Bench* Vol. VII, ed. G. O. Sayles, Selden Society LXXXVIII (London 1971)); to other persons, Edinburgh University Library Ms. 183 *ut supra*; PRO Exchequer Issue Rolls E.403/517 m.2.

[7] It is incorrect to say that the signet was 'ignored' after the appointment of the commission (A. B. Steel, *Richard II* p. 125).

[8] PRO Exchequer Issue Rolls E. 403/517 m.4; Chancery Warrants C.81/495/4278,

without the king, and could not discharge all its functions without consulting the king. The king had left London primarily to avoid an investigation of his household. He was not averse to some contact with the commission whose efforts to keep in touch with Richard show how essential the crown was to government even at this time. Indeed, the evidence suggests, not surprisingly, that the commission was much more anxious to consult the king than the king was to consult them.

The commission, however, had some financial hold over the king, for his household still depended upon income assigned to it by the exchequer in London. Altogether in the ten months Richard was away from Westminster more than £8500 was assigned for the household; there is record of at least part of this sum being carried to the king in the country.[1] The £8500 was somewhat less than usual for household expenses for a period of this length, but the commission had been set up to enforce economies, and it was in a position to insist on some reduction in the income of the household. The income of the chamber was reduced sharply. Between the 9th of February and the 30th of September Richard received only £1755–6–8, less than half the allowance of £4000 a year, and it was paid to the king in a series of instalments none of which was more than 500 marks.[2] Finance was the king's most vulnerable point, the point where the commission could have successfully applied pressure to force him to return to London; but the reduction in chamber income was not disastrous, and may in any case have been a consequence of a decision at the time of the Wonderful Parliament to reduce the allowance to £2000.[3] The commission did not use the financial sanctions available to it, for it was perhaps unwilling even now to deny the king's right to reasonable maintenance. There is, however, some evidence that Richard's income was not sufficient for his needs. In June, Henry Kirkestede, a king's esquire, was sent at the king's order to Northamptonshire, Leicestershire, Lincolnshire, and Rutland to borrow money for the king.[4] It is possible that the king also borrowed money from Nicholas Brembre, a London merchant and former mayor who had made several loans to

---

4284 for evidence that Richard was at Easthampstead; in a letter to the chancellor dated the 14th of August 1387 Richard urged him to issue letters of safe-conduct to a Scots herald 'par manere et selonc ce qe nous vous chargeasmes par bouche a nostre citee de Wircestre' (C.81/1354/1).

[1] PRO Exchequer Issue Rolls E.403/515, 517, 518 *passim*, esp. 515 m. 21.
[2] *ibid.* E.403/515, 517 *passim*.   [3] See pp. 96–8 above.
[4] PRO Exchequer Issue Rolls E.403/517 m.8.

the exchequer up to the point of Richard's departure from London, but none thereafter.[1] He is known to have attended the Nottingham Council,[2] and may have been with the king at other times on his progress. So long as the king could borrow even small sums of money he could make good the shortfall on chamber and household income from the exchequer.

But Richard was not prepared merely to stay in the country and wait for the commission's authority to lapse. The rhetorical extremism of Gloucester and Bishop Arundel at Eltham and the political chains forged for Richard in the Wonderful Parliament bred a similar extremism on the part of the king in the summer of 1387. If Richard was ever motivated by a strong desire for revenge against his political opponents it was now, in the interval between the Wonderful and the Merciless Parliaments. In August, the king began to survey his sources of strength. He sent an agent into Essex and East Anglia distributing money to induce the men of that region to take up arms on the king's behalf when he might call on them to do so. But the agent was arrested and thrown into Cambridge gaol, and his recruiting campaign seems to have had little effect.[3] Richard then embarked upon a policy of consultation. While at Nottingham at the end of August he summoned the sheriffs of the English counties and a deputation of Londoners to ask what support they could give him. According to Walsingham,[4] the Londoners gave a devious answer, designed chiefly to placate the king. He suggests that they had no firm loyalties either to the king or to the commission, and in fact the city was probably divided, with Brembre trying to win it over to the king's side and Exton, the Lord Mayor, trying to keep it out of politics. Early in October the citizens took an oath, probably at Brembre's instigation, to uphold Richard against all his enemies.[5] The oath was sent to the king, who replied thanking them for their efforts to preserve unity and order in the city and warning them that if they failed to elect a mayor 'who could be trusted to govern the city well' he would refuse to recognize their choice.[6] When Richard returned to London the citizens welcomed him and declared their loyalty to him, but as support

[1] A. B. Steel, *The Receipt of the Exchequer 1377–1485* (Cambridge 1954) pp. 46, 56; PRO Exchequer Receipt Rolls E.401/553, 563.
[2] *Knighton* Vol. II, p. 236.   [3] *Westminster* p. 94.
[4] *Walsingham, HA* Vol. II, p. 161.
[5] *Calendar of Letter Books of the City of London* ed. R. R. Sharpe (London 1907) pp. 314–15.
[6] *ibid.* p. 317.

for the nobility grew during October and November, Exton tried to preserve the city's neutrality. When Richard asked whether the citizens would act upon their oath of the previous month, Exton apparently replied that his citizens were for the most part artisans and merchants, inexpert in war, and that they did not engage in war except to defend their city. Despite Brembre's efforts to hold the city for the king, it recognized which side was winning and opened its gates to the victorious barons when they returned after defeating de Vere at the battle of Radcot Bridge on the 20th of December 1387.[1]

From the outset, therefore, Richard cannot have been sure of London. The sheriffs, however, were much blunter than the Londoners. Richard asked them what military support they could command in the shires, and whether it would be possible to prevent the election to the next parliament of any knight not agreeable to the king.[2] But the sheriffs replied that the Commons were all on the side of the barons, and as to elections, they were unwilling to break the established custom of freely electing the knights of the shires. After they had given these answers, the king unceremoniously dismissed the sheriffs; but he had not abandoned all idea of influencing the elections. When the writs for the Merciless Parliament were issued on the 17th of December, the sheriffs were instructed to elect knights who, in addition to the usual qualities, were to be 'neutral in present disputes'.[3] After the Appellant victory at Radcot Bridge and their confrontation with Richard in the Tower, they cancelled these writs and issued others in the usual form, describing the addition of the new clause as 'contrary to the form of election traditionally in use and contrary to the liberties of the lordship and community of the kingdom of England'.[4] But in fact the sheriffs took no notice of the additional clause. Many of them made their return on the first writ and simply noted the second when it arrived. There is no evidence of any new election being held nor of any changes being made in the names of members when the second

[1] Westminster pp. 104, 108–9, 113.
[2] *Walsingham, HA* Vol. II, p. 161; Walsingham is the only authority for Richard's consultation with the sheriffs. H. G. Richardson in 'John of Gaunt and the Parliamentary Representation of Lancashire', *BJRL* XXII (1938) p. 215 suggests that the sheriffs' answers were apocryphal; but such questions were in Richard's mind, as is shown by the wording of the first writs to the Merciless Parliament: see below.
[3] PRO Chancery, Parliamentary Writs and Returns C.219/9/3: the writs were warranted 'per ipsum regem'.
[4] *ibid.* C.219/9/4: these writs were warranted 'per ipsum regem et consilium'.

writ was received.[1] Nor is there anything in the known affiliations of members returned to the Merciless Parliament to suggest that the sheriffs deliberately sought out neutral men or men favourable to the king.[2] In seeking to have his own supporters returned, the king was handicapped by the convention which forbade the election of chamber knights as knights of the shire, and more importantly, he was defeated by the long tradition of freely electing the knights of the shire in the county court.[3] The customary procedure for freely electing the knights was too strong to be affected either by those few sheriffs who were Richard's nominees or by a slight last-minute variation in the wording of the writ.

Richard's attempt to use the sheriffs to mobilize political and military support for the court thus failed; and his failure reveals not only the independent attitude of local officials, but also the extent to which public opinion had hardened against the king during 1386 and 1387. The Westminster chronicler noted that when in the autumn Gloucester, Arundel, and Warwick arrived north of London with their armies, 'a very great multitude of gentlemen flocked to join them'.[4] According to Knighton, the Earl of Northumberland warned Richard about the same time that most people in the country supported the lords.[5] If further proof were required, the temper of the Commons in the Merciless Parliament provides it.[6] Public opinion moved against the king partly because of the success of the commission's war policy. On the 24th of March 1387, the Earl of Arundel defeated the Flemish fleet in a naval engagement off Cadzand. The victory eliminated the threat of invasion for the time being, and although Arundel failed either to bring Ghent into the war again or to

---

[1] The sheriff of Essex, for instance, merely noted on the dorse of the first writ that he had received a second (*ibid.* C.219/9/3 no. 10); the sheriffs of Northumberland and of Oxon and Berks merely noted on the second writ that the return appeared on the first; and many other sheriffs just left the second writ blank, certifying the names of the knights and burgesses elected on the dorse of the first writ. Only three sheriffs made the return on the second writ: Cambs and Hunts, Cumberland, and the Chancellor of the Duchy of Lancaster. Only in the last case may there be political reasons for ignoring the first writ.
[2] Seventeen out of the 74 knights had not sat in parliament before: not an unusually high number (N. B. Lewis, 'Re-election to Parliament in the reign of Richard II', *EHR* XLVIII (1933) p. 366).
[3] H. G. Richardson, 'John of Gaunt' p. 212. Sir James Berners had been disqualified from sitting in 1383 on the ground that he was a knight of the chamber (*RDP* Vol. IV, p. 707), but nonetheless he sat in the parliament of 1386. No other chamber knight sat in the period 1377–89.
[4] Westminster p. 105. [5] *Knighton* Vol. II, pp. 244–5. [6] See p. 126 below

establish an English presence in Flanders, his campaign was the most successful of the past decade. His fortunate capture of about 9000 tuns of wine, which he sold cheaply in London, also added greatly to the commission's short-term popularity.[1] At the same time, on his own initiative, Richard began to explore the possibility of an interview with Charles VI, which would presumably deal with the renewal of the peace negotiations broken off when the commission came to power. Rumours of these proposals reached not only Gloucester and Arundel, who took action against the English intermediaries in the Merciless Parliament, but also the Westminster chronicler, who recorded that the proposals for peace were one of the reasons for the rising of the lords against the king.[2]

Public opinion, however, was also shaped by more diffused and generalized sentiments of hostility to the court. Many of Richard's actions probably aroused the suspicions of all men of property, whether great or small; and although loyalty to the crown was a sentiment widely spread throughout the various classes of the population, it was not a blind or unquestioning loyalty and it generally stopped some way short of adulation. There were probably many who, like Sir Ralph Basset, were quite ready to protest their loyalty to the king but unwilling to risk their heads for the sake of the Duke of Ireland.[3] The court was particularly unpopular because of the youthfulness and apparent effeteness of those around the king, whom Walsingham sneeringly described as 'knights of the bedchamber rather than the battlefield'.[4] Langland's opinion, expressed at the very end of the reign, was much the same:

> The cheuyteyns cheef . that ʒe chesse euerr
> Weren all to yonge of ʒeris . to yeme swyche a rewme.[5]

De Vere above all was disliked, and his divorce and scandalous remarriage to a Bohemian girl in the queen's household gave especial offence. There were other scandals at court, such as John Holland's infatuation with and subsequent marriage to Gaunt's daughter

---

[1] Westminster pp. 92–3; *Knighton* Vol. II, pp. 234–5; J. J. N. Palmer, *England, France and Christendom* pp. 92–8.

[2] Westminster p. 103; J. J. N. Palmer, *England, France and Christendom* pp. 105–119.

[3] *Knighton* Vol. II, p. 244: 'nec intendo me opponere ad fracturam capitis mei pro duce Hiberniae.'

[4] *Walsingham, HA* Vol. II, p. 156.

[5] W. Langland, *Richard the Redeless* Vol. I, ed. W. W. Skeat (London 1886) p. 608, Vol. II, pp. lxxxiii–iv.

Elizabeth, who had earlier been betrothed to the young Earl of Pembroke;[1] but de Vere seemed to epitomize in his person all that was objectionable about Richard's court.

Added to these general sentiments were strong feelings on particular matters, and the grievances of individuals who felt themselves threatened or wronged by Richard's actions. In the north, there was resentment against Archbishop Neville of York, who threw in his lot with the court in 1387 when Richard supported him in his dispute with the canons of Beverley.[2] An anonymous libel[3] against him which circulated in the 1380s accused Neville of doing 'more extorcione and distruccione and disese to the cuntree nor the kyng and al the lordes of Ingelond . . . He makyth to the kyng as he wer a saynt but al the world wot it wel the fayrer he speketh the falser he is.' The author was careful not to implicate the king in his criticism. He began by asserting that 'there is no lond in this world that hath a more rightfull worthier, a more gentill kyng than ʒe have of kyng Richard', and he attributed the king's failure to restrain the archbishop to ignorance, for 'no man dor tellen . . . to him' what the archbishop was doing. This feeling that the king should not be blamed for the misdeeds of his advisers is interesting, and is paralleled by the Appellants in the Merciless Parliament when they kept the king in the background during the trials of the favourites and did not try to blame him for the misdeeds of his associates. In London, too, there were important local reasons for the swing of opinion behind the Appellants in 1387 and 1388. Brembre, one of the king's most prominent supporters, belonged to the oligarchy of victuallers who controlled London's food trade. In the early 1380s John Northampton had tried, with the citizens' support, to free retail trade and exclude the victuallers from office, but had failed and by 1385 the oligarchy of the victuallers had re-established itself. The unpopularity of Brembre in the city thus had little to do with his connection with the court, but the odium in which he was held by the citizens may well have strengthened the mayor and aldermen's decision (taken no doubt on grounds of expediency) to open the city's gates to the Appellants after Radcot Bridge.[4]

[1] Westminster pp. 96–7.
[2] A. F. Leach, 'A Clerical Strike at Beverley Minster in the Fourteenth Century', *Archaeologia* LV, pt. 1 (1896) pp. 1–20.
[3] PRO Chancery, Parliament and Council Proceedings C.49/file 9/22.
[4] For discussion of London politics in this period, see R. Bird, *The Turbulent London of Richard II* (London 1949) and S. Thrupp, *The Merchant Class of Medieval London* (Ann Arbor 1962) pp. 66–80.

The king therefore could count on little support within the political community. Only in the royal earldom of Chester, governed by de Vere in 1387, was the king able to raise any military force; only in Chester was there any generalized commitment to the king, who as earl received the loyalty and support given to other nobles on their inheritances. The king's inquiry into his constitutional rights, however, launched at the same time as his investigation of the extent of his political and military support, brought him more comfort and provided him with an answer to the political arguments of his opponents. At the first assembly of the judges (at Shrewsbury early in August) they declared, according to Knighton, that the king could annul or alter the ordinances of parliament at will, 'quia supra jura'.[1] This was a more explicit, and more royalist, formulation of the relationship between the king and the law than at any time since the conflicts of Edward I's last years, and a direct rebuttal of Gloucester's and Bishop Arundel's view of the constitution. At the end of the month, at Nottingham, the judges set their seals to a series of answers to questions arising out of the events of the previous parliament.[2] The tenor of the answers was that the imposition of the commission on the king was derogatory to his prerogative and regality because it was contrary to his will, and that those who had accroached the king's power in various ways during the parliament deserved to be punished as traitors. The 1352 Statute of Treasons had not included accroaching the royal power as a treasonable offence, which is perhaps why the judges stopped one step short of calling it treason now, but the difference between declaring it treason and stating that those guilty of it should be punished as traitors was unlikely to be taken very seriously by Gloucester and his friends. The narrowness of the distinction the judges made should also be seen in the light of the widening of the definition of treason which had taken place in the previous decade. In the trials which followed the Peasants' Revolt the distinction between treason and mere

[1] *Knighton* Vol. II, p. 236; *Rot. Parl.* Vol. III, p. 238. Knighton is the only chronicler who mentions the Shrewsbury council, but the parliament roll vouches for his accuracy. He suggests that the council was held towards the end of August; record evidence suggests Richard was in Shrewsbury rather earlier in the month (see appendix).

[2] Westminster pp. 99–101; *Knighton* Vol. II, 237–40; *Rot. Parl.* Vol. III, pp. 233–4. The questions and answers have generated a large literature. The best recent discussion is by S. B. Chrimes in *Law Quarterly Review* LXXI (1956) pp. 365–90; W. Ullmann, in *Principles of Government and Politics in the Middle Ages* (London 1961) pp. 182–3 sets them in their context. See also A. B. Steel, *Richard II* pp. 129–34, and D. Clementi, 'Richard II's Ninth Question'

felony had become blurred, and 'juries were happy to call treason what seemed to them to be treason'.[1] The sentences passed in trials arising out of the surrender of English-held fortresses abroad also suggested that there were crimes involving the king's regality and prerogative which constituted treason even though they lay outside the scope of the common law on the subject. The judges' answers at Nottingham, and the Appellants' counter-charges of treason against the king's friends, are consistent with this manner of interpretation. Neither judges nor Appellants were breaking wholly new ground in their view of what constituted treason, but both created a climate of political insecurity which it had been the object of the 1352 statute to avoid.

The judges' answers ensured that the king's opponents would move from constitutional measures to military force. The nobility were now faced with a far more fundamental threat to their interests than the foolish profligacy of a king surrounded by favourites. The political crisis of 1385–6 grew out of the king's manner of government over the previous four years; that of 1387–8 was provoked by the events of the preceding summer—not simply the demonstration that the king was still free to conduct his household as and where he liked, but also the implicit threat to his opponents in the judges' answers. The raising of the cry of treason, and de Vere's move to recruit a military force in Cheshire, provoked Gloucester and the Earl of Arundel to action.[2] They refused to meet the king when summoned to do so the day after he returned to London, perhaps because they were afraid they would be arrested. The Earl of Warwick had probably thrown in his lot with Gloucester and Arundel by this time, for the Westminster chronicler says that Pole urged Richard to have him put to death. Richard ignored this advice, but ordered the Earl of Northumberland, who tried to remain neutral and act as a mediator right through that autumn, to arrest Arundel at Reigate Castle. Reigate was so strongly defended that Northumberland could only have taken Arundel by investing the castle, and this he was not prepared to do. Arundel thereupon marched with his retinue to join Gloucester and Warwick at Harringay, north of London, on the 13th of November, and on the following day all three lords moved to Waltham Cross. The sudden movement of the lords evidently took the king by surprise, and he was momentarily

[1] J. G. Bellamy, *The Law of Treason in England in the Later Middle Ages* (Cambridge 1970) pp. 103–11.
[2] This paragraph is based on Westminster pp. 105–14; *Knighton* Vol. II, pp. 241–52; *Walsingham, HA* Vol. II, pp. 63–8; *Kirkstall Chronicle* p. 126; *Calendar of Letter Book H* p. 321.

unsure what course of action to take. He and his friends seem to have considered various possibilities: seeking help from France, or making a fight of it, or asking the Londoners to provide a force. Northumberland, however, told the king that the lords were loyal subjects who were only opposing the misrule of the favourites, and he advised Richard to send for the three lords and negotiate. Accordingly, a deputation went to Waltham to persuade the lords to meet the king, which they agreed to do. But they waited three days before going to see the king, and in those three days they made sure that their position was understood in London. At their meeting with the king on the 17th of November they presented him with an appeal against Pole, de Vere, Neville, Brembre, and Sir Robert Tresilian, the chief justice of the king's bench, accusing them of various treasons and seeking their arrest. At this stage they probably intended to have the five accused dealt with before the Court of Chivalry, over which Gloucester, as constable, presided. But the king suggested that the matter be referred to a parliament, an intelligent move, for it gave de Vere time to bring his army south and perhaps reverse the whole situation. It also gave the other accused time to escape, and Pole and Neville used the breathing space to flee overseas.

The lords, however, had heard of de Vere's plans. Arundel was kept informed of developments in Cheshire by the officials of his lordship of Bromfield and Yale, and he garrisoned Holt Castle for six weeks at the height of the crisis.[1] Richard's open support for de Vere, reported to a council at Westminster early in December, incensed the lords still further, and Gloucester and Arundel apparently suggested deposing the king there and then.[2] But Warwick more realistically advised them that their first task was to defeat de Vere, so they assembled their forces and set off to block de Vere's route to London. By this time the Earls of Derby and Nottingham had joined the three original Appellants. Derby and Nottingham had been close to the king earlier in the reign, and Derby in particular, as Gaunt's son, had received all the honours that he could reasonably expect in the early years of the reign. Richard's relations with Mowbray had been good in the early eighties, and although they had cooled somewhat in face of de Vere's rapid rise in favour, neither he nor Derby were as disaffected as the three original Appellants, and Derby in particular never enjoyed very cordial relations with Gloucester. Both of them avoided committing themselves to either side in the negotiations which followed Richard's

[1] PRO Ministers' Accounts SC.6/1234/5.   [2] Westminster pp. 109–10.

return to London, but, like Sir Ralph Basset and many others, they had no love for de Vere, and after he took up arms nothing held them back from joining Gloucester, Arundel, and Warwick. The five marched out of London in the middle of December, and on the 20th they decisively defeated de Vere at the battle of Radcot Bridge.[1] De Vere, however, eluded capture and fled abroad.

After their victory the Appellants marched triumphantly to London, and after negotiations in the last week of December, with York, Northumberland, and the Bishops of Ely, Hereford, and Winchester acting as mediators,[2] they confronted Richard in the Tower on the 28th or 29th of December. The *Whalley Abbey Chronicle*[3] states categorically that Richard was deposed for three days, which must be the three last days of December, and this evidence is confirmed by Gloucester's confession in 1397, in which he admitted that he and his fellow-Appellants assented to the king's deposition 'for two dayes or thre and than we for to have done our homage and our oothes and putt him as heyly in his estate as ever he was'. The *Whalley Chronicle* goes on to state that there was support for Gloucester as king, but Derby argued that, as the son of Gloucester's elder brother, he had a better right to the throne. Faced with this disagreement, the Appellants decided to put Richard back on the throne. The story may very well be true. Rumours about Gloucester's designs on the crown were so strong that he had to deny them explicitly and publicly at the opening of the Merciless Parliament, and it is entirely credible that Derby should resist Gloucester's attempt to make himself king. Neither he nor his father would have been prepared to tolerate such a blatant disregard of their own prior claim to the throne.

Saved from deposition merely by Gloucester's ambition, or at the very least cowed by the threat of deposition, Richard submitted to the Appellants' demands. On the 2nd of January they went to Westminster and took over the royal household. They removed some royal servants, arrested others, and required certain of Richard's more prominent followers to abjure the court. They dismissed Burley from his office

[1] For an account of the campaign, see J. N. L. Myres, 'The Campaign of Radcot Bridge in December 1387', *EHR* XLII (1927) pp. 20–33. See also R. G. Davies, 'Some notes from the Register of Henry de Wakefield, Bishop of Worcester, on the Political Crisis of 1386–88', *EHR* LXXXVI (1971) pp. 547–8.
[2] Westminster p. 114; *Kirkstall Chronicle* p. 126; R. G. Davies, 'Some notes' pp. 551, 557.
[3] This discussion is based on Westminster pp. 114–15; Favent pp. 14–15; *Rot. Parl.* Vol. III, pp. 229, 379; M. V. Clarke, *Fourteenth Century Studies* (Oxford 1937) pp. 91–5.

of keeper of Dover Castle and Beauchamp from his position as steward of the household, and gave both offices to Sir John Devereux.[1] A show of force had evidently succeeded where constitutional means had failed. The assembly of parliament was fixed for the 3rd of February 1388, and feeling themselves in complete command the Lords Appellant awaited its opening

[1] Westminster pp. 115–16; *CPR* 1385–9, p. 381.

5

King, Council, and Commons 1388-93

The Merciless Parliament thoroughly deserved its name. Not since the reign of Edward II had there been such a savage and bloodthirsty reaction against the policies and friends of a king. In the course of the parliament, eight of those who were brought to trial were condemned to death and executed, including the chief justice of the king's bench. The other judges who had given their answers at Nottingham in the previous summer were also condemned to death, but were reprieved and sentenced to exile in Ireland. Two bishops found guilty of treason were translated by the pope *in partes infidelium*, and two of the king's closest friends, Pole and de Vere, who had fled overseas, were condemned to death in their absence. But the thoroughness with which the Appellants destroyed the architects and beneficiaries of Richard's personal rule only concealed the weakness of their position and the shakiness of their coalition. Like other magnate groups before them, they had short-term, limited objectives, and to achieve even these they had to overcome weighty and sincerely held legal objections to their proposed course of action. A substantial body of opinion which, while prepared to see the back of de Vere and Pole, was unhappy about the extent of the blood-letting proposed by the Appellants and welcomed by the Commons. Even at the moment of their parliamentary triumph, the Appellants were in reality insecure and divided.

The parliament opened in the White Hall of Westminster Palace on the 3rd of February 1388. Before the appeal of treason was formally read, Gloucester knelt before the king and exonerated himself from the charge of plotting to seize the crown.[1] Rumours of the events of the last days of December had evidently reached the ears of the king and the

[1] Favent pp. 14–15; Westminster p. 118.

other lords, and had created a suspicion that Gloucester had over-reached himself. The king declared that he held Gloucester innocent of any attempt on the crown, and Geoffrey Martyn, a royal clerk, then read the appeal of treason against de Vere, Pole, Neville, Brembre, and Tresilian.[1] The Appellants were now faced with the problem of procedure. The judges, on hearing the appeal, declared in effect that it fell between two legal systems. An appeal was a procedure unknown to the common law, yet the Court of Chivalry, which recognized the procedure, had no jurisdiction over the crimes alleged in the appeal.[2] The judges' reply is most significant, for they were not the men who had returned the answers at Nottingham in August 1387, but those appointed by the Appellants after the arrest of their predecessors. The new chief justice of the king's bench, Sir Walter Clopton, was one of the Duke of Gloucester's retainers,[3] yet the judges put loyalty to their profession above the claims of personal ties—an important illustration of the point that all is not necessarily made clear by an analysis of the personal connections of public figures. Thus baulked, the Appellants fell back upon the old tradition of conducting state trials in parliament, arguing that such serious crimes as those set out in the appeal, touching the person of the king and his realm and implicating some persons who were peers, should be tried in parliament and by the law of parliament.[4] Neither civil law nor the law of any inferior court should apply. This improvisation, for such it surely was, has been unjustly characterized as 'little better than lynch law'.[5] It represents a revival of the belief (for which there were important precedents) that state trials should take place in parliament, and that peers of the realm should stand trial in parliament when accused of a crime as serious as treason.[6]

The appeal of treason[7] contained thirty-nine charges. Most were of a general nature, but a few related to specific incidents. They were arranged in no particular order: the first four dealt generally with the undue influence of the accused over the king; counts 5 to 10, and counts 22, 23 and 36, accused the favourites of abusing their power and their

---

[1] Westminster p. 119; *Rot. Parl.* Vol. III, p. 236; Favent p. 15.

[2] *Rot. Parl.* Vol. III, p. 236.

[3] Clopton was retained by Gloucester at the latest some time between June 1387 and June 1388 (BM Add. Mss. 40859A).   [4] *Rot. Parl.* Vol. III, p. 236.

[5] A. B. Steel, *Richard II* (Cambridge 1941) p. 152.

[6] See for example T. F. T. Plucknett, 'Impeachment and Attainder', *TRHS* 5th series III (1953) pp. 145–58; M. H. Keen, 'Treason Trials and the Law of Arms', *TRHS* XII (1962) pp. 85–103; J. G. Bellamy, *The Law of Treason in England in the Later Middle Ages* (Cambridge 1970).

[7] *Rot. Parl.* Vol. III, pp. 230–36; Westminster pp. 122–40.

influence over the king, 'taking advantage of his tender years'. In effect, they were accused of accroaching the royal power. Counts 15 to 21 and 25 to 32 arose out of Richard's defiance of the commission of 1386, although they are so phrased as to imply that the favourites had persuaded him to subvert its authority. The remaining charges dealt with the events of autumn 1387, purporting to show that the accused had encouraged the king to take military action against the Appellants. Not all the charges in the appeal bear serious examination. Some of them are merely tendentious interpretations of the events of the preceding months; others are propaganda, and others are supported only by the slenderest threads of evidence. Those which can be substantiated, however, include the favourites' use of their influence to obtain grants of land from the king, the bestowal upon de Vere of vice-regal powers in Ireland and power in Cheshire which he used to raise an army, and their participation in the plans made in the previous year for a meeting between Richard and Charles VI of France.[1] The charges throw much light on the reasons for the growth of hostility to Richard's government and the intensification of that hostility in 1387. The issues that emerge as important are the control and direction of patronage, foreign and Irish policy, and in 1387, the sense of insecurity created by the judges' answers and by de Vere's military activity.

Even if some of the charges could be substantiated, however, it was far from clear whether any of them constituted treason. Under the act of 1352, accroachment of the royal power was not a treasonable offence. Although there had been uncertainty in the previous ten years over the precise limits of the treason law,[2] the difficulties which the Appellants experienced in procuring a conviction against Brembre, the one victim of the appeal who stood trial in person, showed that the old definition of treason still had validity for many in parliament. Nonetheless, had some uncertainty about the scope of treason not developed during the past decade it is doubtful whether the Appellants would have used the charge so readily themselves. By their actions they did as much as the judges to widen the concept of treason still further.

The procedure to be followed in a parliamentary treason trial was as troublesome to the Appellants as the definition of treason itself. In dealing with those accused who had absconded, the principle of conviction by default was introduced from the civil law;[3] but in dealing

---

[1] *Rot. Parl.* Vol. III, pp. 230–36.
[2] J. G. Bellamy, *The Law of Treason* pp. 102ff.
[3] *Westminster* p. 148; *Rot. Parl.* Vol. III, p. 237.

with Brembre, the only one of the five accused in custody at the opening of parliament, both common law and civil law procedures were followed.[1] The Appellants exploited the vagueness about procedure to obtain the verdict they wanted. The trial of Brembre showed how shaky the whole legal basis of the Appellants' case was, both procedurally and in substantive law. Brembre throughout denied that parliament had any jurisdiction in the matters alleged against him. In accordance with common law, he was asked how he pled. In reply, he offered to prove his plea of innocence by battle, but although 'more than a hundred gloves were cast against him', he was refused trial by battle on the ground that, in accordance with civil law procedure, it was permissible only when there were no witnesses.[2] Procedurally, the Appellants were up a blind alley and could expect no help from the judges. They therefore set up a committee consisting of the Duke of York, the Earls of Kent, Salisbury, and Northumberland, and eight barons to examine the charges against him, but the committee reported that it could find nothing worthy of death in Brembre's record.[3] York and Northumberland had earlier acted as mediators between the king and the Appellants, and it is clear that neither they nor their associates on the committee were prepared to be browbeaten by the Appellants into reaching a decision inconsistent with their view of the law. This was the Appellants' second defeat: not only the judges but a group of their fellow peers were unwilling to bend the law for their convenience.

The Appellants were in danger of becoming frustrated and isolated, but a welcome diversion was provided when Tresilian, who had already been convicted and condemned to death in his absence, was discovered in sanctuary in Westminster Abbey.[4] Gloucester took upon himself the violation of sanctuary and brought Tresilian to face sentence and execution, despite his protests that the whole process against him had been invalid.[5] After his despatch, the Appellants returned to Brembre's case, and in desperation sought his condemnation from the representatives of the London gilds.[6] They met defeat here too, and turned finally to the mayor, aldermen, and recorder of London, who declared that, on balance, he was more likely to be guilty than not. On this flimsy basis Brembre was condemned to death and executed.[7]

[1] Westminster pp. 148–9; *Rot. Parl.* Vol. III, p. 238.
[2] Westminster p. 149; Favent p. 16.   [3] Westminster pp. 166–7.
[4] Westminster pp. 149–51, 167; Favent p. 17.
[5] Westminster pp. 167–8.   [6] Westminster p. 168.   [7] *ibid.*

The hearing of the appeal had shown the Appellants just how much opposition existed amongst the judges and the lords to their procedure and their charges. They therefore resorted to the process of impeachment to deal with their remaining victims, and in doing so avoided the procedural problems to which the appeal had given rise. John Blake, the serjeant who had drafted the questions to the judges, and Thomas Usk, the under-sheriff of Middlesex and author of the *Testament of Love*, were condemned on charges which were not noted in the record, but which in Blake's case are obvious and in Usk's case probably relate to the king's attempt to hold London in the autumn of 1387.[1] They were both executed. The king's confessor, Thomas Rushook, who had been an object of suspicion as long ago as 1380, was also condemned on unspecified charges and banished to the Clementist See of Kilmore in Ireland.[2] The following day, the 6th of March, the judges who had given the answers at Nottingham were duly condemned to death, but the Appellants had no serious intention of executing them, for they joined the clergy in interceding with the king for their lives, which were readily granted, and their sentence was commuted to loss of property and banishment to Ireland.[3]

Six days later, on the 12th of March, the last trials took place. Four of Richard's chamber knights, Sir Simon Burley, Sir John Beauchamp of Holt, Sir John Salesbury, and Sir James Berners were impeached on sixteen counts.[4] The charges were similar to those in the appeal of treason: nine of them were general accusations that the four had aided and abetted the other favourites in accroaching the royal power, and the others were specific charges against Burley, dealing with his influence over the king and his conduct as constable of Dover and Windsor Castles. There were no specific charges against the other three accused, although the Westminster annalist recorded that there was a special animus against Salesbury because he was thought guilty of treason both within and without the realm, a reference to his participation in negotiations for an interview between Richard and Charles VI. All four accused were condemned to death. No one was prepared to fight for Beauchamp, Berners, or Salesbury, but a bitter and prolonged dispute centred on Burley's fate. In a characteristically vivid phrase, Favent referred to the 'indivisa trinitas' of Gloucester, Arundel, and Warwick

[1] *Rot. Parl.* Vol. III, p. 240; Westminster pp. 150–2.
[2] *Rot. Parl.* Vol. III, p. 240.
[3] *ibid.*
[4] *Rot. Parl.* Vol. III, pp. 241–3; Westminster pp. 140–7.

holding fast to the sentence against him and, with vociferous support from the Commons, demanding his execution.[1] The three lords, however, were isolated amongst their peers; the king and queen, the Earls of Derby and Nottingham, the Prior of the Hospital of St John, and many other lords (amounting in Favent's opinion to a majority) wished to spare Burley. Derby's stand brought into the open the tension between him and Gloucester which was always only just below the surface, and it showed how fragile the unity of the Appellants had been. The king sent York and Cobham to the Commons to beg for Burley's life, but the Commons refused to relent.[2] At this point, however, rumours of a rising in Kent reached the ears of parliament. The men of Kent were apparently demanding Burley's execution, and rather than risk another mob rising, Burley's partisans dropped their plea for mercy and let him go to his death on the 5th of May.[3]

In the end, therefore, the Appellants had their way. But they had achieved their objects only through the exploitation of vaguenesses in legal procedure, the steadfast support of the Commons, and the unenthusiastic acquiescence of their fellow lords, many of whom (including perhaps York and Northumberland) may have thought that the Appellant programme was merely the lesser of two evils. Perhaps sensing that they did not have the whole-hearted support of the political community, the Appellants made strenuous efforts to ensure that the work of the parliament would not be lightly undone. In the middle of March they imposed an oath of loyalty on the leading laymen of each shire;[4] at the close of parliament, on the 3rd of June, lords and Commons together swore to uphold the work of the parliament, and this oath was subsequently imposed upon the community of every shire, laity and clergy alike, and upon the leading citizens and burgesses of each city and borough.[5] The king renewed his coronation oath and the lords renewed their homage,[6] a symbolic reaffirmation of the accepted relationship between the king and the law, and a means of removing the taint of disloyalty and deposition.

The Appellants went further than this, however, and instituted

---

[1] Favent p. 21.

[2] *Walsingham, HA* Vol. II, p. 174; Westminster, p. 176; Favent p. 21.

[3] Favent p. 21; *Knighton* Vol. II, pp. 266–70: a petition included in Knighton's chronicle and apparently submitted to the Merciless Parliament. It hints at a popular rising in the spring of 1388. The petition has not received the attention it deserves.

[4] *Rot. Parl.* Vol. III, pp. 244, 400–3; *CCR* 1385–9, p. 405.

[5] Favent p. 24; PRO Chancery Miscellanea C.49/Roll 24.

[6] Favent p. 24.

certain practical measures for the supervision of the king. The commission's authority was allowed to lapse, and there was evidently no suggestion that it should be revived, but towards the end of March a committee consisting of the Bishops of Winchester and London, the Earl of Warwick, Sir John Cobham, and Sir Richard Lescrope was appointed to attend continually on the king.[1] This committee remained in existence throughout the summer, for Cobham was eventually paid for service from the 1st of April until the 10th of September[2] (the day parliament opened at Cambridge) and in all probability it was the Appellants' intention that the committee should discharge its responsibilities until the opening of the next parliament, the date for which had been fixed at the end of the Merciless Parliament.[3] There is no evidence, however, that the committee was revived at the end of the Cambridge Parliament; the events of that parliament allowed the king to recapture the initiative and isolate his discredited opponents.

The Appellants, however, had seized power not merely to rid the country of the king's favourites and impose yet another committee upon him, but also to reverse the direction which patronage had taken since the early 1380s. Their opportunity to do so was provided by the forfeiture to the crown, as a result of the sentences imposed in the Merciless Parliament, of a vast amount of property. The earldoms and inheritances of Oxford and Suffolk, the temporalities of the Sees of York and Chichester, and the lands, goods, and chattels of the convicted judges, officials, and chamber knights were seized into the king's hands. But the statute passed at the end of the parliament specifically exempted jointures and entails from the scope of the forfeitures, and with very few exceptions the statute was strictly observed.[4] The bulk of the de Vere and Pole inheritances were recovered by their heirs under it, and the same was true of much of the inheritance of John Beauchamp of Holt. The estates of the lesser victims of the parliament, however, had been less carefully safeguarded, and most of them were sold, leased, or given away by the Appellants, to ease the crown's financial difficulties, reward their friends and followers, and create a vested interest in the work of the parliament.

For various reasons, the Appellants appropriated little of the confiscated property. Because of the statute protecting entails and jointures

---

[1] Westminster p. 178.   [2] PRO Exchequer Warrants for Issues E.404/14/96 i.
[3] *Rot. Parl.* Vol. III, p. 246.
[4] C. D. Ross, 'Forfeiture for Treason in the Reign of Richard II', *EHR* LXXI (1956) pp. 560–75. This article corrects the view of Miss M. V. Clarke (*Fourteenth Century Studies* (Oxford 1937) pp. 143–5) that the statute was ignored.

the biggest prizes were either not available at all or capable of exploitation on only a short-term basis. And having been voted £20,000 by the grateful Commons for their 'great expenses in saving the kingdom bringing the traitors to justice',[1] they were perhaps senstitive to the criticism that might arise if they appropriated property which could otherwise have been sold for the crown's benefit. The Duke of Gloucester was the only one of the Appellants who received a substantial amount of the forfeited land. He was granted lands, tenements, and fees to the value of £2000 a year, with the condition that the annual value of the property granted him when he was created Earl of Buckingham should be deducted from that sum.[2] In other words, his income was at last to be given a secure landed base, and one of Gloucester's principal grievances was now satisfied. He also received the keeping of eight manors which Bealknap, the chief justice of common pleas, had forfeited, and de Vere's right of winter venison in the forest of Hatfield Broadoak, near Pleshy.[3] There is some reason to believe that Gloucester also coveted de Vere's duchy of Ireland, perhaps to give himself equality in palatine status with his brother Lancaster, but although the council may have considered bestowing the title on him in January 1389, the Monk of Westminster is surely misinformed when he records that the grant was actually made.[4]

The Appellants ensured that their followers and dependants were not neglected. Sir William Castleacre, Gloucester's chief steward, received a Norfolk wardship; Sir John Lakenheath, a Suffok landowner who was a member of Gloucester's council and deputized for him in the Court of Chivalry in 1389 and 1391, received the keeping of the manor of Benhale, forfeited by Pole; and when this was granted to the Earl of Huntingdon in 1389, he was compensated with the keeping of the manor and hundred of Lowestoft and the hundred of Lothingland, also forfeited by Pole. Another member of the duke's council, John Corbet, picked up the marriage of John Deschalers in May 1388. His clerk Thomas Feriby, described as 'deputy' of the Appellants in June 1388, became Archdeacon of Ely, perhaps to counterbalance John Fordham, Richard's complaisant treasurer, who had been degraded from Durham.[5] Some of Derby's associates also got their reward. John Cope, one of his esquires, was allowed to appropriate £8 worth of Tresilian's goods,

[1] Westminster p. 154; *Rot. Parl.* Vol. III, p. 248.
[2] CPR 1385-9, p. 479.   [3] *ibid.* p. 412.   [4] Westminster p. 203.
[5] PRO Duchy of Lancaster Accounts DL.29/680/11004; BM Add. Mss. 40859A; CFR 1383-91, p. 227; CPR 1388-92, pp. 130, 412; *ibid.* 1385-9, pp. 441, 506.

while Hugh Herle, the earl's chaplain, became Archdeacon of Durham on the 15th of April 1388.[1] The political ascendancy of the Appellants enabled them to display the good lordship which was essential to the maintenance of a magnate's following and his social prestige.

The Appellants, however, were circumspect in their use of patronage. The statute passed at the end of the Merciless Parliament had laid down that the confiscated property was either to remain in the king's hands or to be sold, and in either case the revenue was to be used to pay the king's debts. Members of the royal household and other persons about the king were prohibited from accepting any of the forfeitures as gifts, except for grants made during the Merciless Parliament and offices and benefices.[2] With very few exceptions, the statute was observed, and between July 1388 and September 1389 a grand auction was held. By midsummer 1389, £10,000 had been paid or promised for the forfeited lands, and most of the purchasers were men from the middle ranks of society—merchants, knights, esquires, and clerks.[3] In the southwest, for example, the bulk of Tresilian's lands passed to the wealthy Dartmouth merchant John Hawley. Some of Tresilian's lands were returned to his widow; some of course were concealed; and some were disputed for several years between rival claimants; but in three transactions in 1389, Hawley paid 1100 marks for the bulk of the remainder.[4] Other Devon men, esquires and merchants, purchased lands forfeited by Blake and Cary, and indeed nearly all the property available for sale in the county had gone to local men.[5] The disposal of the property in this way was a powerful practical reinforcement of the oath to uphold the work of the parliament imposed upon the leading men of each shire in June.

This, however, was only one side of the financial picture. Although the crown might expect eventually to receive £10,000 or more from the forfeitures, the Appellants had been granted precisely twice that figure for their expenses in bringing the traitors to justice. The protection of jointures and entails sharply reduced the amount which might have been raised had all the forfeited property been available for sale, and the Commons appear to have had unrealistically high expectations of the income to be derived from the forfeitures. This must go some

[1] PRO DL.28/1/1; *CPR* 1385–9, p. 431; *ibid.* 1388–92, p. 449.
[2] *Rot. Parl.* Vol. III, p. 246.
[3] C. D. Ross, 'Forfeiture for Treason' pp. 570–71.
[4] *CPR* 1388–92, pp. 126, 156, 247; *CMI* V, nos, 134–6, 144, 178, 186.
[5] *CFR* 1383–91, pp. 289, 295; *CPR* 1385–9, p. 531; PRO Exchequer Bille E.207/7/15.

way towards explaining the Commons' criticism of Appellant handling of finance in the Cambridge Parliament in September 1388. Furthermore, very little of the income derived from any of the forfeitures was specifically assigned to any purpose, despite the Commons' request that it should be used to pay the king's debts and maintain his estate. A little was used to repay loans: in the Easter term of 1388, £200 from the sale of goods forfeited by Bealknap and Rushook was assigned to the Bishop of Ely, and £331-3-7 from the sale of Brembre's goods was used to repay Matthew Cheyne. A few small sums were assigned to the captains of Calais and other fortresses in France.[1] But the government's commitment to a war policy was bound to strain its finances. Assignment was practised as extensively as before, a clear sign that the government was living beyond its means; the half subsidy granted in March proved insufficient to cover the costs of Arundel's expedition, and the government had to ask the Cambridge Parliament to grant another subsidy.[2]

The Appellants made some attempt to reduce the size of the household. By 1390 it was not much bigger than it had been in the last years of Edward III's reign. The number of chamber knights was halved, the number of esquires was reduced from 87 to 63, and the number of yeomen of the chamber fell from 26 to 18.[3] The income of the chamber was also reduced—not drastically, for the king had to have a privy purse—but sufficiently to prevent it being developed once again as a source of political power. Its income fell from £3086-13-4 in 1387-8 to £1603-6-8 in 1388-9, and during the period of Appellant rule the exchequer paid over the money in small instalments, none greater than 500 marks.[4] The object of the Appellants and their friends in the offices of state was to eliminate Richard's administrative novelties, rather than to introduce any systematic reforms in the household or the chief departments of government. On the secretarial side, for instance, the Commons in the Merciless Parliament successfully petitioned that letters under the signet or secret seal should not be used to interfere with the course of law or to damage the realm.[5] This may

---

[1] PRO Exchequer Receipt Rolls E.401/571-4 *passim*; Issue Roll E.403/512 *passim*; *Rot. Parl.* Vol. III, p. 246; A. B. Steel, *The Receipt of the Exchequer 1377-1485* (Cambridge 1954) pp. 59-60.
[2] J. A. Tuck, 'The Cambridge Parliament 1388', *EHR* LXXXIV (1969) p. 232; A. B. Steel, *Receipt* pp. 59-60.
[3] PRO Wardrobe and Household Accounts, E.101/401/2, E.101/402/5.
[4] PRO Exchequer Issue Rolls, E.403/18, 19, 21.
[5] *Rot. Parl.* Vol. III, p. 247.

refer to Richard's use of the signet to send instructions to the law courts in the summer of 1387, and this use of the signet ceases after Richard's return to London in October 1387. Chancellor Arundel had already refused to accept the signet as a sufficient warrant for the great seal, and so long as he was in office the regular course for transmitting the king's instructions to the chancery was strictly observed. The signet itself was now regarded with mistrust. In February 1389 a charter of pardon was renewed because it had originally been granted under the signet, and in 1388 even Richard's auditors in Chester refused to recognize it as sufficient warrant for the grant of an annuity.[1] But by autumn 1388 the king was once again using the signet to convey his instructions to the keeper of the Privy Seal, and in all probability throughout the period of Appellant rule he still used it to authenticate his private and personal correspondence.[2]

During the months in which the Merciless Parliament was in session and the weeks that followed its dissolution, the Appellants' main concern (apart from the removal of their political opponents) was foreign affairs. The Appellant strategy, which was almost certainly shaped mainly by Gloucester and Arundel, was to continue the war with France as vigorously as possible and to bring into the war the English forces under Gaunt in Castile and the disaffected Flemish towns.[3] In mid-December 1387 Burgundy had written to Gloucester asking whether he proposed to continue negotiations for a truce, but Gloucester ignored the letter for six months, and Burgundy wisely prepared for war. Gloucester's diplomacy, however, met with little success. His negotiations with the Flemings came to nothing, and in Castile Gaunt ignored Gloucester's objections to his making a separate peace and proceeded to negotiate an agreement which satisfactorily safeguarded his own interests. He also refused to mount an Anglo-Gascon attack on France from Aquitaine, despite the preparations which the council in England made for such an attack. Furthermore, without Gaunt's co-operation, the Duke of Brittany declined to take part in an attack on France and withdrew from his English alliance. The successful prosecution of the war, however, required money as well as allies, and the Appellants were as unsuccessful in procuring the one as the other. The half subsidy voted by the Commons in the Merciless Parliament was quite insufficient to finance an overseas campaign, yet the Com-

[1] *CPR* 1388–92, p. 4; PRO Chester Recognizance Rolls, Chester 2/61 m. 3d.
[2] PRO Privy Seal Office Records PSO.1/1/1, 3, 4.
[3] J. J. N. Palmer, *England, France and Christendom* (London 1971) ch. 7.

mons were as opposed to heavy taxation now as they had been earlier
in the reign, and the exaction of a larger subsidy might have endangered
the political co-operation between the Appellants and the Commons on
which the Appellants' parliamentary power depended. A statute passed
during the Merciless Parliament decreed that the crown lands and
feudal incidents should not be granted out as long as the war lasted, but
this could make little difference to the immediate financial position, for
the income from both was small and came in slowly. In the circumstances it is scarcely surprising that Arundel's naval expedition, which
lasted from the 10th of June until the 3rd of September, was unsuccessful
and marked the final collapse of the Appellant strategy. Indeed, only
two days after Arundel's departure, which had been much delayed
by the long drawn-out arguments in parliament over Burley's fate,
Gloucester made the first move to reverse his strategy by accepting a
conciliar decision to reopen negotiations with the Duke of Burgundy
for a long truce.[1]

The abandonment of an aggressive policy towards France was
necessitated not only by the lack of money and the failure of Gloucester's diplomacy, but also by a Scottish invasion of England which,
according to the Westminster chronicler, was the most serious for
fifty years.[2] England's weakness in the previous ten years had allowed
the Scots to recapture almost the whole of Annandale, Roxburghshire,
and Berwickshire, which though only precariously held by the English,
had served as something of a buffer against a full-scale Scottish invasion
of northern England. But in the summer of 1388 the Scots launched a
two-pronged attack on England, ostensibly in retaliation for the English
invasion of 1385.[3] One force under the Earl of Fife invaded Cumberland and Westmorland, while the other under the Earl of Douglas
entered Northumberland through Redesdale. Douglas burnt parts of
Redesdale and Tynedale, and thoroughly defeated an English army
under Hotspur at the battle of Otterburn on the 5th of August 1388.[4]
The defeat was a severe blow to English prestige, and Hotspur himself
was captured, but the battle was of little strategic significance. Indeed, it
was little more than another encounter in Douglas's perennial feud
with Percy over the lordship of Jedburgh.[5] Douglas himself was killed
in the battle, and the Scots made no attempt to follow up their victory.

[1] *CPR* 1385-9, pp. 502-3.   [2] Westminster pp. 184-7.
[3] Froissart, *Oeuvres* Vol. XIII, pp. 200-01.   [4] *ibid.* p. 209.
[5] For this subject, see J. M. W. Bean, 'The Percies and their Estates in Scotland',
Archaeologia Aeliana 4th series XXXV (1957) pp. 91-9.

The invasion of Cumberland and Westmorland was much more serious Much of the country north of Shap was systematically devastated: Carlisle itself held out, but Appleby was sacked and the villages of the Eden Valley suffered particularly badly. The lay subsidy returns for the tenth and fifteenth granted in the Cambridge Parliament show that scarcely a village in north Westmorland escaped destruction, and Appleby sent no burgesses to the parliament because of the damage done by the Scots.[1] The Appellants' response to the invasion was wholly inadequate: Arundel was ordered to return home and take his fleet to the north, but he ignored the order and spent the summer plundering the French coast.[2] Otherwise the defence of the north was left, as usual, in the hands of the northern nobility, who resisted as best they could.[3] When news of the defeat reached London, the Bishop of Durham was criticized for failing to go to Hotspur's help until it was too late, and a council was held at Northampton to consider reprisals. The king himself was evidently willing to lead an army against the Scots, but the withdrawal of the main invading forces made an immediate expedition unnecessary. Retaliation was left to the local nobility, who successfully repulsed raids on Berwick and Carlisle in October 1388, and burnt Peebles in the summer of 1389.[4]

On almost every count, the Appellants failed to live up to the hopes that had been placed in them, and the financial strains of an unsuccessful war policy created a political situation which Richard could exploit to recapture power for himself. Richard now showed considerable political shrewdness and skill in using the strengths of his position to place his power on new, and perhaps firmer, foundations, and to reassert his personal authority in government. This new approach is first apparent in the Cambridge Parliament of September 1388; Richard maintained it until renewed financial problems and tension with the nobility over the question of law and order compelled its abandonment in 1393.

In seeking to flex his political muscles once again, Richard was bound to benefit from the removal of his friends of the 1380s. Like Edward II before him, Richard felt a strong and bitter sense of personal loss, but

[1] PRO Lay Subsidy Rolls E.179/195/21: roll for Westmorland 1388–9; the roll for Cumberland does not survive. *Return of Members of Parliament* (London 1878) p. 236; *Knighton* Vol. II, pp. 297–8; *Rot. Parl.* Vol. III, pp. 270–1.
[2] J. J. N. Palmer, *England, France and Christendom* p. 133.
[3] *CCR* 1385–9, p. 604.
[4] *Westminster* pp. 205–6; *The Exchequer Rolls of Scotland* Vol. III (Edinburgh 1880) p. 337.

the exile or death of Pole, de Vere, Burley, and Beauchamp could not but be a political gain to him. There was now no obnoxious favourite to give point, unity and popularity to opposition to the king. The men who had tightened their grip on government while the king was still adolescent (some of whom owed their place at court to the king's father and mother) were now gone, and there may be more than a grain of truth in Richard's disavowal (in his speech on the 3rd of May 1389) of responsibility for what had occurred in the 1380s.

Of more immediate importance in helping the king to recover power was the disillusion the Commons felt, by September 1388, with the Appellants' conduct of government. The Commons were unhappy about the Appellants' handling of financial matters, but they also felt a more general dissatisfaction with the lords because of their apparent inability (or unwillingness) to do anything to restrain the activities of disorderly bands of liveried retainers. The Commons' two main pre-occupations, finance and law and order, served to break the alliance with the Appellants which had been the indispensable basis of their political ascendancy in the Merciless Parliament, and made them cautiously inclined to co-operate with a king whose policies seemed to offer some prospect both of a reduction of taxation and of a curbing of the excesses of liveried retainers. Mutual self-interest was to be the basis of relations between the king and the Commons over the next four years. The king's peace policy promised some relief from heavy annual taxation, and the curbing of livery and maintenance might go some way towards undermining the military power of the nobility which had finally brought about Richard's downfall in December 1387.

The parliament which opened in Barnwell Priory, Cambridge, on the 10th of September 1388 revealed how substantially the political climate had changed during the summer. In his opening speech, Chancellor Arundel almost certainly asked for the grant of another subsidy.[1] We do not know how much he asked for, but there is some evidence that the eventual grant, one tenth and one fifteenth, was less than the government wanted.[2] The Commons were not unnaturally reluctant to grant another tax only six months after they had voted one in the Merciless Parliament. They took the view that the Crown's income should have been substantially increased by the sale of forfeited lands and goods, perhaps not realizing how much of the land was recoverable under the statute protecting entails and jointures and how long it took to raise money from the sale of land that was available for disposal. The Commons raised the question of the forfeitures at once, and evidently took the government by surprise, for on the 11th of September a messenger was sent in great haste to Northampton to get a statement on the income from the forfeitures from Walter Malet, one of the remembrancers of the exchequer.[1] Furthermore, the Commons were suspicious of the financial side of Arundel's expedition in the summer. He had originally engaged to serve for four months from the 11th of May, but the unexpected length of the Merciless Parliament delayed his departure until the 10th of June. He returned to England on the 2nd of September and was thus at sea for no more than twelve weeks, but he insisted on receiving payment for the full term of four months for which he had originally been engaged. The Commons were naturally unhappy about this, especially after Arundel had used his ascendancy during the Merciless Parliament to double his fee as captain of Brest, and two of his servants, Sir William Heron and John Stephens, were hauled before parliament at Cambridge and required to explain the delay in the departure of the expedition.[2] But in all probability Arundel managed to prevent the Commons from taking any action against him or his servants, and he was eventually exonerated from responsibility for the delay.[3]

The Appellants had destroyed their credibility by their mishandling of finance and foreign policy; but a *rapprochement* between the king and the Commons was made possible by their collision with the nobility on a more general question, that of livery and maintenance. The Westminster chronicler gave this subject great attention, and evidently thought it was the most important and controversial matter dealt with by the parliament.[4] The Commons petitioned that all liveries, whether of the king or of other lords, which had been assumed since the first year of Edward III, should be abolished; and linked with this was another petition against maintenance, which asked that justices of the peace and of assize should have power to investigate and try cases of maintenance, bribery, or other means of corrupting juries. They asked parliament to establish a penalty for the wearing of livery, and to draw up an ordinance against maintenance under which persons found guilty should be fined, and the plaintiff in the case awarded double damages. But the petition provoked serious opposition from the lords. They first

---

[1] PRO Exchequer Issue Rolls E.403/519 m.21.
[2] PRO Exchequer KR Memoranda Rolls E.159/167 brevia baronibus Michaelmas m. 51.   [3] *ibid*.   [4] Westminster pp. 189–90.

of all promised to punish all offenders, if these could be found, as a warning to others. This, however, failed to satisfy the Commons, who reiterated that law and order could only be restored if liveries were abolished. The king then intervened, taking the initiative for the first time since the Appellants had seized power, and offered to set an example by abolishing his own livery. The lords flatly rejected this offer, and then attacked the Commons for their presumption in raising the matter in the first place. The prospect now opened up of strife between lords and Commons, but Richard seized the opportunity to act as a mediator, and, 'wishing to avoid dissension', managed to persuade both sides to agree that the matter should be shelved until the next parliament, but that in the meantime he and his council would look for a satisfactory solution. This arrangement avoided an open collision between the king and the nobility, which Richard could not afford at this stage, yet it allowed him to demonstrate his sympathy towards the Commons' point of view. He had shown that his personal intervention in political argument might be effective, and the discredit into which the Appellant regime had fallen no doubt inclined the Commons to listen more favourably to the king now that he was no longer under the dominance of the undesirable associates of his youth.

There is no evidence that the committee appointed after the Merciless Parliament to be permanently resident with the king remained in existence after the end of the Cambridge Parliament, and the king's power was now in all probability limited only by the statutory enactments of the Merciless Parliament. These related mainly to finance and patronage, and thus inhibited his immediate reassertion of these aspects of his prerogative. In other matters, however, the king's personal authority in government becomes increasingly apparent in the autumn of 1388. The king's secretary, Richard Medford, had been released from prison in June on condition that he kept away from court, but he seems to have ignored the condition. In August he was described as 'Secretary', and although the signet office may have ceased to function, for John Lincoln was described as 'lately' a clerk in the signet office, Medford himself continued to work, and one or two signet letters survive from autumn 1388 and spring 1389.[1] By the autumn, too, some of the courtiers were beginning to creep back: Sir John Lovell, whom the Appellants had removed from court, witnessed charters at Westminster in mid-November, and two chamber knights, Clanvowe

[1] PRO Exchequer brevia baronibus E.208/10; Privy Seal Office, Warrants PSO.1/1, 3, 4.

and Dagworth, were appointed on the 26th of November, together with Devereux, the captain of Calais, to negotiate with the Count of Flanders. Sir Thomas Blount, another victim of the Appellant purge of the court, was back in favour by February 1389, and Sir John Golafre (who had fled overseas in January 1388 but who had received a pardon at the end of the Merciless Parliament) was acting once again as constable of Wallingford Castle by the spring of 1389.[1]

The Appellants attended the council from time to time in the months after the Cambridge Parliament, but there is no evidence that they attended to the day-to-day business of government.[2] This appears to have been the responsibility of a small group of councillors headed by the great officers of state, and including the Archbishop of Canterbury, the steward, the Bishop of Winchester, Richard Lescrope, and Sir John Cobham. Cobham also acted as an intermediary between the king and the council in dealing with petitions.[3] In all probability this was not a formally constituted committee armed with supervisory powers, such as had held office between the Merciless and Cambridge parliaments. Yet the great officers of state were the Appellants' friends, the men who had come to power in October 1386, and so long as they remained in office, so long as Gloucester and Arundel attended the council frequently, the king could not feel himself completely free.

However, Richard did not now wait long before formally ending the period of Appellant rule. On the 3rd of May 1389 he held a council at Westminster, at which he declared that he was now at an age when 'the meanest heir in the kingdom' was entitled fully to enjoy his rights, and therefore he intended to take the government of the country upon himself.[4] For twelve years, he said, he and his kingdom had been ruled by others, and his people oppressed by heavy taxation, but henceforth he would work to bring peace and prosperity to his kingdom. From now on he would choose his own councillors, and as a first step he ordered Chancellor Arundel to surrender the great seal. On the following day the treasurer and the keeper of the Privy Seal were dismissed, and Gloucester and Arundel were removed from the council. Huntingdon replaced Arundel as admiral and captain of Brest. On the 6th of May

---

[1] PRO Charter Rolls C.53/162 mm. 14, 22; Treaty Rolls C. 76/73 m. 6; *CPR* 1388–92, pp. 10, 23.

[2] PRO Exchequer Issue Rolls E.403/521 m. 6; Charter Rolls C.53/162 mm. 14, 22; *Westminster* pp. 202, 205.

[3] J. F. Baldwin, *The King's Council in England during the Middle Ages* (Oxford 1913) pp. 510–13; *CMI* V, no. 134.

[4] *Westminster* pp. 210–11; *Walsingham, HA* Vol. II, p. 181.

the chief justices of common pleas and king's bench, together with William Thirning, one of the judges appointed by the Appellants, were required to resign and be reappointed. This formal reassertion of Richard's personal authority would hardly have been possible had not the Appellants discredited themselves after they had accomplished their task of destroying the court party and had not Richard's supporters and officials gradually re-established themselves since the previous autumn in positions of influence. In short, the Appellants lost their momentum after the end of the Merciless Parliament. They had achieved their political objects, but in doing so they had removed the main reason for the existence of their coalition. In less than a year, the dominance of the court in politics had reasserted itself.

Gaunt's return from Aquitaine in November 1389 strengthened Richard's position still further. De Vere's fall had removed one of the most serious reasons for hostility between Gaunt and the king, and for the rest of Gaunt's life they remained on the most cordial terms. Gaunt had no sympathy whatever with the political ambitions and beliefs of his younger brother Gloucester. At the most serious crisis of his political career, in 1376, Gaunt had defended royal authority against precisely the kind of attack it had had to face in 1386, and there had been nothing in Gaunt's political activities between 1376 and 1386 to suggest that his views had changed. Gaunt was now an indispensable ally of the king: he was implicitly loyal to the crown and a firm upholder of the royal prerogative, while at the same time he deployed the political and social weight of the enormous Lancastrian inheritance in support of the king's position.

However, despite the strengths of Richard's position he did not seriously try to return to the policies which had led to disaster in 1386 and 1388. De Vere, Pole and Neville had to remain in exile. They themselves never gave up hope of recall,[1] and Richard ensured that de Vere continued to receive the payments of the ransom of John of Blois.[2] In 1392 Richard suggested that de Vere and Neville might be allowed to return home, but the council firmly opposed him and he tactfully let the matter drop.[3] The abandonment of his friends may have been a personal sorrow to him, but it furnished him on at least one occasion

[1] G. S. Haslop, 'Two Entries from the Register of John de Shirburn, Abbot of Selby 1369–1408', *Yorkshire Archaeological Journal* XLI (1964) p. 288.
[2] M. C. E. Jones, 'The Ransom of Jean de Bretagne, Count of Penthièvre: an Aspect of English Foreign Policy 1386–88', *BIHR* XLV (1972) pp. 23–5.
[3] Westminster p. 264.

with a useful propaganda point,[1] and he was not prepared to press the question of their recall to the point of an open breach with the lords of the council. Their surprisingly early deaths fortunately removed another contentious issue from politics, and the touching scene at de Vere's reburial at Colne Priory in 1395, which the nobility boycotted, was one Richard could well afford.[2]

Nor was there any return to the administrative novelties of the 1380s. In the parliament of January 1390 Richard agreed to a formal restriction on the scope of the signet when he accepted a Commons' petition that all signet letters granting pardons for murder, treason, and rape should be sent to the keeper of the Privy Seal, and that the chancellor must have a Privy Seal warrant before a grant could be issued under the great seal.[3] The size of the household was not, at this stage, increased to the inflated figures it had reached in the 1380s; the chamber income remained fixed at £4000 a year, and there is no sign of any attempt to establish independent sources of finance for the chamber. Richard's promise of a new approach in government in his speech of the 3rd of May 1389 may well have accurately described his intentions, and his disavowal of responsibility for the events of the previous twelve years reinforced the impression he wished to create that he was about to make a fresh start.

The most important feature of Richard's government between 1389 and 1393 was his acceptance of some degree of conciliar supervision over his activities. The council from May 1389 onwards was composed of his own nominees, and was thus far more acceptable than a committee appointed by his political opponents and armed with sweeping formal powers of investigation and control. Richard's rights were preserved in theory, even though in practice he sometimes had to give way to his councillors. Furthermore, conciliar supervision of patronage and other acts with financial implications might well be advantageous to the king in that it would serve to deflect parliamentary criticism from him and give the Commons less reason to demand inquiries into the royal finances and the conduct of the royal household. The fear of parliamentary criticism stiffened conciliar resistance to at least one proposal of the king: in October 1389, when the Earl of Nottingham asked for new terms governing his keeping of Berwick Castle and the east march, the

---

[1] Westminster pp. 238–9. The king told Gaunt that if he agreed to his request to recall John Northampton to London he would appear unjust to his own friends in exile. Nevertheless, Northampton was allowed to return.
[2] Walsingham, *Annales* pp. 184–5.   [3] *Rot. Parl.* Vol. III, p. 268.

council refused to negotiate a new agreement until the old one had expired, because, they said, they did not want to be accused in the next parliament of unnecessarily adding to the nation's financial burdens. The king took Nottingham's part and tried to induce the council to agree to his request, but the chancellor, William of Wykeham, speaking for all of them, declined to do so. The king retired angrily to Kennington, but the council held firm and the next day the king suggested that Nottingham's term of office should be prolonged but that he should be paid at the old rate, a settlement which the council accepted.[1]

In the following spring, after Gaunt had returned to England, conciliar supervision of government was put on a more formal basis when it was agreed that no grant which had financial implications was to pass without the advice of the council and the assent of Lancaster, York, Gloucester, and the chancellor, or two of them.[2] There is abundant evidence that the consent of the council was regularly sought for royal grants which affected the revenue, and there is some evidence that Lancaster personally intervened with the chancellor to ensure that royal wishes were put into effect.[3] Lancaster's political standing was very high. Shortly after his return he formally ended his old quarrel with Northumberland, and at the council held at Reading in December 1389 he created an atmosphere of reconciliation which laid the way open to the restoration of Gloucester and Arundel to the council.[4] The closeness between the king and Lancaster was expressed symbolically by Richard's wearing his uncle's collar of SS, and Lancaster's influence in government was recognized as far away as Prussia.[5]

The council with which Richard co-operated in these years gives the impression of being a formal and organized body. In 1389, 1390, and 1391 members were described as 'continually attending the king's council', but the king had control over its membership. Although in the parliament of January 1390 the councillors as a body resigned and were reappointed, the king emphasized that resignation and reappointment in parliament were not to be taken as a precedent, and that he was

---

[1] Nicolas, *POPC* pp. 12b–12d.   [2] *ibid.* pp. 18a–18b.

[3] PRO Ancient Correspondence SC.1/40/190; Issue Rolls E.403/533, 536, 538, 541: grants made 'by the assent of the council'.

[4] Westminster pp. 218–19.

[5] S. Armitage-Smith, *John of Gaunt* (London 1904) pp. 353–5; *Codex Diplomaticus Prussicus* Vol. IV ed. J. Voigt (Kaliningrad (Königsberg) 1853) pp. 140–41: letter from the Grand Master of the Teutonic Knights dated Marienburg the 10th of April 1391 in which he asks the Duke of Lancaster to use his influence with the king to have him attend to an earlier letter asking him to observe the terms of the 1388 treaty. He wrote similarly to Queen Anne (*ibid.* pp. 124–5).

to be free to appoint and remove officers as he pleased.[1] The council met very frequently in these years: Sir Edward Dalingrigg, for instance, attended the council for 207 days between the 8th of January 1392 and the 21st of February 1393; Sir Richard Stury attended for 159 consecutive days in 1392–93; and both men had been described as being 'continually on the king's council' since the autumn of 1389.[2] Under the council's clerk, John Prophete, the habit of keeping systematic records of conciliar attendance and decisions began, and the council was now clearly an organized body entrusted with the day-to-day conduct of government.[3]

The membership of the council shows considerable stability in the four years after May 1389. Although it was afforced from time to time, especially when negotiations with the French were under consideration, by members of the nobility, routine business was handled by a small group of men who had in effect the status of professional administrators.[4] There are two periods for which a systematic body of evidence about membership survives, August 1389 until March 1390, and the 20th of January 1392 to the 21st of February 1393.[5] In all probability the records for both periods were compiled by John Prophete, and may represent the surviving portions of the records he compiled throughout his tenure of the office of clerk of the council.[6] In the first period, the great officers of state were regular in attendance; of the lay lords, York, Northumberland, Nottingham, and Lancaster (after his return) attended most frequently, while Dalingrigg, who had attended continually from the 4th of May to the 24th of August, evidently came less frequently. York has been overshadowed by his more spectacular brothers, yet throughout the troubles of 1387–8 he had sought first to achieve agreement between the king and the Appellants, and then to persuade the Commons to spare Burley. Like Gloucester, part of his income was insecure, dependent on exchequer annuities and customs assignments, yet unlike Gloucester he did not allow this insecurity to drive him to political

[1] *Rot. Parl.* Vol. III, p. 258; PRO Exchequer Issue Rolls E.403/527 m. 23; E.403/536 m. 11.
[2] J. F. Baldwin, *King's Council* pp. 132–4; PRO Exchequer Issue Rolls E.403/527 m. 23, E.403/532 mm. 15, 17, E.403/533 m. 9, E.403/536 mm. 11, 16, E.403/538 m. 5, E.403/541 m. 18, E.403/543 m. 8.
[3] A. L. Brown, *The Early History of the Clerkship of the Council* (Glasgow 1969) pp. 9, 13.
[4] Nicolas, *POPC* pp. 6–18; J. F. Baldwin, *King's Council* pp. 489–504; PRO E.403/530 m. 16, E.403/533 m. 14, E.403/536 m. 14.
[5] Nicolas, *POPC*, pp. 6–18; J. F. Baldwin, *King's Council* pp. 489–504.
[6] A. L. Brown, *Early History* pp. 10–12.

extremism. His military failure in Portugal in 1382 and Gaunt's alleged scorn for his prowess as a general[1] have led to an unduly harsh judgement on him. His moderation in 1387-8 must have earned him Richard's gratitude, despite his membership of the 1386 commission, and he was acceptable to all sides as a member of the council after May 1389. Indeed, in all probability he was as royalist as his brother of Lancaster, and his membership of the 1386 commission might be explained by his status rather than his inclination.

Northumberland, too, had attempted to mediate in the autumn of 1387, and he maintained this role after the Merciless Parliament. In September 1389, for instance, he reported to the council that Gloucester and Arundel wished for peace and affection between them and the king.[2] His quarrel with Lancaster had been settled, and in face of the military facts no one wished to deny him his authority on the northern border. His interests there had not been threatened by the rise of de Vere, Pole, and Burley, and he now shared power on the border with Nottingham. Nor was there any serious talk at this stage of peace with Scotland. Northumberland had no reason to oppose Richard, and was ideally placed to act as a political mediator. His own best interests, too, were served by the maintenance of his influence and good reputation at court.

If York and Northumberland were the honest brokers of politics in 1388 and 1389, Nottingham was a self-seeking renegade. Richard seems to have found little difficulty in detaching him from his allies of 1387-8 and restoring him, now that de Vere was out of the way, to a place of favour at court. As evidence of his favour, the king supported him in his negotiations for an extension of his custody of Berwick and the east march on more favourable terms than those contained in the indenture of the 2nd of March 1389.[3] It is possible that Richard never entirely trusted him, but for a moment their relations were once again close.

The other frequent attenders at the council in 1389-90 were the chamberlain and the steward, Sir Edward Dalingrigg, and a group of chamber knights, Sir John Clanvowe, Sir William Neville, Sir Nicholas Sharnesfeld, Sir Lewis Clifford, and Sir Richard Stury. The household, in fact, was powerfully represented on the council, and this too helped to ensure that it maintained good relations with the king. The majority

[1] S. Armitage-Smith, *John of Gaunt* p. 422.
[2] Nicolas, *POPC* p. 12.
[3] *Rot. Scot.* Vol. II, p. 96.

of its members were men whom the king could trust. But the chamber knights who attended the council received nothing like the lavish rewards of their predecessors in the 1380s. They obtained their wages but little else, and they have more the status of professional administrators attached to the household than courtiers participating in government. This did much to ensure their acceptability to all shades of opinion. In all probability, the great officers of state and these chamber knights, together with Sir Edward Dalingrigg, formed the nucleus of the council throughout the period from 1389 to 1393. When Prophete's journal begins, in January 1392, the names of Dalingrigg, Stury, and Clifford occur regularly in the lists of attendance, and the other chamber knights were present from time to time. The steward continued to attend, but the under-chamberlain, Sir Thomas Percy, replaced the chamberlain. Percy was the only member of the council at this time to benefit markedly from royal patronage. He received two castles in South Wales, the office of justice of South Wales, and, for a time, the office of forester of Inglewood in Cumberland.[1] In February 1393, when Devereux died, he became steward of the household, while Sir William Lescrope succeeded him as under-chamberlain. Lescrope, too, climbed high in royal favour in these years, being endowed with land in Wiltshire which formed the nucleus of the earldom he was to receive in 1397.[2] In Percy, Lescrope, and the chamberlain, the Earl of Huntingdon, Richard had the nucleus of a new party of household officials whose potential was to be fully realized in the last three years of the reign. But in the early 1390s they had only a small share in government, and their rewards, though extensive by comparison with those of their colleagues on the council, were insufficient to arouse either the alarm of the Commons or the jealousy of the nobility. In essence, the composition of the council in the early 1390s suggests that the political situation had returned to normal. The king was not required to accept an imposed council, nor were influential nobles excluded from what they took to be their rightful position. The council in the early 1390s was in no sense a hostile body, and Richard was quite ready to work with it. Its occasional conflicts with the king should be set against the large body of evidence for harmonious co-operation between the two.

Relations between the king and the Commons, too, remained good in the early 1390s. The council showed considerable sensitivity towards

[1] CPR 1391–6, pp. 208, 413–14, 507; 1388–92, p. 249.
[2] CPR 1391–6, pp. 270, 309.

the Commons' concern for probity and economy in financial administration, and Richard's restrained use of his powers of patronage gave
the Commons no reason to revive their complaints of undue liberality
towards courtiers and favourites. Even more important, however, was
a lessening of the pressure of taxation. After the subsidy granted by the
Cambridge Parliament, no further direct parliamentary tax was
granted until November 1391, when the Commons agreed to levy a
half-tenth and fifteenth, with another full tenth and fifteenth if the king
went to war. This was followed by another respite of over a year, until
the January parliament of 1393, when the Commons granted one and a
half tenths and fifteenths under conditions similar to the 1391 grant.[1]
The virtual cessation of the war, of course, provided the main reason
for the decrease in the scale of taxation; no longer could the Commons
complain that they were being taxed beyond endurance to pay for an
unsuccessful war. The infrequency of direct taxation between 1388 and
1393 brought political benefits, and the low level of borrowing in these
years does not suggest that the crown needed the revenue it forewent.
On the other hand, however, there is some evidence that the crown was
exploiting other sources of revenue. In May 1389, for instance, as
evidence of his goodwill when he formally assumed personal power,
Richard ordered the postponement of the collection of part of the
subsidy granted by the Cambridge Parliament. This gesture had to be
paid for three months later by the sale of some of the forfeited lands
which the crown had hitherto kept in its own hand.[2] Although there
was no war, Richard's diplomacy was expensive, while Aquitaine,
Ireland, and the northern border still had to be defended. Some of the
burden of defence could be sustained out of the customs revenue which
parliament regularly granted, but the king also had to raise money
from other sources. Financial pressure on the king's lands outside the
realm increased; a subsidy of 1000 marks was levied in North Wales in
the winter of 1389-90, and the men of Cheshire granted the king 2000
marks in the autumn of 1391.[3] In the summer of the same year the
king sought loans from a wide variety of individuals and borough
communities; the response does not appear to have been particularly
good.[4] In 1392 the council raised money by distraint of knighthood,

[1] *Rot. Parl.* Vol. III, pp. 285, 301.
[2] *Foedera* Vol. VII, pp. 620–21; *CPR* 1389–91, p. 107.
[3] PRO Exchequer Issue Rolls E.403/536 m. 12, E.403/532 m. 16.
[4] *ibid.* E.403/533 m. 8. The following were approached: Bishop of Worcester;
Earl of Warwick; dean and chapter of Lichfield; persons (unspecified) in Devon
and Cornwall; Abbot of Thornton, Lincs; mayor, bailiff and community of

and the king made repeated requests to London to lend him money, all of which were turned down.[1] The Londoners' refusal to advance money provides the real reason for the quarrel with the city which Richard instigated in 1392 and which ended with the king better off by £10,000.[2]

An understanding with the Commons, however, was possible not only because of the reduction in the burden of taxation, but also because of the king's evident intention to curb the disorderly behaviour of gangs of armed liveried retainers. Violent interference with the course of justice had provided material for complaint for at least a century and probably longer, and legislation against the intimidation of juries had been passed from time to time since the reign of Edward II, but had proved ineffective. The reasons both for the existence of the problem and the ineffectiveness of measures against it are complex and poorly understood. The answer lies as much in the inadequacy of common law procedure as in the establishment by the nobility of permanent private armies. Until 1382, the enforcement of legislation against livery and maintenance lay in the hands of the justices of the peace, but they encountered great difficulties in bringing offenders to justice.[3] Few of those who were indicted by the justices ever stood trial before the justices of gaol delivery, and the great majority of those who were tried were acquitted. The justices and the king's bench could only deal with an offender if the sheriff could force him to appear before them, and many (perhaps a majority) of offenders could not be made to appear. Even if a trial took place and an offender was found guilty, there was a good chance that he would be pardoned. There was a great trade

---

York; Abbot of St Augustine's Canterbury; John Roper 'and others in Kent, Surrey and Sussex'; Bishop of Norwich; mayor, bailiffs and community of Colchester 'and others of Norfolk, Suffolk and Cambridgeshire'; Bishop of Hereford, Abbot of Osney 'and others in Hereford and Gloucestershire'; 'abbots, priors, barons and other persons, and towns', presumably, from the context, in the west Midlands. If any loans were made, they have left no trace on the receipt rolls.

[1] J. F. Baldwin, *King's Council* p. 494; Westminster p. 270; *Walsingham, HA* Vol. II, pp. 207–8.
[2] Caroline M. Barron, 'The Quarrel of Richard II with London 1392–7', in *The Reign of Richard II* ed. Barron and F. R. H. du Boulay (London 1971) pp. 173–201.
[3] *Rolls of the Warwickshire and Coventry Sessions of the Peace 1377–97* ed. E. G. Kimball, Dugdale Society Vol. XVI (London 1939) p. lxvii; *Some Sessions of the Peace in Lincolnshire* ed. E. G. Kimball, Lincoln Record Society Vol. XLIX (1955) p. lvii; *Proceedings Before the Justices of the Peace in the 14th and 15th Centuries* ed. B. H. Putnam, Ames Foundation (London 1938) p. cxxviii.

in pardons in the fourteenth century, to produce revenue, and the implications of this trade for the judicial system were not lost on the Commons, who complained in the January 1390 parliament about the undue freedom with which pardons were granted.[1] There was a very high degree of probability, therefore, that the guilty would escape punishment, and the inadequacy of the judicial methods of the fourteenth century did as much as anything to encourage disorder.

The ineffectiveness of common law procedures led, not unnaturally, to the extension of the jursidiction of other courts of law which were thought to be more effective. In default of a remedy before local justices, injured parties petitioned the chancery or the council for justice.[2] The chancery then issued writs of *quibusdam certis de causis, praemunire,* or *subpoena,* ordering the accused to appear before the chancery or council without specifying the charges against him. When he appeared, he was dealt with by a procedure that owed more to the civil than the common law, an inquisatorial rather than an adversary system. Although the difficulties of compelling a defendant to appear must have applied to the chancery and the council as well as to the king's bench and the local courts, it was evidently thought that powerful men would obey a command to appear before the council. In 1377 it was enacted that the council should have jurisdiction in cases of maintenance involving 'such high personages that right cannot be done elsewhere'.[3]

The council, of course, embodied the king's prerogative of justice, and it had long been accepted that it had jurisdiction when a petitioner could not obtain right elsewhere. But men also sought justice in Richard's reign in two other courts, the Court of Chivalry and the Court of Admiralty, which had developed in the second half of the fourteenth century to deal with cases that arose beyond the common law's geographical jurisdiction.[4] In the 1370s and 1380s, however, the Court of Chivalry extended its jurisdiction to cover offences committed within the realm which were properly triable at common law: it heard cases of debt, breach of contract, trespass, and homicide. In the 1390s,

[1] *Rot. Parl.* Vol. III, p. 268; see also in general N. D. Hurnard, *The King's Pardon for Homicide before 1307* (Oxford 1969).
[2] *Select Cases Before the King's Council 1243–1482* ed. I. S. Leadam and J. F. Baldwin Selden Society XXXV (Cambridge Mass. 1918) pp. xv–xlvi.
[3] *Rot. Parl.* Vol. III, p. 40.
[4] *Select Pleas in the Court of Admiralty* ed. R. G. Marsden, Selden Society VI (London 1892); G. D. Squibb, *The High Court of Chivalry* (Oxford 1959) pp. 1–21.

the Court of Admiralty similarly extended its jurisdiction, hearing cases of debt and breach of contract which arose in areas outside the proper jurisdiction of the admiral.[1] The procedure of both courts resembled that of the chancery and the council, and it may be that the extension of the judicial work of all four courts was a response to a genuine popular demand. The encroachment of the Courts of Chivalry and Admiralty could not have taken place had some litigants not preferred to seek justice there, and the same applies to the council. In 1391, for instance, the Abbot of Croyland complained that the council was so preoccupied with political business that it had no time to attend to the affairs of individual petitioners.[2]

Dissatisfaction with the lawlessness which the defects in common law procedure permitted found expression in parliament in 1384, when the lords declined to do anything about it,[3] in a petition presented to the Merciless Parliament and in the Cambridge Parliament,[4] when the king realized that here lay an opportunity to forge an alliance with the Commons. The lords again baulked any effective action, but the king at least secured agreement that the council should be asked to devise a remedy. However, the pressure of magnate opinion ensured that nothing was done, and the Commons returned to their campaign against retaining in the January parliament of 1390. Meanwhile, the king excluded all magnates from the commissions of the peace issued in July 1389, a move calculated to gain the sympathy of the knightly class, who had shown that they had little confidence in the willingness of the lords to uphold law and order. In November the justices were once again empowered to hear cases of felony and maintenance, powers which they had lost in 1382; and the sheriffs were appointed by the king and his council rather than by the chancellor and the treasurer, perhaps in order to impress upon them the king's personal concern that they should carry out their duties efficiently.[5] In 1389–90 the king may have been looking for a new power base among the knightly class. His policies towards both taxation and retaining were calculated to appeal to that social group. By implementing a programme which was attractive to them, he hoped to prevent their alliance with the nobility which had

---

[1] G. D. Squibb, *Court of Chivalry* pp. 17–18; *Select Pleas in ... Admiralty* ed. Marsden, pp. 1–26.
[2] J. F. Baldwin, *King's Council* p. 294.
[3] See p. 94 above.
[4] See pp. 135–6 above.
[5] R. L. Storey, 'Liveries and Commissions of the Peace 1388–90', in *The Reign of Richard II* ed. du Boulay and Barron, pp. 131–52.

led to disaster in 1386 and 1388. In his speech in May 1389 Richard emphasized his intention to do justice to all his subjects. His propaganda now skilfully dwelt upon the duties as well as the rights of kingship, and he made much of his obligation to protect all his subjects impartially.

In the parliament of January 1390, the chancellor went out of his way in his opening speech to emphasize the king's desire to suppress lawlessness. The Commons, given this lead, once again demanded the total abolition of all liveries and the adoption of effective measures to deal with disorder. The king's eventual response was an ordinance which only partially met the Commons' demands.[1] The keeping of liveried retainers was to be restricted, not forbidden, and no precise procedure for enforcing the ordinance was laid down. The king, however, granted a Commons' petition that there should be new commissions of the peace and that their members should be chosen from knights, esquires, and lawyers. But the statute embodying the acts of the parliament laid down that lords' stewards were no longer to be excluded from the commissions of the peace, and five of the new justices of the peace appointed in June 1390 have been identified as officials of John of Gaunt.[2] The king was clearly facing opposition to his attempts to curb the excesses of liveried retainers, and it may well be that some of the opposition came from Gaunt, who had made his position on the subject quite clear in 1384.[3]

The king, however, was not yet prepared to abandon his policy completely. In December 1390 lords were restored to the commissions of the peace—Gaunt himself was appointed to eighteen commissions—but this was done at the request of the Commons, who had perhaps come to the conclusion that it was impossible for the justices to carry out their tasks without the help of the nobility.[4] Richard's chosen instrument for enforcing the law against maintenance was the council, as provided in the statute of 1377. Most of the records of the council's jurisdiction have perished, but in 1392 it heard the case of Esturmy v. Courtenay, a case which has not received the attention it deserves.[5] The Earl of Devon was accused of intimidating justices of the peace and jurymen who were to hear an indictment of murder against one of the earl's retainers, Robert Yeo. On behalf of his fellow justices, William

---

[1] *Statutes of the Realm* Vol. II, pp. 61–75; *Rot. Parl.* Vol. III, p. 257.
[2] R. L. Storey, 'Liveries and Commissions' pp. 148–9.
[3] See p. 94 above.
[4] R. L. Storey, 'Liveries and Commissions' pp. 149–50.
[5] *Select Cases* ed. Leadam and Baldwin pp. 77–81.

Esturmy complained to the king, and on the 23rd of January 1392 the council (attended by the great officers of state, the Bishops of Winchester, Durham, and Lichfield, Devereux, Sir Thomas Percy, Dalingrigg, Stury, and the king's judges) ordered a writ of *subpoena* to be served on the earl. While the case was pending, Devon attended an afforced session of the council—some indication, perhaps, of the leniency with which the other lords regarded his alleged crime. When he appeared before the council, Devon admitted his guilt and threw himself on the king's mercy. The council committed him to prison until he made fine and ransom; but immediately after judgement was delivered the lords prayed the king to excuse the earl his offence. The king granted him a full pardon the same day. The most solemn means of law enforcement had been used, yet in effect the earl had got away with it. It is clear that the lords were not prepared to tolerate the enforcement of the law against one of their own number who had had the misfortune to be charged with an offence of which they were all probably guilty, and they were fearful lest the king should use the council to proceed against those who had taken part in the Radcot Bridge campaign. This fear was made more acute by the king's request in the same council for the recall of de Vere and Neville.[1] The king had to be content with a declaration of good intentions from the lords and an agreement to act within the law. The king for his part promised not to proceed against any lord for anything he might have done in the past[2]—a scarcely veiled reference to the events of 1387 and 1388. These events had made it impossible for the nobility to accept with equanimity the use of the council to deal with the illegal para-military activities of their retainers.

The nobility were the real victors in the case of Esturmy v. Courtenay. Their resistance to the effective measures against lawlessness which the Commons demanded and to the use of the council to curb overmighty subjects did much to bring about the collapse of Richard's policy of law enforcement and the growth of his belief that the military power of the nobility could be checked most effectively not by statute, ordinance, or conciliar jurisdiction but by the creation of his own armed retinue. The distribution of his livery of the white hart, which perhaps began in October 1390,[3] became much more widespread from

---

[1] Westminster p. 264.
[2] J. F. Baldwin, *King's Council* pp. 494–5.
[3] *Evesham* p. 122; the Issue Rolls record that the knights and esquires of the king's retinue were ordered to be in London on the 6th of October; this may have been the occasion to which the Monk of Evesham refers (PRO. E.403/530 m. 16).

1392 onwards. The expenditure of the great wardrobe, responsible for the giving of liveries, rose from £8000 in the period from November 1390 to September 1392 to almost £16,000 in the period between September 1392 and September 1394.[1] The expenses of the household, too, doubled in much the same period.[2] The collapse of the law and order policy led to a renewed, and expensive, emphasis upon the household, and now the household became organized for military rather than political or administrative activity.

Richard's campaign against livery and maintenance, however, failed not only because of the resistance of the nobility but also because the Commons themselves mistrusted the new procedures the king proposed to use. Inadequate though the common law undoubtedly was, the Commons in parliament displayed much zeal in defending it not only against the council but also against the Courts of Chivalry and Admiralty. They were prepared to will the end but not the means. In the parliament of January 1390 the Commons petitioned that no one should be summoned before the council by writs of *quibusdam certis de causis* to answer for any matter which was justiciable at common law. The king did not accept the petition, simply replying that his regality was to be saved.[3] They also complained in the same parliament about the encroachments of the Court of Chivalry, and this met with more success.[4] Parliament passed a statute limiting the court's jurisdiction to matters which could not be dealt with at common law and providing a remedy for any person summoned before the court who thought his case ought to be tried by common law. There is some evidence that the statute was observed, and that for some time the court's jurisdiction was subject to conciliar scrutiny.[5] The jurisdiction of the Admiral's court was regulated by the same statute, and the chancellor evidently had the power to determine which cases that came before it were properly triable at common law. But the Commons were even reluctant to see the procedures of the common law used to their fullest extent. In February 1389 the Earl of Arundel had held a trailbaston inquiry in Wales, and in the following November a similar inquiry took place in Essex and Kent. Yet in the parliament of November 1391 the Commons petitioned that no further trailbaston inquiries should be ordered, and at the same time they sought an assurance that no general eyre

---

[1] Tout, *Chapters* Vol. VI, p. 108.
[2] *ibid.* pp. 97–101.
[3] *Rot. Parl.* Vol. III, p. 267.   [4] *ibid.* p. 265.
[5] *Statutes of the Realm* Vol. II, pp. 61–2; *CCR* 1392–6, p. 153.

would be held before another parliament had met, and they repeated this request in the next parliament.[1] The use of exceptional judicial procedures, with the expense and inconvenience they entailed, was evidently more objectionable to the Commons than the evils the procedures were intended to curb.

The reasons for the Commons' attitude are not entirely clear. Many of them were, of course, retainers or clients of the great nobles, and might find themselves compromised by really effective measures against disorders. In April 1385, for instance, eight knights were removed from the commission of the peace in Yorkshire because they were 'of the household, livery, counsel and retinue' of Alexander Neville Archbishop of York.[2] The system of clientage bound nobility and gentry together, and Richard was perhaps flying in the face of social facts in seeking to drive a wedge between knights and nobles. On an issue as complicated and far-reaching as that of retaining, the Commons' general view was likely to conflict with a multiplicity of individual interests and personal ties with members of the nobility.

This does not, however, provide the sole explanation. There was undoubtedly a widespread suspicion of the civil law, which governed the procedure of the council and the Courts of Chivalry and Admiralty. In 1384 the Commons in parliament had said that they did not understand the terms of the civil law; in 1388 the judges had stated that England was not governed by the civil law; and a petition in 1393–4 appears to imply that the common law was thought to be consonant with right and reason.[3] Several of the most frequent attenders at the council, however, had received their training in civil rather than common law. The Bishop of Lichfield, for instance, who attended the council regularly in the period covered by Prophete's journal, had received the degree of Doctor of Civil and Canon Law by 1379; Walter Skirlaw, Bishop of Durham from 1388, was a BCL of Oxford University, and many of the king's clerks were civilians, graduates of that seminary for civil servants, King's Hall Cambridge.[4] The study of the civil law expanded rapidly in the fourteenth century. About half of those who entered King's Hall studied the subject, and Bishop Bateman of Norwich founded Trinity Hall with the explicit purpose of

[1] *Rot. Parl.* Vol. III, pp. 286, 302; Westminster pp. 205, 218.
[2] *CCR* 1381–5, p. 635; and more generally, *Proceedings Before the Justices of the Peace* ed. Putnam.
[3] *Rot. Parl.* Vol. III, pp. 170, 236; J. F. Baldwin, *King's Council* p. 281.
[4] A. B. Cobban, *The King's Hall* (Cambridge 1969) pp. 280–82, 286; A. B. Emden, *A Biographical Register of the University of Oxford* Vol. III (Oxford 1959).

increasing the number of students of civil and canon law.[1] The number of Cambridge graduates in the subject steadily increased in the second half of the fourteenth century.[2] It may be that Cambridge's reputation in that period rested upon its civil law studies and the close relations it enjoyed with the government and civil service. This may also be one reason why the university showed little interest in Wycliffite ideas. The growth of civil law studies and the development of courts whose jurisdiction was parallel and rival to those of the common law must have alarmed the common lawyers. How influential they were in parliament is unknown, but they may have sat for borough seats, and some knights of the shire may have received some elementary education in the common law in the Inns of Chancery.[3] The defenders of the common law had a powerful, though embarrassing, ally in Wycliffe, who took the view that the study of civil law should be forbidden in the universities, that civil law was no better than common law, and that therefore the king ought to encourage the study of common law at the universities.[4] The common law survived, but suspicion of the king's intentions lived on long after his deposition; it can only have been to Richard II that Fortescue referred when he said that certain kings of England had sought to introduce the civil law into England and thereby to diminish the liberty of their subjects.[5] This belief must have been intensified by Richard's use in the last three years of his reign of the council and the Court of Chivalry as instruments of political discipline, but it was in the early 1390s that Richard first realized the potential of these institutions.

The political peace which prevailed in the years after the Cambridge Parliament rested, therefore, on fragile foundations. The Commons gradually lost confidence in the king's ability, or willingness, to stamp out disorder, and they came to realize that some of his methods had unacceptable implications. The infrequency of taxation pleased them, but created problems for the king elsewhere. Neither Wales nor London forgot the financial demands the king made upon them in the early 1390s. The nobility for their part had little reason to complain

[1] J. P. C. Roach, 'The University of Cambridge', *VCH* Cambridge Vol. III (1959) pp. 362–3; A. B. Cobban, *The King's Hall* pp. 54–5.

[2] A. B. Cobban, *The King's Hall* pp. 255–6.

[3] *The Pension Book of Clement's Inn* ed. C. Carr, Selden Society LXXVIII (London 1960) pp. xviii–xix.

[4] J. Wycliffe, *De Officio Regis* ed. A. W. Pollard and C. Sayle, Wycliffe Society (London 1887) pp. 188, 193, 237.

[5] Sir John Fortescue, *De Laudibus Legum Angliae* ed. S. B. Chrimes (Cambridge 1942) pp. 79–80.

of the king's handling of his government. The law and order issue had resolved itself to their satisfaction, despite a moment of alarm in the council of February 1392. The king was not so far using his powers of patronage to build up another court party, and the household was neither unduly expensive nor unduly politically influential. It may be, as has sometimes been suggested, that Lancaster's presence on the council inhibited open hostility to the king; but it is hard to find any issue in domestic politics in the early 1390s which might have united the former Appellants in opposition to the king.

Gloucester especially felt his interests best served by remaining on good terms with the king. In the Martinmas parliament of 1390 he and York jointly presented a petition which the king accepted and which finally put their income on a secure hereditary basis.[1] Gloucester had returned to the council in January 1390 and shared with his royal brothers the duty of supervising royal patronage. In 1389 he had evidently coveted de Vere's Duchy of Ireland, but he does not seem to have pressed his ambition with either the king or the council. In the autumn of 1391 he began preparations to go on a crusade in Prussia, whither Derby had gone in 1390.[2] Derby's crusade had been both a social and a military success, and Gloucester was spurred to go partly no doubt by the sense, which never entirely left him, that his young nephew was overshadowing him. The cessation of the French war meant that there was no outlet nearer home for Gloucester's military energies, and this was a very important reason for his proposed expedition. The crusade in Prussia was highly popular at the end of the fourteenth century. It offered an opportunity to display chivalric virtues against an enemy less powerful and less well organized than the Turks in the Holy Land or the Balkans, and it avoided any need to co-operate with the French nobility, whose crusading interests lay in southeastern Europe, the Levant, and North Africa.[3] This must have increased its appeal to Gloucester. From the government's point of view, too, the participation by English nobles in the wars of the Teutonic Knights brought political and economic advantages, for the profitability of the English cloth trade with the Baltic ports depended upon the maintenance of good relations with the ports themselves and with the Grand Master of the Teutonic Knights. In 1388 a series

[1] *Rot. Parl.* Vol. III, p. 278.
[2] Westminster p. 260; *Walsingham, HA* Vol. II, p. 202.
[3] *Expeditions to Prussia and the Holy Land made by Henry Earl of Derby* ed. L. Toulmin-Smith, Camden New Series LII (London 1894); A. Goodman, *The Loyal Conspiracy* (London 1971) p. 57.

F

of long-standing problems between England and the Teutonic Knights were resolved in the treaty of Marienburg, perhaps the sole diplomatic success of the Appellant regime, and both Derby and Gloucester were given power to negotiate with the Grand Master when they reached Prussia.[1] Frequent personal contacts obviously served the interests of both sides in smoothing over the disputes which perennially occurred between English and Prussian shipping and trading interests.

Unhappily, however, Gloucester came nowhere near emulating Derby's success. He unwisely chose to set out in mid-October, intending no doubt to follow Derby's route across the North Sea and through The Sound, but bad weather forced him to put in first in Denmark and then in Norway. He lost some of his ships and eventually struggled back to Scotland a little before Christmas.[2] As if to rub salt in the wound, Derby began preparations in the following spring for another crusade in Prussia. He left England on the 24th of July 1392, and after a rather less successful campaign than he had enjoyed on the previous occasion, he left Prussia and went to the Holy Land, returning to England on the 28th of June 1393 having made many useful political contacts.[3]

Meanwhile, events in Ireland had claimed the king's attention. Sir John Stanley, who had been appointed lieutenant in Ireland in July 1389, had made himself unpopular with the Dublin government, and Richard sent out a committee to inquire into allegations being made against him.[4] Perhaps acting on their report, Richard removed Stanley from office on the 11th of September 1391, and gave the Bishop of Meath responsibility for the government of the country.[5] Meath's administration, however, was no more satisfactory than Stanley's had been, and early in 1392 the citizens of Dublin wrote to the king urging him to do something about the government of Ireland.[6] Richard now revived the proposal to send Gloucester out. On the 29th of April 1392 he declared that he intended to appoint Gloucester lieutenant in Ireland, and early in May preparations for his expedition began.[7] Gloucester's indenture with the king specified that he was to hold office for

---

[1] *The Loyal Conspiracy* p. 57; for the Treaty of Marienburg, see PRO Treaty Roll C.76/74 m. 16.
[2] Westminster p. 262; *Walsingham, HA* Vol. II, p. 202.
[3] *Expeditions to Prussia* ed. Toulmin-Smith.
[4] PRO Accounts, various, E.101/247/1 mm. 2–7.
[5] J. Otway-Ruthven, *A History of Medieval Ireland* (London 1968) p. 323.
[6] BM *Cotton Titus* B XI f. 11.
[7] *CCR* 1388–92, p. 463.

five years, and that for the first three years he was to receive 32,000 marks from the English exchequer. Thereafter the government of the country was to pay for itself.[1] But on the 23rd of July his appointment was cancelled. By this time he had received £6333–6–8 towards the costs of his expedition, mostly from the parliamentary subsidy granted for the purpose, and he had spent over £1250, including £225 on the purchase of artillery.[2] It is not clear whether he himself sought release because he had concluded that the lieutenancy would be too expensive and unrewarding, or whether the king discharged him because he wanted him to join Gaunt in the peace negotiations due to be resumed with the French. Gloucester played an important part in these negotiations, and for the moment at least took a constructive view of them. The men of Cheshire thought that he was as responsible as Gaunt for their apparently successful progress. His attitude to the peace proposals was perhaps ambiguous; he seems to have blown hot and cold about them, and in 1392–3 he seems to have been quite happy to work with Gaunt for a settlement.[3]

The events of the early 1390s showed that there was no enduring community of interest amongst the Appellants. Once they had achieved their political objects in 1388, each went his separate way. Derby found fame abroad and Gloucester looked for it; Warwick faded once again from the political scene on to which he had so briefly emerged in 1387, and the sycophantic Nottingham threw in his lot with the king and the court. Only Arundel remained disaffected; only he of all the Appellants failed to make his peace with the king, and his potential for trouble-making was soon to be revealed. However, it was not Richard's handling of affairs at home that was to give rise to the renewed dissension which culminated in his tyranny and deposition, but his policies towards France, Scotland, and Ireland.

[1] BM Cotton *Titus* B XI f. 19; J. T. Gilbert, *The Viceroys of Ireland* (Dublin 1865) pp. 552ff.
[2] PRO Issue Rolls E.403/538; BM Add. Mss. 40859A; PRO Indentures of War E.101/74/1; J. A. Tuck, 'Anglo-Irish Relations 1382–1393', *Proceedings of the Royal Irish Academy* LXIX (1970) pp. 15–31.
[3] Walsingham, *Annales* p. 159.

6

The Revival of Dissension 1393-7

The domestic harmony which prevailed for more than four years after the end of the Merciless Parliament rested upon Richard's avoidance of the manner of rule which had provoked the opposition to him between 1386 and 1388. Yet domestic peace was fragile: the alliance with the Commons rested upon an avoidance of heavy taxation which may have contributed to unpopular financial exactions elsewhere, together with an attempt to curb disorder which broke down in the face of aristocratic hostility and the Commons' own doubts. The more open political dissension of the years after 1393, however, arose in the first place from opposition to the king's policies towards France and Scotland and a lack of enthusiasm about his plans for Ireland. The French chroniclers who wrote of Richard's deposition were of one mind in attributing the revival of political tension to the king's successful pursuit of a *rapprochement* with France, and they provide a most convincing explanation of the reasons for the deterioration in relations between the king and the Duke of Gloucester. There seems little reason to believe that throughout the early 1390s Richard was planning to revenge himself on his opponents of 1388 and was merely waiting until the moment was right to strike. There is no contemporary warrant for such a belief: the Kirkstall chronicler, for instance, went no further than to say that in 1397 Richard 'recollected and newly recalled to mind' the injuries he had suffered earlier.[1] Richard's concern to bring justice, peace, and good government to his subjects in the early 1390s was in all probability genuine; his policies towards Scotland, France, and Ireland are consistent in this respect with his domestic policy. But his pursuit

[1] *Kirkstall Chronicle* pp. 125-9.

of these unexceptionable goals aroused mistrust and suspicion to the point where, in 1397, Richard felt it necessary to preserve his own security by making a pre-emptive strike against his opponents. The events of July, August, and September 1397 derive not from a long-premeditated scheme of revenge but from the political developments of the previous four years.

On the 8th of July 1389 a truce between England and France was publicly proclaimed. It brought to an end the hostilities of 1385–8 (in which the Earl of Arundel had played so prominent a part) and through its renewal in 1392, 1393, 1394, and 1396 it brought to an end a whole phase of the war, a phase which had been more bitterly fought and more expensive than any so far.[1] Although England and France came to the brink of war at least once in the 1390s, the rest of Richard's reign passed in peace between the two countries. By 1393 a provisional peace treaty had been agreed which settled most of the important points at issue between England and France, and by the summer of 1394 a formal public proclamation of peace was clearly very close.[2] Yet by 1396 the negotiations for a final peace had been abandoned, and the two sides contented themselves with a twenty-eight years' truce and a marriage alliance. Recent work on the failure of the negotiations for a permanent peace has rightly stressed the part played by the Gascons, who refused to accept the separation of their duchy from the English crown and its grant to John of Gaunt and his heirs, to hold of Richard as king of France, or in the likely event of Richard renouncing his French title, of the Valois kings.[3] Territorially the terms proposed for Aquitaine were most generous to Gaunt, giving him about two-thirds of the land Edward III had won on paper by the treaty of Brétigny, but the constitutional arrangements were unacceptable to the Gascons. They rightly held that the proposal to alienate the duchy to Gaunt and his heirs was a violation of many earlier agreements and understandings whereby English kings had promised to alienate Gascony only to their eldest sons, heirs to the English throne. Yet the Gascons did not believe that Gaunt was ever likely to succeed to the throne, for they (like the English) no doubt expected Richard to have children. The House of Lancaster would become a French princely dynasty, and the Gascons thought that their liberties and their

[1] J. J. N. Palmer, *England, France and Christendom* (London 1971) pp. 2, 142–3.
[2] *ibid.* pp. 146–50.
[3] J. J. N. Palmer, 'The Anglo-French Peace Negotiations, 1390–1396', *TRHS* 5th series XVI (1966) pp. 81–94.

commercial interests, safeguarded by the English connection, would be lost. To many of the nobility of Aquitaine, furthermore, the war had become a way of life, a means of profit and an excuse to act like independent potentates. They resembled the magnates of the northern border in their vested interest in war, and the prospect of the restoration of order by a permanently resident duke was far from an unmixed blessing. The Gascons could neither be persuaded nor coerced into accepting the Anglo–French agreement, and their hostility did much to compel the two governments to abandon the scheme and agree instead upon a lengthy truce which maintained the traditional status of Aquitaine.

Gascon opposition to the peace proposals was strong and persistent, yet it is important not to underrate domestic English discontent with the terms as they had been agreed by 1394. The attitudes of the various sections of English society to the prospect of an end to the war were confused and often contradictory. For men from the lower ranks of society, especially those who came from the parts of the country which tended to produce a larger population than they could sustain, peace with France and Scotland threatened their prospects of employment as soldiers. The fear that their livelihood might disappear does much to explain the revolt by men of Cheshire in 1393.[1] The knightly class, the class which was represented in the House of Commons, had a more ambiguous attitude to peace. On the one hand, as the chancellor pointed out in the January parliament of 1394, the continuance of the war meant the continuance of heavy taxation, and it is clear that the Commons had no stomach for that.[2] On the other hand, the terms on which the end of the war was proposed were not immediately acceptable to them. They objected to the grant of Aquitaine to Gaunt on the grounds that it amounted to disinheritance of the crown and entailed the breach of undertakings given by Edward III.[3] The French certainly thought that the Commons were opposed to peace. The Duke of Burgundy said as much in 1399, and Froissart made it clear several times that the other French nobles shared Burgundy's view, which he himself believed was true.[4] The portrait Froissart gives of Gloucester is strongly coloured by his belief that Gloucester sympathized with and played upon the Commons' preference for war. In 1391 he makes Gloucester oppose the continuance of peace negotiations with the

---

[1] See pp. 165–67 below. [2] *Rot. Parl.* Vol. III, p. 309.
[3] Westminster pp. 266–7, 281–2; Froissart, *Oeuvres* Vol. XV, pp. 79–80.
[4] Froissart, *Oeuvres* Vol. XV, pp. 80, 108–9; see p. 213 below.

argument that the prosperity of the 'poor knights and esquires of England' depended upon war.[1] Gloucester's argument, if he actually put it forward, was of course propagandist in intent, but like all good propaganda it had an element of truth in it. Individuals of all social rank had made money out of both the French and the Scottish wars, either by strokes of good fortune or by the more systematic but less spectacular supply of war materials. The burgess element among the Commons, who were in a numerical majority but who have left little mark in the records, must have included at least some men who were involved in war contracting and who stood to lose if peace were agreed.

It is impossible to say whether the war was on balance profitable or unprofitable to England. The Commons accepted that any substantial expedition by land or sea required a subsidy, but they expected the money they voted to be well spent[2] and it was not surprising that they linked their complaints about taxation with complaints about corruption and inefficiency in the management of the war. But they were not concerned simply with material considerations; they were also anxious that the honour and integrity of the crown should be upheld and that no peace should be concluded which seemed to disinherit the crown or which might gratuitously surrender the gains that Edward III had made. Perhaps, too, in an only half-felt way, the Commons were afraid of the unknown. To all of them, war, not peace, was the natural and seemingly permanent state of affairs. It was by no means self-evident that peace was preferable to war, as Sir Thomas Grey had pointed out forty years earlier in his *Scalacronica*,[3] and the effect on their lives, their income, and their self-respect if the war were brought to an end on the terms proposed in 1394 was incalculable. However, a sense of deference, or perhaps a desire to keep out of trouble, inhibited the Commons from offering too determined an opposition to the terms. Finally, in the 1394 parliament, they accepted the draft treaty even though they evidently disliked it, and they confined themselves (so far as can be deduced from the record) to expressing their concern about one or two general points.

The nobility shared many of the preconceptions of the Commons,

[1] Froissart, *Oeuvres* Vol. XIV, p. 314.
[2] K. B. McFarlane, 'England and the Hundred Years' War', *Past & Present* 22 (1962) pp. 5-9, 3-13; M. M. Postan, 'The Costs of the Hundred Years' War', *Past & Present* 27 (1964) pp. 34-53.
[3] *Scalacronica of Sir Thomas Grey of Heton* ed. J. Stevenson (Edinburgh 1836) pp. 197-8.

though their attitudes varied more sharply as their individual interests were affected. There is little doubt, for example, that Gaunt was whole-heartedly in favour of the terms which he had done so much to nego-tiate. He stood to gain personally from them, and although his trans-formation into a French aristocrat would raise problems both for the duchy of Lancaster and possibly for the succession to the crown of England, he was completely committed to the Gascon policy. As Froissart pointed out, too, peace offered security for his daughters who were married into the royal houses of Castile and Portugal, and might lead to an equally advantageous marriage for his eldest son Derby, whose first wife Mary Bohun died in 1394.[1]

Gloucester, on the other hand, was said by Froissart to have been in general opposed to the peace negotiations, yet his attitude was evi-dently not without its ambiguities. Froissart had formed the opinion that Gloucester was more inclined to war than peace, and his policy during his brief period of power leaves no room for doubt that at that time he was wholeheartedly in favour of renewing the war as vigor-ously as possible. Froissart also suggests that Gloucester was suspicious of French intentions, and unhappy about the terms upon which peace was to be concluded.[2] He apparently told Robert the Hermit in 1394 that in his view the French were calling the tune in the negotiations, and that no peace between the two countries ought to be concluded until England received all that was due to her under the treaty of Brétigny. He did not object to peace in principle, but merely to the terms.[3] Froissart had some grounds for believing that the treaty of Brétigny represented Gloucester's sticking point. In their speech to the king at Eltham in October 1386, he and Bishop Arundel had ar-gued that it was folly to throw away all that had been won at such cost in the time of Edward III.[4] In effect, according to Froissart, Gloucester wanted a peace which made it clear that the English had won the war. Yet in fact Gloucester's attitude to the peace terms seems to have been less clear-cut and consistent than this; it changed from time to time, and had in it elements of realism and of self-interest. He was perhaps suspicious of French intentions, and saw French designs on Italy and Burgundian expansion into the Low Countries as real dangers to English interests. This was an entirely understandable point of view and one which the English government at times showed signs of

[1] Froissart, *Oeuvres* Vol. XV, p. 81.
[2] *ibid.* pp. 120–21.   [3] *ibid.*
[4] *Knighton* Vol. II, pp. 218–19.

sharing.[1] France, Gloucester may have thought, stood to benefit more than England from an end to the war, and for the English, Ireland was a poor substitute for France as an outlet for martial enterprise and as a source of wealth. When he went over in 1394 Gloucester was not in the least bit impressed by what he saw of Ireland. He is said to have described it as a land of no profit, not worth conquering, for it was likely to be lost again with great speed.[2] Nor did Gloucester show much interest in the proposals being extensively canvassed in the 1390s for an Anglo–French crusade against the Turks. Perhaps he took the quite realistic view that the crusade in the north was a much more worthwhile venture for the English than the uncertainties of campaigning in the Balkans, even though he showed willing by joining Robert the Hermit's Order of the Passion,[3] established to promote a crusade against the Turks. However, Gloucester apparently greeted the news of the French disaster at Nicopolis in 1396 with pleasure, feeling that it presented a chance to fall upon France (now shocked by the loss of so many of her nobles) which a more opportunist and warlike king than Richard would have eagerly grasped.[4] He was fully aware, from his own military experience, that English armies could still march through France unopposed, and that the English had not been defeated in the field. His assessment of the military situation was more optimistic than that of some of his contemporaries, but it contained an element of truth.

On the other hand, two of Froissart's informants, Jean de Grailly and Sir Richard Stury (both of whom were in a position to know the facts) thought in 1395 that Gloucester favoured the grant of Aquitaine to Gaunt.[5] Their view rested on the somewhat crude belief that Gloucester wanted his brother out of the country, because he thought he was too powerful. He also argued, evidently, that Gascon rebels ought not to be allowed to overturn a grant made by the king and accepted, however reluctantly, by the English parliament. Again, there is probably some truth in Grailly's and Stury's accounts. Gaunt's presence in England cramped Gloucester's style and ensured that neither his political nor his military ambitions were likely to be fulfilled. But with Gaunt out of the way, Gloucester might hope to recreate for himself the political dominance he had enjoyed between 1386 and 1388. This

[1] J. J. N. Palmer, *England, France and Christendom* pp. 219–20.
[2] Froissart, *Oeuvres* Vol. XVI, p. 5.
[3] J. J. N. Palmer, *England, France and Christendom* p. 190.
[4] Froissart, *Oeuvres* Vol. XVI, pp. 1–3.
[5] *ibid.* Vol. XV, pp. 149ff., 163–5.

may help to explain Gloucester's ambiguous attitude towards the peace negotiations. In 1392–3 he had co-operated with Gaunt in negotiating with France, but in 1394 his attitude seems to have hardened. On the other hand Stury's account of his views in 1395 may well be correct. Froissart's portrait of the duke is too simple, and implies a consistency of outlook which the duke did not show until, perhaps, 1396, when the peace negotiations had broken down.

The Earl of Arundel also had doubts about the settlement with France. In 1387–8, when the commission had renewed the war, he had led two naval expeditions, one of which had brought him great popularity. He objected to the renewal of negotiations in 1391, according to Froissart,[1] and three years later, in the parliament of January 1394, he objected to the whole peace treaty, and particularly criticized the proposal to grant Aquitaine to Gaunt.[2] Arundel's objection seems to have been couched in general terms. Perhaps he regretted the passing of any opportunity for personal military glory; perhaps he thought that the proposed terms constituted a betrayal of all that he and his father had fought for, and, in his father's case, made money out of. Nor is there any evidence that he favoured Ireland as an alternative theatre of war, though relations between him and the king were so bad in 1394 that it is doubtful whether the king would have wanted him to participate in the expedition even if he had been eager to do so.

Much less is known of the attitude of the other nobles towards the peace proposals. The Earl of Derby appears to have supported his father, and Nottingham by the 1390s had fallen in with Richard's views. Yet there is some evidence that Gloucester and Arundel were not the only lords who had reservations about the peace treaty. Froissart thought in 1391 that many barons shared Gloucester's view that the treaty of Brétigny ought to be enforced.[3] while the Westminster chronicler suggests that in the January parliament of 1394, the lords as well as the Commons objected to the proposal to grant Aquitaine to Gaunt.[4] This suggestion is borne out by Sir Richard Stury's report of the council at Eltham in 1395, when some of the lords again seemed uneasy about the Gascon proposals, though they did not press their views to the point of open opposition to Gaunt and

[1] Froissart, *Oeuvres* Vol. XIV, p. 314.
[2] *Rot. Parl.* Vol. III, pp. 313–14.
[3] Froissart, *Oeuvres* Vol. XIV, p. 314.
[4] Westminster pp. 281–2.

the king.[1] The most significant clue to the motives for their objection to the settlement is provided by the Westminster chronicler, who reported that they believed that the grant of Aquitaine to Gaunt would disinherit the crown.[2] This was evidently a deeply held conviction which it would be foolish to underrate. It may well have been more powerful in influencing the attitude of both lords and Commons than any more subtle calculation of the relative advantages of war and peace. The careful formulation of policy on the basis of an assessment of the advantages and disadvantages likely to flow from a particular course of action was foreign to their way of thinking. Their approach was more rhetorical, more concerned with upholding particular principles which were held to be fundamental. The maintenance of the integrity of the crown was the most important of all such principles, and it was closely followed in some men's minds by the need to enforce the treaty of Brétigny which had been won at great cost from the French.

The negotiations with France were the principal foreign preoccupation of Richard and his council in the 1390s, but the gradual movement towards a settlement with France necessarily entailed a reconsideration of Scottish policy. There is no reason to believe that Richard's intentions towards Scotland were as consistently pacific as they were towards France. The Scottish kings, Robert II (who died in 1390) and Robert III, hoped to include their country in a general peace between England and France, but English policy up to 1394 was to make a separate peace with France, isolate Scotland, and then presumably deal with her.[3] Richard and his advisers may not have contemplated a full-scale invasion of the country, but they evidently calculated that if she were deprived of French protection, she could be induced to offer substantial territorial concessions and a recognition of English overlordship in return for peace. The ambassadors whom Richard sent to Scotland in February 1394 to negotiate a treaty were instructed to demand that the king of Scotland should do homage to the king of England for his kingdom, that the prelates and magnates of Scotland should recognize the English king as their sovereign lord, and that the Scots should hand over to England all the land ceded to Edward III by Edward Balliol in 1334—in effect, the whole of southeastern Scotland. The English council recognized the unreality of this proposition by instructing the envoys to settle if necessary for the land held

[1] Froissart, *Oeuvres* Vol. XV, p. 163. [2] Westminster pp. 266-7.
[3] J. A. Tuck, 'Richard II and the Border Magnates', *Northern History* III (1968) pp. 45-6.

by the English in 1369;[1] this amounted only to the border counties.
These terms were as tough as any put forward by the English in the
previous twenty years. The only concession Richard was prepared to
make was to drop his demand for the outstanding portion of David II's
ransom. At the same time, Richard and his council put pressure on the
Scottish king from other directions. They opened negotiations for an
alliance with the Lord of the Isles, a substantial naval power and the
effective political authority in the western Isles from Skye to Islay,[2]
and they also attempted to attract the Earls of Douglas and March,
the most powerful lords of the border region, into the English allegiance.[3]

Neither Robert III nor his magnates could possibly accept England's
terms for peace; they amounted to dismemberment of the kingdom and
recognition of English suzerainty. But the French successfully insisted
upon Scotland's inclusion, first in the abortive peace treaty, and then in
the twenty-eight years' truce.[4] The ending of the war with France
thus entailed an ending of the war with Scotland without securing the
grandiose concessions demanded by the English in February 1394.
Richard quickly recognized the reality of the situation and by April
1394, at the time when an agreement with France may have been
secretly accepted,[5] he adopted a more pacific attitude towards Scotland,
going so far as to propose a marriage alliance between the two royal
houses.[6] The birth of a son, the future James I, to Queen Annabella
early in 1394 may have provided the occasion for such a proposal,
but the negotiations never came to anything, and Richard contented
himself with attempting to enforce the truce along the northern
border.

Yet the ending of the war with Scotland ran counter to the interests
of the northern nobility, especially the Percy family, headed by the
Earl of Northumberland. Northumberland in particular stood to
lose important possessions in Roxburghshire if the English eventually
agreed, as the price of a settlement, to surrender their territorial claims
in Scotland;[7] and despite the harshness of English terms in February

[1] *Rot. Scot.* Vol. II, p. 121; BM Cotton *Vespasian* F VII ff. 29, 36.
[2] *Rot. Scot.* Vol. II, p. 94; *Foedera* Vol. VII, p. 626.
[3] *Rot. Scot.* Vol. II, p. 122.
[4] J. A. Tuck, 'Richard II and the Border Magnates' p. 46.
[5] J. J. N. Palmer, *England, France and Christendom* p. 150.
[6] BM Cotton *Vespasian* F VII f.39; *Rot Scot.* Vol. II, p. 126.
[7] J. M. W. Bean, 'The Percies and their Estates in Scotland', *Archaeologia Aeliana*
4th series XXXV (1957) pp. 91-9.

1394, Richard's instructions to Gaunt in 1383 had shown that such a step might not be entirely out of the question.[1] More generally, the dominance which the noble families of the north enjoyed in Cumberland and Northumberland rested upon their control of military office on the border, which allowed them to recruit and maintain what amounted to private armies publicly financed and which gave them prestige and extensive powers of patronage.[2] Their social position depended upon the maintenance of the system for the defence of the border which had come into existence as the war with Scotland became institutionalized. Furthermore, the war with Scotland had become a way of life to many of the inhabitants of the northern counties. Lords, and sometimes lesser men, made money out of ransoms and booty; the proximity of a hostile country meant that a ready refuge was available to all who fell foul of the law, and forces from the other side of the border might be useful in the furtherance of private quarrels. The burgesses of Newcastle and York made money out of supplying cloth, food, weapons, and means of transport for the armies stationed on the border, and the economic benefits of constructing and maintaining the fortifications in the northern counties must have spread themselves widely through the population. There is some reason to believe that Scottish raids into the north of England were not as destructive as has sometimes been suggested, at least in the period after 1332, and it may be that the benefits and pleasures of war were more obvious than its disadvantages.

Opposition from certain nobles to Richard's foreign policies had played an important part in the growth of hostility towards the court in the 1380s, but although, according to Froissart, Gloucester, Arundel, and many other lords, together with the Commons, opposed the negotiations with France in 1391,[3] the first open demonstration against Richard's peace policy in the 1390s came from outside the political community. In the spring of 1393 a rising broke out in Cheshire under the leadership of Sir Thomas Talbot, a king's knight who had enjoyed a successful career as a soldier in both France and Scotland. This rising has been linked, in both contemporary and modern accounts, with a series of disturbances in Yorkshire which had dragged on since 1387, but the only connection between the two appears to be that

---

[1] *Rot. Scot.* Vol. II, p. 51.
[2] J. A. Tuck, 'Northumbrian Society in the Fourteenth Century', *Northern History* VI (1971) pp. 22–39.
[3] Froissart, *Oeuvres* Vol. XIV, p. 314.

Lancaster successfully suppressed both of them.[1] Walsingham took the view that the Cheshire rising arose directly out of Richard's proposals for peace with France.[2] The rebels, he states, nailed their manifesto to church doors, and in it they proclaimed that Lancaster, Gloucester, and Derby were intent on giving away the king's title to the throne of France, and that they also intended to abolish the ancient liberties of Cheshire. The leaders of the revolt quickly gained a large following, and they announced that they intended to kill Lancaster, Gloucester, Derby, and other kinsmen of the king if they got the chance. There seems no good reason to reject Walsingham's interpretation of the revolt. For over a century Cheshire had been a recruiting ground for soldiers.[3] Edward I recruited 1000 archers there for his Welsh campaign in 1277, almost twice as many as any other county, and in 1361 Cheshire sent three times the average number of soldiers raised from each county to Ireland: throughout the fourteenth century there was a high proportion of Cheshire men in the army. The tradition of military service probably arose originally from the county's proximity to Wales. It was strengthened by the advowry system, which allowed criminals from elsewhere to seek refuge in the county and they then became an obvious source of military manpower; and it was carried on during the war with France by the Black Prince's tenure of the earldom of Chester, which gave the county a personal connection with the most prominent soldier of the century. It may be, too, that the county's economy, which was mainly pastoral, meant that there was no alternative to military service for many young men. If the county suffered from overpopulation in relation to its resources, military service was a vital source of employment. The peace proposals of the 1390s thus constituted a most serious threat to the traditional occupation of a considerable proportion of the men of Cheshire, and the discontent engendered by the levying of a very large subsidy in the county in 1391 perhaps eroded the loyalty to the king as earl which might otherwise have inhibited a rising. Though in their manifesto, the rebel leaders were careful to blame Gaunt, Gloucester, and Derby for the peace policy, rather than the king.

The rising took the government by surprise. The council instructed Huntingdon and Sir John Stanley to go to Cheshire to express the

---

[1] J. G. Bellamy, 'The Northern Rebellions in the Later Years of Richard II', *BJRL* XLVII (1964–5) pp. 254–74; A. B. Steel, *Richard II* (Cambridge 1941) p. 201; Walsingham, *Annales* pp. 159–61.
[2] Walsingham, *Annales* p. 159.
[3] H. J. Hewitt, *Medieval Cheshire* (Manchester 1929) pp. 157–60.

royal displeasure and to suppress illegal assemblies and gatherings of troops.[1] They were also told to promise redress of grievances against the king's officials in the county. The choice of Stanley, one of the most prominent Cheshire knights in royal service, was shrewd; but the government's fairly mild reaction proved insufficient. The rising spread, and Gaunt and Gloucester were recalled to England and instructed to suppress it.[2] They set about their task with considerable tact and sensitivity, using force only on one occasion, reassuring the people about the king's intentions, and recruiting many of the rebels into the army Gaunt was forming to take to Aquitaine, a measure which went some way towards eliminating the main reason for the rising. The rebel leaders were treated most leniently; many received immediate pardons, and although Talbot himself was taken into custody he had little difficulty in escaping and was never brought to justice, despite pressure from Gaunt and Gloucester in the January parliament of 1394.[3] Richard evidently did not wish to take any action which might jeopardize the loyalty that the men of Cheshire felt towards their earl, a direct personal loyalty which the king received nowhere else within the kingdom. Indeed, he went so far as to remove Gloucester from his position as Justice of Chester and appoint Nottingham in his place.[4] Outside Cheshire, however, the rising had more complicated repercussions. With memories of Radcot Bridge still fresh in men's minds, it was inevitable that some should see the hand of the king behind a rising which was directed against Gloucester as well as Gaunt, and which was led by one of the king's retainers. So seriously did the king take this reaction that he issued a proclamation denying that it was his intention to destroy the magnates of the realm.[5] None the less, his lenient treatment of Talbot in face of repeated protests by Gaunt and Gloucester can have done little to diminish suspicion. The Earl of Arundel, meanwhile, whose lordships of Oswestry, Chirk,

---

[1] PRO Chancery Miscellanea C.47/14/16 no. 44.

[2] Walsingham, *Annales* pp. 160–61; *Foedera* Vol. VII, p. 746.

[3] *Rot. Parl.* Vol. III, p. 316. Talbot was arrested and imprisoned in the Tower on the 16th of May 1394, but on the 19th of May the king ordered all proceedings against him to be suspended until further notice. On the 28th of September he was transferred to Windsor Castle, but some time thereafter he was allowed to escape. In the January parliament of 1397 Gaunt again demanded his punishment, but in April 1397 he was pardoned and his annuity restored with full arrears (*CCR* 1392–6, pp. 208, 294, 316; *CPR* 1391–6, p. 560; 1396–9, p. 109; *Rot. Parl.* Vol. III, p. 338; PRO Exchequer Warrants for Issues E.404/14/96 ii no. 88).

[4] *CPR* 1391–6, p. 391.

[5] *Foedera* Vol. VII, p. 746.

Bromfield, and Yale bordered upon Cheshire and who might have been expected to join Gaunt and Gloucester in putting down the revolt did nothing at all and sat in his castle of Holt waiting to see what happened,[1] a surprisingly passive reaction in view of the damage which men from Cheshire had inflicted on his lordship of Bromfield and Yale.[2] No doubt Arundel was quite happy to see one of the chief negotiators of peace embarrassed by a revolt against his policy. Gaunt took the view that Arundel was guilty of disloyalty, and said as much in the parliament of January 1394.[3]

The proposed terms for peace with France were laid before this parliament. The chancellor read the treaty in his opening speech,[4] and pointed out that since parliament had given its consent to the war in the first place, it was bound to go on financing it if no better course emerged—a clear indication to the Commons that the continuation of their freedom from heavy taxation depended upon their acceptance of the peace. Nonetheless, the Westminster annalist recorded that both lords and Commons were displeased by the treaty, the main ground of their objection being the grant of Aquitaine to Gaunt, which they thought would disinherit the crown.[5] He noted that at first the nobles and Commons flatly refused to accept the treaty; however, the official record of the proceedings makes it clear that in the end both lords and Commons gave way, although they expressed their concern about certain provisions in the treaty, notably those relating to liege homage, sovereignty and resort.[6] The government's carrying of the treaty was apparently a fairly sophisticated political manoeuvre. According to Westminster, Gaunt bought off Gloucester's opposition by promising him lands, perhaps those in Aquitaine to which he had a title but which the French had conquered.[7] Winning Gloucester's silence may have been made easier by his ambiguous attitude to Gaunt's grant of Aquitaine, but his defection cost him the support of the Commons: the Westminster annalist says he 'lost the voice of the people'.[8] At the same time, it is likely that the speaker, Sir John Bushy, was using his arts of persuasion to bring the Commons round. Bushy was both a royal and a

---

[1] Walsingham, *Annales* p. 162.
[2] PRO Ancient Petitions SC.8/8/88 no. 4387, probably to be dated in the early 1390s.
[3] *Rot. Parl.* Vol. III, pp. 313–14.   [4] *ibid.* p. 309.
[5] Westminster pp. 281–2.   [6] *Rot. Parl.* Vol. III, pp. 315–16.
[7] Westminster p. 282. In 1368 Gloucester held the lordships of Melle, Chizée, and Civray in Poitou (A. Goodman, *The Loyal Conspiracy* (London 1971) p. 88).
[8] Westminster p. 282.

Lancastrian retainer. He was an experienced parliamentarian, 1394 being his sixth consecutive parliament, and he evidently so handled the Commons that he was able before the session concluded to present their acceptance of the treaty to the council.[1]

The Earl of Arundel, meanwhile, had launched a characteristically crude and ill-judged attack upon Gaunt.[2] He accused him of over-familiarity with the king, and criticized both the grant to him of Aquitaine and the peace treaty in general. The king reacted indignantly, saying that the duchy of Aquitaine had been given to Gaunt with the consent of all the estates assembled in parliament, and that there was nothing in the peace treaty which was not acceptable to the king and his council. As for his relationship with Gaunt, it was as cordial as was proper between an uncle and a nephew. Arundel was thoroughly squashed, and had to make a public apology to Gaunt. Gaunt for his part accused Arundel of plotting to aid the Cheshire rebels during the rising in the previous year, and perhaps Arundel's inactivity at the time still rankled with Gaunt. But Arundel's outburst can have had little to do with the Cheshire rising. By attacking Gaunt and the peace proposals, he may have been trying to gain the support and popularity of the Commons which Gloucester had just lost, and to stiffen their resistance to the peace proposals. But the plan completely misfired, and Arundel succeeded only in making himself look a fool. He revenged himself in a petty-minded manner in the following summer by de-liberate and tasteless rudeness to the king at Queen Anne's funeral. According to Walsingham,[3] Richard retaliated by hitting Arundel on the head with a rod. There is no other authority for this, though it is consistent with a violent and impetuous streak in Richard's character. The same day he sent Arundel to the Tower, where he stayed for a week, and he was released only by mainperning for the very large sum of £40,000 that he would make no riots or unlawful assemblies in future.[4] Perhaps the king believed, or had been persuaded by Gaunt, that Arundel had somehow been implicated in the Cheshire rising, yet had the earl not made himself look foolish in parliament and then dis-graced himself at the queen's funeral, it is very doubtful whether (after the Earl of Devon's case) Richard would have felt able to take so strong a line against his disorderly conduct.

[1] *Rot. Parl.* Vol. III, p. 316.
[2] *ibid.* pp. 313–14.
[3] Walsingham, *Annales* p. 424: 'Rex . . . accepta lictoris canna, percussit eum violenter in capite.'
[4] *CCR* 1392–6, p. 368.

Richard and Gaunt had won a notable victory in the parliament of January 1394. Gloucester had been persuaded, momentarily at least, to accept the peace proposals; the Commons had been successfully managed; and Arundel had been humiliated. Had it not been for the Gascon revolt, the peace would in all probability have been formally proclaimed. Well content with the success of his French policy, Richard turned in the spring of 1394 to the preparation of an expedition to Ireland. Richard's motives in going to Ireland have been the subject of remarkably varied explanations. Steel gave Richard credit for attempting to come to grips with the Irish question, but suggested that he embarked upon it in the autumn of 1394 as a reaction to the death of Queen Anne.[1] Perroy argued that the expedition took the form of a crusade against the Clementist Irish,[2] while Tout saw it as an opportunity for Richard to test his military strength.[3] Yet Richard said many times in his correspondence that he was going to Ireland to restore justice and good government.[4] There is no reason to disbelieve this, and indeed if he had not made a major military effort in Ireland, the English lordship there would in all probability soon have ceased to exist. There had long been pressure from the English colony in Ireland for the king to go over in person; equally, Richard had been anxious for some years to restore order in Ireland and end its drain on English financial resources.[5] He also hoped to revive the English settlement in Leinster by removing the native Irish and bringing over new English colonists. He intended that Leinster should be an English land, firmly under the control of the government in Dublin.[6] There is no reason to believe that Richard's view of the Irish situation was any more complicated than this. If, in addition to restoring the English lordship he could persuade the Irish church to recognize Rome and provide 'the young knights and esquires of England' with an opportunity for war which they no longer had in France, so much the better. It does not appear that at this stage Richard entertained any far-reaching

[1] A. B. Steel, *Richard II* p. 205.
[2] E. Perroy, *L'Angleterre et le Grand Schisme d'Occident* (Paris 1933) pp. 102–3.
[3] Tout, *Chapters* Vol. III, pp. 487–95.
[4] See for instance *Anglo-Norman Letters and Petitions* ed. M. D. Legge, Anglo-Norman Text Society III (Oxford 1941) pp. 47–8, 51–2.
[5] See for example the terms of Richard's grant of Ireland to de Vere in 1385 (*RDP* Vol. V, pp. 76–7) and in general, J. A. Tuck, 'Anglo-Irish Relations 1382–1393', *Proceedings of the Royal Irish Academy* LXIX (1970).
[6] E. Curtis, 'Unpublished Letters from Richard II in Ireland', *Proceedings of the Royal Irish Academy* XXXVII (1927) pp. 276–303. For the plantation scheme put forward in 1399, see J. T. Gilbert, *The Viceroys of Ireland* (Dublin 1865) p. 561.

military plans for which the Irish expedition was a preparation; the army was disbanded on its return to England. Nor is there any evidence, despite the temptations of the theory, that Richard and his council thought that the loss of Ireland would be strategically disadvantageous to England and would threaten her with encirclement. There is no sign of this view, which became an obsession with later English governments, before the reign of Henry VI.[1] Richard went to Ireland to prevent his inheritance being entirely eroded by the Irish chiefs.

The preparations for the reassertion of the English lordship were long-drawn-out, and they reveal something of the politics of the court in the mid-1390s.[2] When Gloucester was discharged from the lieutenancy of Ireland in July 1392, Richard wrote to the Irish council informing them that in his place he had appointed Roger Mortimer Earl of March, who was only nineteen. As a temporary measure, until Mortimer could come over, the Earl of Ormond was appointed justiciar. However, Ormond held office for much longer than he anticipated; more than two years elapsed before Mortimer actually arrived in Ireland. The explanation for the long delay is almost certainly to be found in a controversy between the Earl of Kent on the one hand and the Earls of Arundel, Warwick, and Northumberland on the other, over the terms on which Mortimer was to leave the country while still under age. Kent was the guardian of the young earl himself, but Arundel, Warwick, and Northumberland had received custody of the March inheritance after a dispute over its control in 1382. This divided control was almost bound to create tension, and Mortimer's appointment as lieutenant led to a direct clash. In a document probably drawn up soon after the announcement of Mortimer's appointment, Kent put to the council certain articles concerning Mortimer's proposed expedition to Ireland.[3] The first and most important of these was that Mortimer should have livery of his inheritance even though he was under age. But in another document laid before the council,[4] Arundel, Warwick, and Northumberland opposed this proposal on the grounds that they were the lawful guardians of the inheritance, and saw no reason why they should be ousted without their goodwill and assent. They were also doubtful about the propriety of Mortimer using the resources of his inheritance to finance the expedition. This was another

[1] *The Libelle of Englyshe Polycye* ed. G. Warner (Oxford 1926) p. 37. I have been guided on this point by Dr J. F. Lydon of Trinity College Dublin.
[2] J. A. Tuck, 'Anglo-Irish Relations' pp. 29–31.
[3] BM Cotton *Titus* B xi f. 8.
[4] *ibid.* f. 25.

of Kent's proposals, and might well have received a favourable reception from the council, for it would have saved the exchequer, and thus the taxpayer, some of the costs of the expedition. The three earls protested that their only interest was to safeguard the inheritance from waste and destruction, and administer it for the profit of the young Earl of March. They took their obligations as custodians seriously, and were praised by the Wigmore chronicler for their administration of the inheritance.[1]

The matter remained in dispute for some time. On the 13th of June 1393 the king gave Mortimer livery of his Irish lands,[2] but the three earls had never had custody of these, and they were not referred to in either of the documents submitted to the council. Not until the following February did the king give him livery of his English and Welsh inheritance.[3] It is possible that Richard deliberately delayed any decision on Kent's proposals until Mortimer was nearly twenty and a royal expedition to Ireland imminent, so as not to antagonize either side more than was inevitable. Kent was Richard's half brother, and prominent at court, but Northumberland was a man of moderate views whom the king did not wish to alienate. By February 1394, when their custody of the inheritance had little more than a year to run, he and his co-guardians may have somewhat moderated their objections to Kent's proposals. But even so, when the king and council finally made their decision it went against the three earls. They were 'ousted from their estate' and, so far as is known, no special arrangements were made to protect the Mortimer inheritance while the earl was in Ireland with the king. Their opposition had, perhaps, prevented Kent's proposals being implemented in 1392 or 1393, but in the long run they failed to carry the day on the council. It was a small, but unmistakable, sign of the gap that was again beginning to emerge between the king and some of the more prominent members of the nobility.

Mortimer's retinue formed merely a part of the royal expedition to Ireland which got under way in the late summer of 1394. In the organization of the expedition, Richard departed from the methods of the early years of his reign, when he himself had not been in command of his armies. The expedition was financed through the wardrobe, as was normal when the king took command in person, but on this

---

[1] *Monasticon Anglicanum* Vol. VI, part 1, by Sir W. Dugdale, ed. J. Caley, *et al.* (London 1817–30) p. 354.
[2] *CPR* 1391–6, p. 284.
[3] *ibid.* p. 375.

occasion, although several magnates brought their retinues, the main body of the army over 5000 men, was a household force of the kind which had been familiar in Edward I's Welsh and Scottish wars.[1] The king had learnt not to rely solely on the military power of the nobility but instead to organize his own army. The household character of the Irish expedition is in keeping with this policy, and more generally with the emphasis on the household which characterizes the whole of Richard's reign. Within the household he was safe from magnate pressures, and need not depend upon armed forces whose loyalty lay to their lord as much as to the king.

The composition of the aristocratic contingent in the army, however, is as significant as its mainly household character. Of the older generation of nobles, only Gloucester joined the expedition. Lancaster was in Aquitaine; York remained in England as keeper of the realm; and Arundel and Warwick evidently preferred not to take part. The majority of the nobles who went with Richard were the young men of his own generation who had formed the court circle in the previous few years. The Earl of March went, of course, as the greatest landowner in Ireland and as the man who would be left in charge as lieutenant after the king's return home. But the other nobles were Richard's close friends: the Earl of Nottingham, the Earl of Rutland, the Earl of Huntingdon, the heir to the Earl of Kent, Sir Thomas Despenser, Sir Thomas Percy, Sir John Beaumont, and Sir William Lescrope. Huntingdon was chamberlain, Lescrope under-chamberlain, and Percy steward of the household; few of them had the experience of campaigning in France which enabled Gloucester, and perhaps Arundel, to take so disparaging a view of a campaign in Ireland, and there is no evidence that any of them had offered any opposition to the king's policy of negotiating peace with France and diverting resources to the reassertion of the English lordship in Ireland.

The surviving letters which describe the actual conduct of the expedition suggest that these men played a dominant part in the campaign.[2] In a night raid Nottingham nearly captured Art MacMurrough, self-styled king of Leinster and the Irish chief whose submission and departure from Leinster Richard was especially anxious to achieve. Rutland, marching into Munster captured a MacCarthy chief and forced Taig MacCarthy Mór, leader of the MacCarthys of Desmond,

[1] J. F. Lydon, 'Richard II's Expeditions to Ireland', *Journal of the Royal Society of Antiquaries of Ireland* XCIII (1963) p. 141.
[2] E. Curtis, 'Unpublished Letters' pp. 283–8.

to submit. There is very little evidence, on the other hand, about Gloucester's activities. He developed a low opinion of Ireland, and he may have been quite pleased to return home at the turn of the year as Richard's envoy to the parliament which assembled in January 1395.[1]

In military terms, the campaign was a remarkable success.[2] With a strategy reminiscent of Edward I's in Wales, Richard surrounded the Wicklow Mountains, where MacMurrough's power lay, with a series of garrisons and a naval blockade. In the few pitched battles which occurred, the English archers were more than a match for the Irish armed with double-headed axes. On the 7th of January 1395 MacMurrough met Nottingham near Tullow and agreed to leave Leinster together with his people and his vassal tribes. After Mac-Murrough's submission, the other Irish chiefs gradually came in and recognized the English overlordship. The king received most of the submissions in person, and much of the preliminary negotiation was handled by the Earl of Ormond and the Archbishop of Armagh, both of whom spoke Irish fluently and who had experience in dealing with the native Irish.[3] But the beneficiaries of the removal of the Irish from Leinster were, for the most part, Richard's noble companions. Gloucester was granted part of the land to be vacated by O'Byrne, one of MacMurrough's urraghts, but he correctly assumed that it would be of no value to him and that he would never be able to gain possession.[4] Beaumont received a large area of southern Wicklow and northern Wexford;[5] William Lescrope was granted a part of O'Byrne's country;[6] and Nottingham was allowed to assume the title of Lord of Carlow, even though it was not due to come to him until the death of Margaret Marshall, his grandmother.[7] Outside Leinster the king made fewer grants, and although he bestowed the title Earl of Cork on Rutland it is not clear how much, if any, land went with the grant.[8] He had to be careful lest he create too large a patrimony within the region dominated by the Earls of Ormond and Desmond, the only Anglo-Irish

[1] Froissart, *Oeuvres* Vol. XVI, p. 5.
[2] J. F. Lydon, 'Richard II's Expeditions' pp. 146–7.
[3] E. Curtis, *Richard II in Ireland* (Oxford 1927) *passim*; *idem*, 'Unpublished Letters' p. 287.
[4] E. Curtis, 'Unpublished Letters' pp. 281–2; Froissart, *Oeuvres* Vol. XVI, p. 5.
[5] *CCPRI* pp. 152–3.
[6] E. Curtis, 'Unpublished Letters' p. 282; *CCPRI* p. 154.
[7] E. Curtis, 'Unpublished Letters' p. 269; J. Otway-Ruthven, *A History of Medieval Ireland* (London 1968) p. 327; A. Goodman, *The Loyal Conspiracy* p. 62.
[8] GEC XII part 2 pp. 900–91; E. Curtis, 'Unpublished Letters' pp. 123–4. No patent of creation survives, but Rutland used the title 'Earl of Cork' until he died.

lords with any effective authority in Munster. The direction of patronage, however, was unmistakable, and Richard's diplomacy was designed to ensure that these nobles could enjoy their lands in peace by securing the removal of the Irish from Leinster.

In the north of Ireland, the position was rather different. The Earl of March was nominally Earl of Ulster, and the submission of Niall óg O'Neill opened up the prospect of a settlement in Ulster which would allow March to recover some of his inheritance. The Irish of Munster and Connacht had urged O'Neill not to submit,[1] but through the mediation of the Archbishop of Armagh he did so, expecting that he would be confirmed in his lordship of the Irish of Ulster.[2] Yet when he submitted, he found that the king proposed to reserve this question for his later judgement and that his Irish would be expected to take an oath of loyalty to Mortimer.[3] The king, whom O'Neill had looked to as an impartial judge, appeared to be upholding Mortimer's feudal claims in Ulster, and the suspicion that was engendered even at the time of submission goes far towards explaining the rapid breakdown of the settlement in Ulster. March for his part could not have been entirely happy about the situation: too much was left in doubt, and he may well have felt that his peers in Leinster had achieved a more satisfactory settlement.

Before Richard returned to England on the 15th of May 1395 he had received the submissions of most of the Irish chiefs. Even those of Connacht had come in and done homage either in person or through the Bishops of Kilfenora and Kilmacduagh.[4] It had evidently been Richard's intention to stay in Ireland until the Irish of Connacht and Ulster had submitted, for although parliament in England had urged him in early February to return home because of the threat that the Scots were about to break the truce and 'for other important reasons which would be explained more fully to the king on his return,' he remained in Ireland for another three months.[5] There seems no reason whatsoever to accept Walsingham's story that Richard hurried back to England to save the Church from the menace of the Lollards.[6] The manifesto which a group of Lollards produced in January 1395 was not, as Walsingham thought, presented to parliament or sponsored by a group of knights in parliament.[7] The government under York seems

---

[1] E. Curtis, *Richard II in Ireland* pp. 143–4.   [2] *ibid.*
[3] *ibid.* p. 146.   [4] *ibid.* pp. 90–93, 113–14.   [5] *ibid.* pp. 137–9.
[6] Walsingham, *Annales* p. 173.
[7] *ibid.* p. 174; *Rogeri Dymmok Liber Contra XII Errores et Hereses Lollardorum* ed. H. S. Cronin, Wycliffe Society (London 1922) pp. xxvi–xlii.

to have dealt calmly and satisfactorily with the Lollard outburst, and Richard did not make plans to leave Ireland until he was satisfied that the most important Irish lords recognized his overlordship.

To all outward appearances, Richard had achieved a military and political triumph in Ireland. He had persuaded the Irish to agree to leave Leinster and he had received the submission of the great majority of the Irish chiefs elsewhere; only those of the far north west held out.[1] Yet the settlement broke down almost at once. MacMurrough and his urraghts refused to leave Leinster, and war broke out in the north between Mortimer and O'Neill. The Irish annals give no reason for MacMurrough's breach of his undertaking. They merely state that he broke faith with Richard, but the reason may be that the king refused to grant him his wife's inheritance, the Barony of Norragh, which the Statutes of Kilkenny disqualified him from holding, despite the fact that he had been promised it under the 1394 agreement.[2] Faced with the prospect of having to conquer what land they could outside Leinster, it was only to be expected that MacMurrough and his followers would exploit whatever pretext they could find to stay. In Ulster, O'Neill's faith in Richard collapsed even before he left for England. When he heard that the king was planning to depart, he wrote to him predicting that as soon as he had gone 'my lord the Earl of Ulster will wage bitter war against me, and if I make no resistance he will crush me without pity'.[3] O'Neill was in a real difficulty: if he did not resist Mortimer he would, as he put it in an earlier letter, 'be held to scorn by all the Irish and Scots',[4] yet if he took arms against him he would 'become rebel and traitor to your majesty, which, God be witness, I never intended to be'.[5] There is no reason to doubt O'Neill's good faith. From his point of view, Richard could have ruled Ulster through him, and he would gladly have recognized Richard as overlord. He could also have had at his disposal the gallowglasses of John MacDonald, brother of the Lord of the Isles with whom Richard already had an understanding.[6] Yet to confirm O'Neill in his lordship was in effect

---

[1] The O'Donnells of Tír Connaill did not submit to Richard, nor did they do homage to Mortimer.
[2] E. Curtis, 'The Barons of Norragh, Co. Kildare, 1171–1660', *Journal of the Royal Society of Antiquaries of Ireland* LXV (1935) pp. 89–90; *Annals of the Four Masters* Vol. IV, ed. J. O'Donovan (Dublin 1851) p. 739: 'Although MacMurrough had gone into the King's house, he did not afterwards keep faith with him.'
[3] E. Curtis, *Richard II in Ireland* pp. 214–15.   [4] *ibid*. pp. 143–4.   [5] *ibid*. p. 215.
[6] *ibid*. pp. 87–8; *Foedera* Vol. VII p. 626; *Diplomatic Correspondence of Richard II* ed. E. Perroy, Camden Series XLVIII (1933) pp. 103–4; A. McKerral, 'West Highland Mercenaries in Ireland', *Scottish Historical Review* XXX (1951) pp. 1–14.

to disinherit Mortimer, a step Richard could not contemplate taking. O'Neill did not understand, or would not accept, the English feudal concept that lordship over men and lordship over land were inseparable and that submission to Mortimer implied acceptance that ultimate lordship over the land of Ulster belonged to Mortimer. To the Irish chiefs, lordship over persons was acceptable and common, but the land was the inalienable property of the clan and lordship over it could not be granted away. In the end, Richard's Irish settlement broke down in the face of this fundamental and unbridgeable difference between English and Irish social assumptions.[1]

It seems likely, furthermore, that Richard had no very clear intentions towards either Ulster or Connacht. He presumably accepted the inevitability of inter-tribal war if MacMurrough and his followers were expelled from Leinster and compelled to find lands elsewhere, and he never sorted out the matters in dispute between Mortimer and O'Neill, though he promised to do so. In the end he seems to have been quite happy to leave Mortimer and O'Neill to fight it out. The arrangements Richard made for the government of the country tend to confirm this interpretation. Sir William Lescrope was appointed justiciar and the Earl of March lieutenant, and their spheres of authority were carefully demarcated. Lescrope was to govern Leinster, Munster, and Louth, while Mortimer was in charge of Ulster and Connacht.[2] Lescrope in fact occupied the office by deputy, though he was allowed to draw the usual fees from it,[3] but Richard's intention was that he should rule nominally in the peaceful southeast of Ireland, the region the king was most interested in, while to Mortimer fell the task of making war upon the Irish of Ulster and Connacht. Leinster was to be reinvigorated with settlers from England; it was to become an English land, and its lords and governors were to be drawn from Richard's courtier nobility.

At home, Richard's Irish expedition does not seem to have made much impact. Parliament was impressed with his achievement, but thought that he could well afford to come home and leave his deputies

---

[1] Little has so far been written on this subject. Two useful accounts are: D. B. Quinn, *The Elizabethans and the Irish* (New York 1966) and K. Nichollas, *Gaelic and Gaelicised Ireland in the Middle Ages* (Dublin 1972). An interesting but neglected contemporary account of O'Neill's court is given by the Catalan Count John de Perelhos, who went on pilgrimage to Lough Derg in 1397 (J. P. Mahaffy, 'Two Early Tours in Ireland', *Hermathena* XVIII (1914) pp. 1–9).
[2] PRO Indentures E.101/69/1 nos. 292, 293.
[3] PRO Exchequer Warrants for Issues E.404/14/96 ii no. 25.

in charge once most of the Irish chiefs had submitted.[1] Though couched in highly diplomatic language, the tone of the letter parliament sent to the king in Ireland is unmistakable. They thought he had spent long enough over there, and they may well have been encouraged in this view by Gloucester, whom Richard sent to parliament as his envoy and who had developed a sour view of Ireland in his months there. The lords of parliament thought that Scottish and probably Gascon affairs were more important than Ireland. Walsingham suggests[2] that public opinion was more concerned by the Lollard propaganda of January 1395 than by events in Ireland, even though the king was not; and when Froissart came to England in April 1395 he found the king's council preoccupied with the problem of Aquitaine.[3] Ireland faded very rapidly from the consciousness of the English political community, yet Richard himself kept it in mind and as early as December 1397 he had made up his mind to go back there and enforce the 1395 settlement.[4] His concern with Ireland was a constant element in his policy, but his emphasis on it after 1394 can only have intensified the feeling of some of the nobility that his interests and priorities were not theirs.

In all probability the 'other business' which parliament asked the king to attend to on his return to England was the revolt in Gascony against the proposed peace treaty. Gaunt proved unable to bring the Gascons into line, and the unpopularity of the proposed treaty at home meant that a policy of coercion was unlikely to be acceptable to either nobles or Commons.[5] It would be almost impossible to persuade the Commons to pay for the imposition on Gascony of a treaty which they themselves disliked. The breakdown of the peace proposals compelled the government to seek an alternative settlement with the French. By 1397 Gaunt had abandoned Aquitaine, and his eldest illegitimate son, John Beaufort, ruled there as his seneschal; the formal status of Aquitaine remained as it had been. But the two governments agreed in 1396 upon a twenty-eight years' truce,[6] cemented by a marriage alliance between Richard and Charles VI's seven-year-old daughter Isabella, and the truce brought both countries many of the advantages of a final peace. The fighting ceased, and there now appeared the pros-

---

[1] E. Curtis, *Richard II in Ireland* pp. 137–9.
[2] Walsingham, *Annales* pp. 173–4, 183.
[3] Froissart, *Oeuvres* Vol. XV, pp. 149ff.
[4] PRO Indentures E.101/69/1 no. 296.
[5] J. J. N. Palmer, *England, France and Christendom* pp. 160–63.
[6] *Foedera* Vol. VII, pp. 820–30.

pect of a generation's freedom from heavy war taxation. Under the
terms of the truce, England surrendered Brest to the Duke of Brittany,
and this, together with the surrender of Cherbourg to the King of
Navarre in 1393,[1] marked the abandonment of the barbican policy
which had been developed at the beginning of the reign. There was a
remarkable atmosphere of harmony between England and France in
these years[2] and much sympathy on both sides of the Channel for a
crusade against the Turks in the Balkans. Richard and Charles planned
a joint expedition against Milan.[3] Rather more ominous, at least from
Gloucester's point of view, was a clause in the king's instructions to the
ambassadors sent to negotiate the marriage alliance in 1396.[4] They were
to ask that the King of France and his royal uncles should aid and sustain Richard 'with all their power against any of his subjects'. Such an
undertaking was not embodied in the final treaty, and Richard evidently did not set much store by it; it cannot be taken as evidence of
his despotic intentions. Yet it may well have created some sense of
insecurity in those nobles who had opposed the king in 1387–8 and it
suggests a certain insensitivity on the king's part. What Gloucester
thought about the clause is just as important as Richard's abandonment
of it, but unfortunately his reaction is not recorded.

There was little to Gloucester's liking, however, in the settlement
with France which was reached in 1396. The collapse of the Gascon
proposals meant that Gaunt was likely to spend the rest of his life in
England and the alliance between the crown and the Lancastrian interest was likely to hold firm. Yet although there was no final peace
there was no war either, and two important ports of entry into France
had been surrendered. Gloucester's attitude to the peace proposals
had not been entirely hostile, and he had accepted them in 1394, but
the truce of 1396 gave him the worst of both worlds. The chroniclers
of the French court were unanimous in believing that it was Gloucester's dissatisfaction with the terms of the 1396 settlement that precipitated his downfall.[5]

---

[1] *ibid.* pp. 756–7.
[2] A. B. Steel, *Richard II* pp. 188–9; J. J. N. Palmer, *England, France and Christendom* pp. 149–50.
[3] A. S. Atiya, *The Crusade of Nicopolis* (London 1934); D. M. Bueno de Mesquita,
'The Foreign Policy of Richard II in 1397: Some Italian Letters', *EHR* LVI (1941)
pp. 628–37.
[4] *Foedera* Vol. VII, p. 811: 'Et auxi de lui aider et susteigner ovec tout lour pouvoir
encontre aucune de ses subgiz.'
[5] *Traison* p. 1; *Chronique du Religieux de Saint Denys* Vol. II, ed. M. L. Bellaguet
(Paris 1839) pp. 476–7.

Gloucester and Arundel, furthermore, had little reason to be content with the direction of the king's favour from 1394 onwards. Those who now had the ear of the king were the same nobles who had benefited, on paper at least, from the settlement of Leinster: Rutland, Nottingham, and Lescrope, together with Huntingdon and Thomas Percy. These men obtained numerous pardons and grants for their dependants, and their favour with the king ensured that men lower in the social scale would look to them for good lordship:[1] in this respect Rutland, Nottingham, and Lescrope replaced de Vere, Burley, and Pole. The social consequences for a noble who did not enjoy access to the king were the same now as they had been in the 1380s. Richard's patronage of his new nobility, however, was less lavish and more calculating than it had been in the first decade of the reign. In the first place, there could be little of the social prejudice that had helped to arouse opposition to the favourites of the 1380s. Rutland was York's eldest son; Holland and Kent were Richard's half-brothers, while Nottingham was heir to the vast Norfolk inheritance and Thomas Percy was the younger brother of the Earl of Northumberland. Only Lescrope came from below the topmost social rank, and, perhaps partly for this reason, he attracted a disproportionate amount of opprobrium.[2] Such men had little need of lavish endowment, for most of them had either already been provided for or had great expectations. His patronage of them was therefore unlikely to arouse such bitter opposition on financial grounds as it had in the 1380s. Here, too, Richard's awareness of the need to avoid a head-on collision with the Commons over finance weighed heavily with him.

Richard's grants to his aristocratic friends in the years after 1394 look as though they are part of a policy of strengthening royal power in his hereditary lands, the earldom of Chester and the principality of Wales. In doing this, of course, Richard was merely behaving like an ordinary magnate in exploiting the potential of his inheritance, and in its beginnings his Cheshire retinue bears comparison with a magnate's liveried retinue. After 1397, Richard recruited men from Cheshire on a scale which surpassed that of all his magnates, and no magnate recruited a retinue which consisted to such an extent of humble archers. But although he went further than any magnate, his policy of deploying the manpower and wealth of his inheritance in support of his position bears comparison with the policies of many magnates. Richard carried

[1] See for example *CPR* 1391–6, pp. 404, 471, 508, 576, 594, 721.
[2] See p. 199 below.

out his policy with remarkable thoroughness. William Lescrope became constable of Beaumaris Castle in 1394 and of Caernarvon and Pembroke Castles in 1396; he also held the lordship of the Isle of Man, and exercised authority in Leinster by deputy.[1] He was the key official in the crown lands in the west. But others received office there as well. Thomas Percy held the lordship of Haverford and the office of Justice of South Wales; Mowbray was appointed Justice of Chester and North Wales in 1394, ousting Gloucester in Chester;[2] and Huntingdon was given Conway Castle in the same year.[3] Royal authority in Cheshire and Wales must have appeared highly organized, and it is not surprising that rumours spread in 1399 that Richard intended to rule England from his lordships outside the realm.[4]

Hostility to the king grew sharply in the months after the twenty-eight years' truce with France was agreed. In the parliament which opened in January 1397, the Commons expressed misgivings about the king's proposal to send an expedition to Milan against Giangaleazzo Visconti in conjunction with Charles VI, though they offered no objection if he chose to mount the expedition at his own cost.[5] The king asserted his right to do so, but in the end, for reasons which probably had little to do with parliamentary opposition, he abandoned the idea and indeed reversed his whole Italian policy.[6] The Commons also presented a bill which subsequently turned out to have been presented to them by one Thomas Haxey[7] in which, among other points, they revived their complaints about liveried retainers and criticized the excessive costs of the household, singling out for particular mention the 'multitude of bishops' who were advanced at court by the king even though they had their own lordships, and the number of ladies staying in the royal household. The complaint about liveries merely repeated those of the early 1390s, and the king met the Commons' wishes by agreeing to yet another statute forbidding persons of lower rank than esquire from wearing their lords' livery. The enforcement of the statute was, as usual, left to the justices of the peace, and it is difficult to resist the conclusion that by this time Richard had lost interest in the whole problem of retaining. His reaction to the Commons' criticism of the cost of the household, however, was strongly hostile.[8] It is difficult to be sure how much justification the Commons

---

[1] *CPR* 1391-6, pp. 371; 1396-9, pp. 10, 36; GEC XII part 2, pp. 730-31.
[2] *CPR* 1391-6, pp. 307, 391, 404.   [3] *ibid.* p. 501.
[4] Walsingham, *Annales* pp. 239-40.
[5] *Rot. Parl.* Vol. III, pp. 337-8.
[6] *ibid.* p. 338.   [7] *ibid.* p. 339.   [8] *ibid.*

had for their complaint. The expenses of the household may have risen since 1395,[1] yet the petition does not read as though it was based on any very precise financial analysis. It is more probable that the impression created by the court had changed over the previous year or two. The number of bishops with connections at court had certainly increased,[2] and it may be that the court was becoming more luxurious. The Commons' sensitivity towards the cost and character of the court had evidently been aroused again. Their complaint, however, must have seemed to the king suspiciously like a renewal of the grumblings in the early years of the reign which had so often led to the establishment of commissions of inquiry. It may also have reminded him of the moves which had led to the dismissal from court in 1381 of his confessor, Thomas Rushook, later bishop of Chichester, and the removal of certain ladies from court in January 1388.[3] He was outraged by the Commons' presumption in questioning his conduct of the household, and he said that the Commons had given 'great offence'. The lords then declared that whoever engaged in such criticism was guilty of treason. The king insisted that the author of the petition should be brought before him: the Commons humbly apologized for their presumption and produced the unfortunate Haxey, who was sentenced for treason but pardoned because of his cloth. The episode showed that the king enjoyed considerable command over parliament: the lords had been smoothly deployed to declare criticism of the household treason, and speaker Bushy handled the Commons to great effect in getting them to apologize and produce Haxey.

It has been suggested that Haxey was merely a man of straw, put up by a noble or even by the king to provoke an incident.[4] But this is hard to believe: a noble who wished to criticize the king would not choose such a roundabout way of doing it. Although Arundel had maintained in 1394 that the nobility were too frightened by Gaunt's overbearing attitude to speak their mind in council or parliament,[5] there is no good reason to think that the Commons enjoyed greater freedom of speech than the nobility. The petition embodies the traditional preoccupations of the Commons: the appointment of sheriffs, the defence

[1] Tout, *Chapters* Vol. VI, pp. 98–9, 108.
[2] R. H. Jones makes this point (*The Royal Policy of Richard II* (Oxford 1968) p. 169), but the whole subject requires fuller examination.
[3] See p. 56 above for Rushook. The ladies required to abjure the court in 1388 were Lady Ponynges, Lady Mohun and Lady Molyns: Westminster p. 116.
[4] R. H. Jones, *Royal Policy of Richard II*, pp. 72–3.
[5] *Rot. Parl.* Vol. III, pp. 313–14.

of the northern border, the cost of the household, and retaining. The latter issue was one on which lords differed radically from Commons, and the appointment and conduct of sheriffs was not a matter in which they took much interest. The contents of the petition suggest that it arose, somehow, from within the Commons, and further research into Commons' procedure may throw light on the means by which the petition was presented and drafted. The affair demonstrated that the good relations which had existed between king and Commons in the earlier 1390s had broken down, yet the king could still control the Commons effectively through a competent speaker. It also showed that the king was still extremely sensitive to criticism of his household and that he was still prepared, perhaps insensitively and unwisely, to allow the cry of treason to be raised. The episode resembled the disputes of the 1380s too closely for king, Commons, and lords to feel anything but uncomfortable, and Richard's recall of the judges from exile in Ireland by an act of the same parliament can only have intensified suspicion.[1]

The cumulative effect of the domestic and foreign policies Richard had pursued since 1395 was to create a climate of mistrust between him and Gloucester and Arundel. Richard felt his security threatened by the renewed Commons criticism of his household and by Gloucester's opposition to the truce with France. Gloucester and Arundel, for their part, may have felt their security endangered by the king's ready resort to the accusation of treason in the parliament of January 1397, and more generally, by Richard's reliance upon Gaunt and upon his young noble friends at court. If Froissart can be believed, Richard's suspicions of Gloucester grew sharply from 1395 onwards, and he went to some trouble to find out, through people visiting Pleshy, what the Duke was thinking.[2] When Robert the Hermit visited Gloucester in 1395, he found him still adamantly opposed to peace with France, and Froissart suggests that Richard may have questioned Robert about Gloucester's attitude after his visit to Pleshy. Other visitors also reported that Gloucester was irreconcilable, and again according to Froissart, Richard's courtiers were pressing the king to act against him—as well they might, in view of the fate of their predecessors in 1388.[3] No one had ever forgotten how Gloucester had treated Burley. The author of the *Chronique de la Traison et Mort de Richart II*, in common with the

---

[1] *Statutes of the Realm* Vol. II, p. 94; however, the statute explicitly declared that the conviction of the judges still stood.
[2] Froissart, *Oeuvres* Vol. XV, pp. 196–201.   [3] *ibid.* Vol. XVI, p. 6.

French historiographer–royal, believed that Gloucester was particularly incensed at the surrender of Brest and the arrival home of the garrison, which had been poorly paid and which now had nothing to do.[1] In fact, the garrison had been paid, the Duke of Brittany made a payment of 120,000 francs for the return of the fortress, and the retention of it would have been a needless drain on the country's resources once the truce came into effect.[2] Yet the effect on public opinion of its surrender was bound to be unfortunate, and when the Count of St Pol visited England in 1396 it was rumoured in London that he had come to negotiate the surrender of Calais.[3] There was no truth whatsoever in the rumour, but it was only natural that those who believed it, and those who objected to the surrender of Brest, should look to Gloucester for support. He was bound to become the focus for all who were dissatisfied or alarmed at Richard's rapprochement with France.

It was perhaps an unwise move for Gloucester and Arundel to refuse to attend a council in February 1397[4] and thereby incur the king's annoyance. Their refusal followed speedily on the Commons' criticism of the expense of the king's household, and can only have intensified Richard's suspicions that the events of 1386 were about to repeat themselves. The French chroniclers believed that in the summer of 1397 Gloucester and Arundel actually hatched a plot against the king.[5] The author of the *Traison* reported that at a feast given by the Abbot of St Albans (Gloucester's godfather) Gloucester promised to remedy the surrender of Brest, and invited all present to meet at Arundel in a fortnight's time. At Arundel, he goes on to relate, Gloucester, Arundel, Warwick, Derby, Nottingham, the Archbishop of Canterbury, the Abbot of St Albans, and the Prior of Westminster prepared a plan to seize and imprison the king, Lancaster, and York. Nottingham then betrayed the plot to the king, who thereupon ordered the arrest of Gloucester, Arundel, Warwick, and the archbishop. As it stands, this story is unacceptable. There are one or two plausible circumstantial details. Gloucester and the Abbot of St Albans were on good terms and the political attitude of the St Albans scriptorium was sympathetic to the nobility.[6] Yet it is hard to believe that had a plot been prepared

[1] *Traison* p. 1; *Chronique . . . Saint Denys* Vol. II, ed. Bellaguet, pp. 476–7.
[2] M. C. E. Jones, *Ducal Brittany 1364–1399* (Oxford 1970) pp. 138–9.
[3] Froissart, *Oeuvres* Vol. XVI, pp. 15–16.
[4] *Evesham* p. 129.   [5] *Traison* pp. 3–6.
[6] *ibid.*; V. H. Galbraith, *Roger Wendover and Matthew Paris* (Glasgow 1944) p. 20 'The St Albans history is, as it were, an *apologia pro baronibus*.'

Nottingham and Derby would have been parties to it, for both were high in favour with the king in 1397. It is even harder to accept that the king knew of the plot but failed to make use of it in his charges against Gloucester, Arundel, and Warwick in September 1397. Furthermore, there is very little independent confirmation of the story. In a proclamation on the 15th of July, the king declared that the three lords had not been arrested for their part in the events of 1387–8, but he described their arrest in very general terms as being 'for great number of extortions, oppressions, grievances etc. committed against the king and people, and for other offences against the king's majesty which shall be declared in the next parliament'.[1] There is no specific suggestion of a plot in the wording of the proclamation, and it may have been made to lull the retainers of the arrested lords into a sense of false security and thus prevent disorder. The *Traison* and the French chronicles which repeat the story of a plot are interrelated sources, and the whole literary purpose of the *Traison* required that Richard should have a good reason for his arrest of the three nobles. Of the English sources, only Usk reports anything that could be regarded in the remotest way as confirmation when he has Warwick say, during his trial, that he had been encouraged to join the other lords 'by the Duke of Gloucester and by the then abbot of St Albans and by a monk recluse of Westminster',[2] but this may refer to the events of ten years earlier rather than to a plot in the summer of 1397. In all probability, the *Traison*'s story is no more than a highly coloured account of normal social contacts between members of the nobility on occasions when politics would certainly have been discussed and criticisms expressed, but it is straining credulity to accept that a plot against the king was actually prepared in the spring or summer of 1397.

However, it is unnecessary to go to the opposite extreme and assume, with the Kirkstall chronicler, that Richard was deliberately planning revenge for the humiliations of 1387–8.[3] In all probability, neither side plotted against the other, but in the tense atmosphere which developed in 1396 and 1397, each side was afraid of the other and suspicious of its intentions. The king may well have thought that he could only ensure his security by striking at Gloucester and Arundel before they struck at him, and the events of 1386–8 gave him a good case against them. He could make himself secure and gain his revenge at one and the same time.

---

[1] *CCR* 1396–9, p. 208.
[2] *Usk* p. 16.   [3] *Kirkstall Chronicle* p. 129.

G

Gloucester was arrested at Pleshy on the 10th of July 1397. He was dispatched to Calais, where he was probably murdered.[1] Arundel and Warwick were arrested at the same time but held in custody to await their trial in parliament.[2] Richard took no chances with the followers of the three nobles: he ordered the justices in those counties where their principal estates lay to arrest and imprison anyone protesting against the arrests and to take precautions against any armed demonstrations by their retainers.[3] At the same time he ensured that he had sufficient force at his disposal to quell any more general risings on their behalf. On the 13th of July he ordered his sheriff in Cheshire to recruit 2000 archers, and a month later, perhaps to help recruiting, he forbade any archer from taking service with anyone else until he had the number he required.[4] The retinue was to muster at Kingston-upon-Thames on the 15th of September, two days before parliament was due to open at Westminster. From Kingston, the retinue was to ride with the king to London. Lancaster, York, Derby, and the seven nobles who were to bring a new appeal of treason against Gloucester, Arundel, and Warwick were licensed to come armed and to bring their retinues to parliament.[5] The military force at the king's disposal was enormous, and must have been intended to overawe London as well as to protect the king and the Palace of Westminster. Richard's preparations were characteristically thorough, and effective as well. There were no serious disturbances after the arrest of the three lords, and London remained quiet. Richard was not risking any of the setbacks of 1387. In complete command, he awaited the opening of parliament.

[1] Walsingham, *Annales* pp. 203–6; R. L. Atkinson, 'Richard II and the Death of the Duke of Gloucester', *EHR* XXXVIII (1923) pp. 563–4; A. E. Stamp, 'Richard II and the Death of the Duke of Gloucester', *EHR* XXXVIII (1923) pp. 249–51; H. G. Wright, 'Richard II and the Death of the Duke of Gloucester', *EHR* XLVII (1923) pp. 276–80; J. Tait, 'Did Richard II Murder the Duke of Gloucester?' in *Historical Essays* ed. T. F. Tout and J. Tait (Manchester 1907).
[2] Walsingham, *Annales* pp. 202–3.
[3] *CCR* 1396–9, p. 147.
[4] PRO Chester Recognizance Rolls, Chester 2170 m. 7d.
[5] *CCR* 1396–9, pp. 192, 210.

7

Richard's Tyranny and Deposition

Parliament opened on St Lambert's Day, the 17th of September 1397. London and Westminster were occupied by a larger military force than can ever have been assembled there in time of peace; the wardrobe of the household was supplied with weapons of war, and the king himself was protected by a personal bodyguard of 312 Cheshire archers, divided into seven watches each under the command of a Cheshire knight or esquire.[1] The chroniclers reported that the open-sided building in which parliament met was surrounded by archers, who were evidently ready to fire at the slightest provocation.[2] It was clear to all that Richard rested his power, ultimately, upon overwhelming military force. It was inevitable that there should be incidents of misbehaviour among so large a force, and the Londoners, unused to the presence of numerous troops, resented their presence.[3] Richard's retinue rapidly became more unpopular and more vilified than the retinues of his nobles, in many of which discipline was probably no better maintained.

The sermon at the opening of parliament was preached by the chancellor, Edmund Stafford Bishop of Exeter, and in it he set out the ideology which was to inform the proceedings of the parliament.[4] Taking his theme from Ezekiel XXXVII 22, 'One king shall be king to them all', he 'kept his discourse to the one point, that the power of

[1] PRO KR Memoranda Roll. E.159/175 brevia baronibus Hilary 21 RII rot. 9; Accounts, various, E.101/42/10.
[2] *Usk* p. 11; *Evesham* p. 134.
[3] B.M. Harleian Ms. 565 f. 63—*A London Chronicle 1089–1483* printed by J. Nichols (London 1827): 'Chestreshire men maden a grete fray in Fryday Strete on a nyȝt in here innes, the whiche weren well beten and hurte with arowes.'
[4] *Rot. Parl.* Vol. III, p. 347.

the king lay singly and wholly in the king, and that they who usurped or plotted against it were worthy of the penalties of the law'. The unlawfulness of the 1386 commission was clearly implied, and from the outset it must have been obvious that this was to form the basis of the charges against Gloucester, Arundel, and Warwick, together with Archbishop Arundel, who was arrested after parliament met, The subsequent proceedings of parliament show every sign of having been planned with thoroughness and care. The king proclaimed, through the chancellor, that fifty persons were to be excluded from the general pardon which he would grant to all persons implicated in the events of 1386–8.[1] These fifty persons were not named, and the implied threat was an obvious means of political discipline. On the following day, the commission of 1386 was declared to have been null and void, and the king revoked both the general pardon of 1388 and the pardon granted to Arundel in 1394. In doing so he earnde himself the charge of deceitfulness in the articles of deposition.[2] All the members of the 1386 commission except Gloucester, Arundel, Warwick, and the archbishop were, however, immediately exempted from the revocation of the pardon. Two days later the first victim was dealt with: Archbishop Arundel was impeached on a charge of treason, and on the 25th of September he was sentenced to forfeiture and exile.[3] Despite Richard's personal assurance to Arundel that his exile would be short, he soon afterwards wrote to the pope abusing the archbishop and insisting that he should not be given any benefice in any land under the king's jurisdiction, another instance of the king's duplicity.[4]

On the day after Archbishop Arundel's appearance before parliament, the Earls of Rutland, Kent, Huntingdon, Nottingham, Somerset, and Salisbury, together with Lord Despenser and Sir William Lescrope, formally appealed Gloucester, Arundel, and Warwick of treason, in deliberate imitation of the procedure followed in the Merciless Parliament. Arundel's trial followed immediately. According to Adam of Usk, he indignantly denied the charges against him, and claimed the benefit of his pardon.[5] Lancaster, who as high steward of England conducted the trial, replied that the pardon was revoked, and Bushy, the Speaker of the Commons, added obsequiously that it had been

---

[1] *Rot. Parl.* Vol. III, p. 347.
[2] *ibid.* pp. 350, 418.
[3] *ibid.* p. 351; Margaret Aston, *Thomas Arundel* (Oxford 1967) pp. 368–73.
[4] A. L. Brown, 'The Latin Letters in All Souls Ms. 182', *EHR* LXXXVII (1972) pp. 565–71.
[5] *Usk* pp. 13–14; Walsingham, *Annales* pp. 214–15.

revoked by the king, the lords, and the faithful Commons, thus provoking Arundel's famous retort that 'the faithful Commons are not
here'. This was probably just a rhetorical outburst, in resentment at
Bushy's ability to manage the Commons and, perhaps, at their change
of political attitude since 1388, for although the House contained a
number of experienced knights closely connected with the king, there
is no evidence that the king had made any *systematic* attempt to interfere with the elections, despite the charge in the articles of deposition.[1]
Arundel's bitter and abusive defence was of no avail, however, and he
was condemned and executed the same day. Walsingham recorded that
Arundel was venerated as a martyr by the Londoners and that pilgrim-
ages were made to his tomb. Usk said that his body was 'most glori-
ously worshipped with deep reverence and with abundant offerings by
the people'.[2] Even allowing for the exaggeration of both these anti-
Ricardian chroniclers, the popular attitude to the execution of Arundel
must have been a warning to Richard of the temper of London, and a
confirmation of his judgement that his security necessitated filling the
city with troops.

After Arundel's execution, Warwick was produced before parliament. He broke down, confessed his guilt, and had his death sentence
commuted to exile in the Isle of Man, where he would be under the
eye of William Lescrope.[3] But when Gloucester was ordered to
appear to stand trial, it was reported that he was already dead. It is
generally accepted that he had been murdered at Calais, probably
earlier in September, and that Nottingham, the captain of Calais,
may have been implicated.[4] It is, however, just conceivable that, since
he was apparently a sick man at the time of his arrest, he died a natural
death, though one hastened by the rigours of his imprisonment.
Assuming that Richard did have him murdered or, at least, that he
did not try to prevent nature taking its course, the explanation must
be that he dare not bring him to trial. The risk of popular demonstrations in his favour was too great, and Gaunt might have been much
less ready to pronounce sentence upon his own brother than upon
Arundel, with whom he had had a bitter quarrel in 1394. Before
Gloucester died, however, he had apparently put his seal to a confession, in which he made it clear that he thought that he had been

[1] *Rot. Parl.* Vol. III, p. 420; Tout, *Chapters* Vol. IV, p. 23n.; A. B. Steel, *Richard II*
(Cambridge 1941) pp. 232-3.
[2] Walsingham, *Annales* pp. 218-19; *Usk* p. 15.
[3] Walsingham, *Annales* p. 220; *Rot. Parl.* Vol. III, p. 380.
[4] *Rot. Parl.* Vol. III, pp. 377-9; see p. 186 n. 1 above.

arrested and imprisoned for his part in the events of 1386–8, and admitted his guilt.[1] Like those of Arundel and Warwick, his lands and goods were forfeited.

Thus far, Richard had been notably more humane than the Appellants in 1388. Although fifty unnamed persons had an unspecified threat hanging over them, and although Richard was equipped to meet any resistance with military force, only two lords had suffered death and two exile. There was to be no repetition of the bloodbath of 1388, for not only was it unnecessary, but it would have sharply diminished the force of the one count on which Gloucester had been widely unpopular, his treatment of Burley. The moderation of Richard's measures, in this first session of parliament at least, may be one of the reasons why he encountered no opposition from parliament. But equally important was the support he steadfastly received from Gaunt, whose political attitude inclined him to side with the king when any question of accroaching the royal power arose. There was little likelihood of any opposition from any of the other peers. York closely identified with his brother of Lancaster; March was in Ireland; Northumberland was unlikely to abandon his attitude of moderation, or neutrality, unless his interests on the northern border were threatened more seriously than they had been by the ineffective truce with Scotland; and most of the other titled nobles were either too young and inexperienced or too firmly attached to the king to offer any objection to what he was doing.

The position with regard to the Commons, however, was rather more complicated. In the articles of deposition, Richard was accused of influencing the elections to the 1397 parliament so as to secure a complaisant house.[2] The charge as it stands is unproveable, but there are certain pieces of circumstantial evidence which suggest it may have some substance. The number of members for whom this parliament was their first was thirty-three, more than any parliament since January 1377, which has attracted similar suspicions.[3] However, the mere number of newcomers is less significant, in an assembly where some members carried more weight than others, than the affiliations of particular individuals. Several of the king's most prominent servants,

[1] *Rot. Parl.* Vol. III, p. 379: 'I. . . knowleche, that I was on with steryng of other men to assente to the makyng of a commission; in the which commission I amonges other restreyned my Lord of his fredom. . . '.

[2] *Rot. Parl.* Vol. III, p. 420.

[3] N. B. Lewis, 'Re-election to Parliament in the Reign of Richard II', *EHR* XLVIII (1933) p. 366.

among them Sir John Bushy, Sir William Bagot, and Sir Henry Green, were elected; Bagot's brother sat for Staffordshire, and members of the household were elected in several counties. Eight members held office as sheriff from November 1397 onwards, and it is most unlikely that they would have been appointed had they not already shown their reliability.[1] This nucleus of trusted men provided the king with the political base he needed in the Commons. Bushy, the most experienced parliamentarian of all, acted as speaker, and he and his colleagues could be relied upon to control the Commons. There is no good evidence that the sheriffs were given any special instructions: Richard's methods had become subtler since 1387, and the great majority of those sheriffs whose terms of office were prolonged in 1398 and who were members of the household or otherwise connected with the king were not appointed until after parliament opened.

In the first session of parliament, therefore, the proceedings went well for Richard, yet there were already clear signs of the manner of government that was to lead to his downfall. Although he managed parliament effectively, his ascendancy there and the docility of London rested in the last resort upon military force deployed on a scale unknown in England at least since the battle of Boroughbridge. His proclamation in July, denying that Gloucester, Arundel, and Warwick had been arrested for their part in the events of 1387–8, now appeared false and he had laid himself open to the charge of deceit in revoking Arundel's pardon. He may have thought his security necessitated such measures, yet they were bound to provoke further hostility and mistrust; and the more Richard felt himself threatened, the more extreme and tyrannical his government became.

The condemnation of Gloucester, Arundel, and Warwick entailed the forfeiture of their lands and goods, and in the winter of 1397–8 the king granted much of their inheritances to his friends, the new Appellants. On this occasion, entailed as well as unentailed land was forfeited.[2] The rights of the widows of Gloucester and Arundel were protected,[3] but even so there was far more land available for redistribution than there had been in 1388. In making his grants, Richard deliberately divided up each of the three inheritances so that they ceased

[1] *Return of Members of Parliament*, part 1: *Parliaments of England 1213–1702* (London 1878); PRO Lists & Indexes IX, List of Sheriffs; A. B. Steel, 'Sheriffs of Cambridgeshire and Huntingdonshire in the time of Richard II' (typescript in Cambridge University Library 1934).
[2] *Rot. Parl.* Vol. III, pp. 377, 380.
[3] *CCR* 1396–9, pp. 77–83.

to exist as social or economic units.[1] Nottingham, for instance, received the Arundel lordship of Lewes, but the honour of Arundel itself went to Huntingdon. Warwick's castle with his manors in Warwickshire was granted to the Earl of Kent, but his lands in the Welsh marches were entrusted, significantly, to Sir William Lescrope. Richard's purpose was to change entirely the territorial pattern which had developed over the previous seventy years and to ensure not only a vested interest in the 1397 settlement, but also the creation of a new territorial order so different from the old that restoration of the forfeited lands would be impossibly complicated. There had been nothing like it since 1265, perhaps since 1066. Those who received lands received titles as well: Nottingham, Rutland, Huntingdon, and Kent received the dukedoms of Norfolk, Albemarle, Exeter and Surrey; Lescrope became Earl of Wiltshire; Sir Thomas Percy became Earl of Worcester; and Thomas Despenser, a descendant of Edward II's favourite, was created Earl of Gloucester. Others shared in the distribution of titles: Derby became Duke of Hereford and Gaunt's eldest son by Katherine Swynford, John Beaufort, who had been created Earl of Somerset in February 1397, now became Marquis of Dorset. Ralph Lord Neville received the earldom of Westmorland, a title which gave him equality in status with his neighbour and rival in the north, the Earl of Northumberland. Neville's elevation was deserved and, probably, expected; but never before had so many dukes been created at one time. This cheapening of a hitherto carefully guarded title provoked scorn in some quarters, and according to Walsingham the new dukes were derisively called "duketti" by the common people.[2]

With the confiscation and redistribution of the lands of the three former Appellants, Richard's territorial strategy became abundantly clear. The Arundel lordships in Shropshire and North Wales were annexed to Chester, and the whole area was elevated into a principality which was intended to become a patrimony for the king's eldest son.[3] In the short run, however, the new principality was to form a military bastion for the king. The castles of Chester and Holt were stuffed with weapons and large garrisons were maintained there. Throughout 1397 and 1398 the king gave his livery to Cheshire men who wished to serve in his army, and their loyalty was rewarded by displays of favour

---

[1] *CPR* 1396–9, pp. 200–10, 280–81.
[2] *RDP* Vol. V, pp. 117–20; Walsingham, *Annales* p. 223.
[3] R. R. Davies, 'Richard II and the Principality of Chester' in *The Reign of Richard II* ed. F. R. H. du Boulay and Caroline M. Barron (London 1971) pp. 256–79.

towards the whole county.[1] The creation of the principality of Chester and the recruitment of the Cheshire army was not simply an expression of his special relationship with the county: it must be seen against the background of the consolidation of royal authority in Wales which had taken place since 1394. The principal castles were all in friendly hands; the marcher lordships of the forfeited Appellants, with the exception of those annexed to Chester, were entrusted to entirely reliable men such as Lescrope; and Richard went to some trouble to support his friend the Earl of Salisbury's claim to the lordship of Denbigh, held by the Earl of March.[2] When March died, custody of the lordship during the heir's minority was entrusted to Lescrope,[3] who played a key role in the administration of both Chester and North Wales, for in addition to his other offices he was appointed justice of the new principality of Chester.

Yet such an impressive scheme had many defects. There can be little doubt about the loyalty of the men of Cheshire itself: it had a basis in their traditional affection for the king or his eldest son as earl, and Richard had most carefully fostered their loyalty to him. He had treated the leaders of the Cheshire rising with great leniency. Those who sought a career in military service now had the opportunity to join the king's retinue; and he set aside the sum of 4000 marks to be distributed among those who had fought for de Vere at Radcot Bridge.[4] Elsewhere, however, Richard's position was much less secure. In the Arundel lordships, the former officials and servants of the earl were dismissed and a carpet-bagger administration from Chester introduced, which fell eagerly on the offices available, but which was bound to create a sense of resentment among local men with a tradition of service to Arundel.[5] The new ministers imposed a harsh financial discipline on the lordships,[6] and nothing was done to win the loyalty of either the English or the Welsh inhabitants. To this extent, the creation of the enlarged principality of Chester looks suspiciously like an attempt to increase the financial and territorial resources of the old county, and make the former Arundel lordships carry some of the burden of supporting the Cheshire army.

[1] PRO Chester Recognizance Rolls, Chester 2/71, 72, 73 *passim*; Accounts, various, E.101/42/10.
[2] *Rot. Parl.* Vol. III, pp. 352–3; *Usk* pp. 15–17.
[3] *CPR* 1396–9, p. 408.
[4] PRO Miscellanea of the Exchequer E.163/6/12.
[5] R. R. Davies, 'Richard II' pp. 263–4.
[6] *ibid.* p. 277.

Similarly, in Wales the impressive presence in castles and lordships of the king and his closest supporters concealed tensions which limited the efficiency of the principality as a bastion of royal authority. Few if any Welshmen received the king's livery or served in his army; there was no lavish display of favour towards the king's Welsh subjects as there had been towards the men of Cheshire, and they had to bear heavy financial burdens. Anglesey and Caernarvonshire were required in 1395 to agree to a subsidy totalling £1002–4–8, to be paid in instalments over the next four years,[1] and subsidies on a similar scale were granted by the counties of Cardigan and Carmarthen.[2] These grants may have helped to ease the burdens on the English exchequer, but they were unlikely to produce much loyalty towards the king who sought them, and there is evidence of unrest in various parts of Wales in these years.[3] It may be that the financial burdens Richard imposed upon his Welsh subjects contributed to the discontent which Glendower was to exploit so effectively in the next decade. In the end, the Welsh refused to fight for Richard, and although, according to Creton, they took this attitude because they believed the king was dead[4] the growing discontent in the principality may have played some part.

Richard's construction of a new power base for himself outside the kingdom, where he thought he was secure, went hand in hand with the oppression of his subjects within the kingdom. One of the most serious problems that Richard had to face was that of ensuring a regular supply of money, to maintain the huge military organization which he had developed, as well as to finance the more ordinary and regular expenses of government. It appears to have been Richard's intention to escape from the financial insecurity which the short-term parliamentary grant of the customs revenue necessarily engendered. Earlier in the reign the Commons had strongly resisted any suggestion that the king might have the customs revenue as of right, and by granting it for short periods they preserved at least the fiction that it was a permanent tax.[5] But now that there was no prospect of war with

[1] PRO Receivers' and Ministers' Accounts SC.6/1215/6, 7, **8.**
[2] PRO SC. 6/1222/6, 7.
[3] R. A. Griffiths, 'Gentlemen and Rebels in Late Medieval Cardiganshire', *Ceredigion* V (1964–7) pp. 154, 166; R. R. Davies, 'Owain Glyn Dŵr and the Welsh Squirearchy', *Transactions of the Honourable Society of Cymmrodorion* (1968) pp. 150–69.
[4] 'A Metrical History of the Deposition of Richard II', *Archaeologia* Vol. XX (1824) p. 317.
[5] *Rot. Parl.* Vol. III, p. 104.

France for a generation, Richard may have been afraid that the Commons would resist his requests for renewal of the customs revenue.

Furthermore, the need to summon parliament regularly to obtain the grant of customs exposed the king to the risk of parliamentary criticism and the possibility of parliamentary intervention in the financial side of royal government. To get his way, Richard once again relied upon the psychological pressure which his promise of a pardon at the opening of the Westminster session of parliament imposed on the Commons. At the opening of the second session of parliament, held at Shrewsbury in January 1398, the promised pardon was made conditional upon the Commons voting the customs revenue for the king's life; and if the Commons went back on their grant at any time, the pardon was to lapse.[1] This grant, rather than the more famous establishment of the committee to deal with business left over after parliament came to an end, threatened the position of parliament in the country's political life. In time of peace, as Richard had shown in the early 1390s, he could manage with only an occasional parliamentary subsidy, provided he had the customs revenue and provided he could exploit other sources of revenue effectively. With the customs revenue his for life, therefore, parliament would, he hoped, need to meet less frequently. It was certainly not the king's intention to eliminate parliament altogether. Such a view is too extreme and is belied by the king's own words, but it is consistent with his search for security and immunity from criticism and control that he should seek to diminish the frequency with which it met and the financial power it could wield.

The parliamentary grant of the customs for life might alleviate Richard's long-term financial difficulties, but he also needed to mobilize revenue quickly to pay his army and, in the spring of 1399, to finance his second expedition to Ireland. To do so he fell back upon the well-tried device of the obligatory loan.[2] Royal serjeants-at-arms were sent round the country with letters under the Privy Seal in which the king asked for a 'notable' sum, and when a loan was negotiated an indenture was sealed between the serjeants-at-arms and the lender. Richard indeed raised a 'notable' sum, much of it very quickly. He received over £22,000, much of it before the end of 1397, and the size of the loan and the speed with which it was raised suggest not only

---

[1] *ibid.* p. 368.
[2] PRO Exchequer Receipt Rolls E.401/608; Patents for Loans E.34/1B/40; Caroline Barron, 'The Tyranny of Richard II', *BIHR* XLI (1968) pp. 2–6.

that the king's methods were effective but also that resistance was not very widespread. Some prospective lenders offered excuses which were accepted; others who refused had to appear before the council and explain themselves. There was nothing improper or unprecedented about raising money in this way; there is no evidence that the serjeants-at-arms used threats or intimidation to obtain money, and very many refusals were accepted. The articles of deposition make no mention of the method Richard used to raise the money: they merely accused the king, correctly, of failing to repay most of the loans by the specified date.[1] There is, however, some evidence that resistance to the loan was higher in the north of England than elsewhere. The Earl of Northumberland and the Bishop of Durham both asked to make their excuses before the council; Sir William FitzWilliam, Lord Greystoke, Thomas Ughtred, John Savill, Sir John Hotham, Sir William Melton, Sir Stephen Lescrope, and Sir Henry FitzHugh of Ravensworth all lent nothing: these men form a sizeable proportion of the men approached in Yorkshire and the northeastern counties.[2] This may imply that Richard's government was widely unpopular in the north. The unpopularity which it had incurred in Yorkshire in the 1380s had perhaps not abated, and it becomes all the easier to understand why the north went over so readily to Henry in 1399.

Richard also raised money by requiring those who had been implicated in the rising of 1387–8 to pay for the pardons they sued out. By implying that the general pardon granted in parliament might be only temporary, the king created a climate of insecurity in which 'the need to seek individual charters of pardon became even more pressing'.[3] Men who had been associated with the Appellants in the Radcot Bridge campaign were summoned before the council, and were required to pay a fine before receiving their pardon. If they failed to agree with the council about the size of the fine, they were liable to imprisonment.[4] The session of the council to which such men were summoned was attended only by the chancellor, the treasurer, the keeper of the Privy Seal, and Bushy, Bagot, and Green.[5] The powers these six had to determine the size of a fine or to order imprisonment are sufficient in themselves to explain the animosity towards

---

[1] *Rot. Parl.* Vol. III, p. 419.
[2] PRO Patents for Loans E.34/1B/40/214.
[3] Caroline Barron, 'Tyranny' p. 7.
[4] PRO Issue Rolls E.403/561 m. 10; Receipt Rolls E.401/608, 609 *passim*.
[5] Nicolas, *POPC* Vol. I, pp. 75–6.

them and the pleasure expressed when Henry executed Bushy, Green, and Lescrope at Bristol in July 1399. The king also granted the men of Essex and Hertfordshire a general collective pardon in return for the sum of £2000, and anyone who refused to contribute his share of what was in effect a huge collective fine was liable to be imprisoned.[1] Richard's oppression of entire communities was greatly extended in the spring of 1398 when the inhabitants of London and sixteen south-eastern counties were required to admit their complicity in the rising of 1387–8 and submit to his grace.[2] Each county appointed proctors who sealed charters on behalf of their counties submitting themselves and their goods to the king's pleasure, giving him *carte blanche* to do what he wished to them; and from this basis in fact grew the legend that Richard extorted 'blank charters' from his subjects. There is a consensus among the English chroniclers that the king also exacted sums of money as large as £1000 or 1000 marks from the sixteen counties, but if he did so the exactions have left no mark in the financial records of the government.[3] The pardons and collective fines gave him some useful income, but their primary purpose was almost certainly political, not financial. At the first sign of disaffection the king now had the power to move against both the persons and the goods of those who had submitted to him.

The council was the instrument Richard chose to deal with individuals who had taken the Appellants' side in 1387–8, but criticism of the regime the king had now imposed upon the country was to be repressed by the Court of Chivalry. In the articles of deposition Richard was accused of having people who slandered or disparaged the king arrested, imprisoned, and brought before the Court of Chivalry.[4] There is some substance in the charge. On the 15th of March 1398 Albemarle and Surrey, the constable and marshal, were given power to arrest all traitors found within the realm, and after they had been convicted they were to be punished 'at discretion according to their deserts'.[5] Six months later, on the 10th of September, Albemarle was given power to hear cases involving the king—presumably slander and disparagement—and to deal with them in the Court of Chivalry.[6] At

[1] *CPR* 1391–6, pp. 311–12; *CFR* 1391–9, pp. 250–52.
[2] Caroline Barron, 'Tyranny' pp. 10–13.
[3] Walsingham, *Annales* pp. 234–5; *Eulogium Historiarum sive Temporis* Vol. III, ed. F. S. Haydon, Rolls Series (London 1863) p. 378; *Evesham* p. 146; Caroline Barron, 'Tyranny' p. 12.
[4] *Rot. Parl.* Vol. III, p. 420.
[5] *CPR* 1396–9, p. 365.
[6] *ibid.* p. 505.

least one case brought under this order has come to light.[1] On the 3rd
of December 1398 Sir William Lescrope and the other members of
the council accused John Dyne, Richard French, and William Pilkyngton
of slandering the king. They were imprisoned, and the king eventually ordered their appearance before the constable and the marshal.
The three denied that the Court of Chivalry had any jurisdiction in the
matter, and the case was still in progress when Richard was deposed
and it was abandoned. The article of deposition goes on to allege that
persons brought before the court were required to defend themselves
by battle, so that the old and feeble were vanquished by the young and
strong. This is unlikely to have been true of every case heard by the
court, for in accordance with its procedure, trial by battle took place
only when there was no evidence. But apart from the famous abortive
duel at Coventry no record survives of any combat ordered by the
court. Richard's use of the Court of Chivalry in this way was de-
nounced by the article of deposition as contrary to clause thirty-nine
of Magna Carta, and it is difficult to believe that the power given to
Albemarle and Surrey to take traitors and punish them at their discretion was consistent with the undertaking to deal with offenders 'by
the lawful judgement of their equals and the law of the land'. Men
believed that they were being denied their fundamental rights at
common law by the use of the civil law procedures of the Court of
Chivalry, and this added substance to the argument that Richard had
broken his coronation oath to uphold the laws and customs of the
realm. Richard's government in this period was not only harshly
oppressive, but threatened to undermine the legal system which men
believed protected their rights and their property. Richard's security,
it seemed, could be purchased only at the price of the insecurity of
his subjects.

The directing force of Richard's government from 1397 until his
deposition was the council, which was composed of his officials and
most trusted friends and which met regularly to deal with all aspects of
government business. In this, Richard was making use of a system
of administration which had developed during the early 1390s, and
which at that time had helped to promote domestic harmony. The
councillors then had been men who commanded the confidence of
king, nobles, and Commons; but in the last two years of Richard's
reign they were men who, although trusted and intimate servants of

[1] PRO Exchequer KR Memoranda Roll E.159/176 brevia baronibus Michaelmas I
HIV rot. 7.

the king, became detested by all those who suffered from their oppressive activities. There is no detailed record of conciliar business and membership for the last two years of the reign such as the journal Prophete compiled in 1392 and 1393, but there is sufficient evidence from a variety of sources to indicate the composition of the council. The three officers of state together with Bushy, Bagot and Green sat in special session to deal with persons suspected of association with the Appellants in 1387-8, and the counter-signatures to petitions suggest that it was Lescrope, Bushy, and Green, together with Russell, Laurence Dru, and Ralph Selby, who were responsible for the day-to-day business of government, with the chancellor and the keeper of the Privy Seal sometimes taking part.[1] Bushy, Bagot, Green, and Lescrope, together with Albemarle, Norfolk, and Exeter, were singled out by Walsingham as the king's principal advisers, and Usk described Lescrope, Bushy, and Green as 'the king's most evil councillors and the chief fosterers of his malice'.[2] Finally, when about to leave for Ireland in May 1399, Richard is said to have appointed Lescrope, Bushy, Bagot, and Green as commissioners to administer the country under the authority of the Duke of York as keeper of the realm.[3] Lescrope in particular played a key part in Richard's policies—whether as keeper of castles and justice in Chester and North Wales, justice in Leinster, keeper of confiscated property, member of the inner group of the council responsible for dealing with petitions or commissioner in the last months of Richard's rule, he was present either in person or by deputy. Modern historians have not fully recognized the pervasiveness of his power, but it was all too apparent to contemporaries. In 1399 it was rumoured that he was plotting the deaths of several leading nobles so that he could exploit their escheated property, and that he was about to be granted all the escheats in England for three years.[4] It is scarcely surprising that his execution in July 1399 was received with great joy.

The council even went so far as to maintain a close watch on letters sent overseas and arriving in this country from abroad. On the 16th of March 1398 the king ordered that no letters, except those dealing with purely commercial matters, were to be taken abroad without licence, and all letters coming into the country addressed to 'lords and great men' were to be sent to the council.[5] The following year the

---

[1] PRO Exchequer Council and Privy Seal Records E.28/4/60–65; E.28/5/22–24.
[2] Walsingham, *Annales* pp. 223–4; *Usk* p. 25.   [3] *Traison* p. 24.
[4] Walsingham, *Annales* p. 240.   [5] *CCR* 1396–9, p. 288.

censorship was extended, and on the 19th of March 1399 the king forbade anyone to send letters abroad before they had been seen by the king and council.[1] Effective censorship on this scale was clearly impossible, and there is little if any evidence to suggest that the council exercised its powers of censorship at all systematically. The purpose of the proclamation was presumably to prevent communication between exiles, notably Archbishop Arundel and, after September 1398, Hereford and Norfolk, and their sympathizers at home. Richard may also have feared, not without reason, that certain French nobles might have an interest in exploiting England's domestic troubles. However, the censorship evidently had little effect in preventing Hereford from communicating with his English supporters after he had gone into exile, and it served merely to create hostility without bringing any compensating gain in political security.

The council controlled government at the centre, and dealt with men of standing who were politically unreliable, while the Court of Chivalry had a general power to deal with traitors found anywhere within the realm. But there remained the problem of supervising local government. There is some evidence that a number of the sheriffs who held office from November and December 1397 onwards were chosen either by the king personally or by the council on the basis of political reliability. The sheriff of Herefordshire, for example, was Sir Thomas Clanvowe, a chamber knight; the sheriff of Cambridgeshire and Huntingdonshire was Andrew Newport, who had been a royal serjeant-at-arms and was now a king's esquire; and Sir John Golafre, another chamber knight, was appointed sheriff of Oxfordshire and Berkshire.[2] These three sheriffs, together with twelve others who were presumably reliable, had their terms of office prolonged for a further year in November 1398, an unusual move and one contrary to statute.[3] Richard's purpose in choosing as sheriffs men whom he could trust was probably military rather than parliamentary. He did not intend parliament to meet as frequently as it had done in the past, and in any case he had found little difficulty in securing the election of a nucleus of reliable knights to the Commons in September 1397, before these sheriffs were appointed. In 1387, however, he had asked the sheriffs whether they could raise forces on his behalf and had received an

---

[1] *CCR 1396–9*, pp. 488–9.
[2] *List of Sheriffs of England and Wales from the Earliest Times to 1831* PRO (1898); A. B. Steel, 'Sheriffs of Cambridgeshire and Huntingdonshire'.
[3] *List of Sheriffs*.

unfavourable answer. This time he hoped for a more satisfactory response if the need arose, and the events of July 1399 were to show that his confidence was not entirely misplaced. Richard attended to his military resources with characteristic thoroughness, and throughout the second half of his reign he showed great awareness of the military problems facing the crown. So far as supervising local government was concerned, however, Richard was perhaps more interested in the commissions of the peace than the sheriffs. He ensured their co-operation in his policies by appointing his closest and most powerful supporters as justices in large numbers of counties. Gaunt, upon whose support so much still depended, was a member of the commission in twenty-four counties in 1397, Exeter in eleven, Albemarle in eighteen, Surrey in twelve, and Norfolk in nine.[1] It was almost certainly out of the question that these nobles should sit in person on all the commissions to which they were appointed, but the mere fact of their appointment may have been enough to keep the other justices in line.

In the north, where the need to defend the Scottish border gave the local nobility exceptionally wide influence, royal surveillance extended to the wardenships of the march and the commissions to keep the truce, positions traditionally held by the border magnates. Between 1390 and 1396 the Percy family had monopolized the office of warden of the marches, Northumberland being warden of the east march and his son Hotspur of the west, and the supervision of the truce was entrusted to Northumberland himself and local landowners of lesser importance.[2] On the 1st of June 1396, when Northumberland's term of office expired, Hotspur succeeded him as warden of the east march, but at the same time Richard appointed one of his friends, Sir John Beaumont, to the vacant wardenship of the west march. Beaumont died in September 1396 and was succeeded on the 16th of February 1397 by Huntingdon, who in turn gave way on the 10th of February 1398 to Albemarle.[3] Albemarle soon recognized the difficulties of his position and in June wrote to the king asking him to divide the east march and appoint Northumberland warden of a middle march, the region which lay against the Earl of Douglas's lands in Roxburghshire.[4] This arrangement had been tried before, in the 1380s, when it had served to keep

---

[1] *CPR* 1396–9 *passim*.
[2] J. A. Tuck, 'Richard II and the Border Magnates', *Northern History* III (1968) pp. 48–9.
[3] *Rot. Scot.* Vol. II, pp. 131, 135, 140; *Calendar of Documents Relating to Scotland* Vol. IV, ed. J. Bain (London 1886) no. 474.
[4] *Calendar of Documents, Scotland* ed. Bain, Vol. IV, no. 506.

a precarious peace between Northumberland and Gaunt, but this time the king and council ignored Albemarle's request. Indeed, Richard undermined Northumberland's influence still further in July when he appointed Gaunt lieutenant in the marches for the duration of the truce,[1] a move which was bound to antagonize Northumberland, for Gaunt's tenure of a similar position in 1381 had led to the quarrel between the two in which Northumberland shut Gaunt out of Bamburgh during the Peasants' Revolt. At the same time, Richard appointed Albemarle keeper of the truce in the west march and Exeter in the east, while in October he commissioned Bushy, Green, Ferriby, and Dru to deal with violators of the truce. In November, Exeter received a similar commission, while in the following April the king entrusted the task to Albemarle, the Bishop of St Asaph, the Earl of Salisbury, Bushy, Green, and Dru.[2] The Earl of Westmorland replaced Exeter as keeper of the truce in the east march in November 1398,[3] but Richard allowed no other northern magnate any share in its enforcement. At no previous time had there been such a thorough-going exclusion of the northern magnates from authority in their own region, and Richard's policy there goes far towards explaining why Northumberland readily supported Henry in 1399.

Westmorland's position was rather more complicated. He had recently received his title from Richard together with a number of grants of land which suggest that Richard intended to build him up as a counterweight to Northumberland. But in making one of these grants the king miscalculated. He transferred to him the office of sheriff of Westmorland together with the cornage of the free tenants of the county, both of which belonged by hereditary right to John Lord Clifford, who was under age at the time. The pretext for the grant was that the Cliffords held the office and the cornage under a misinterpretation of a charter granted by king John to their ancestors, the Viponds.[4] But the grant looks like a thinly disguised attempt to disinherit Clifford, and some considerable pressure must have been applied, for Clifford received back all he had lost in May 1398, only four months after the grant to Neville.[5] The king's actions served to make both families insecure, and in all probability to alienate Neville. Like his rival Northumberland, he went over to Henry when he landed in July 1399.[6]

[1] *Rot. Scot.* Vol. II, p. 140.   [2] *ibid.* pp. 142–3, 145, 149.   [3] *ibid.* p. 145.
[4] PRO Patent Roll 21 RII part 3 C.66/349 m. 1.
[5] *ibid.* m. 16. I owe these references to Mrs V. Rees.   [6] *Kirkstall Chronicle* p. 132.

Both locally and nationally, Richard's measures in the last two years of his reign were motivated above all by his search for security. In this respect his policy is consistent and continuous throughout his reign. Feeling himself threatened by hostile magnates and by commissions of inquiry or of government which infrined the freedom he thought his predecessors had enjoyed, he reacted by seeking to develop a basis for his power which would put it beyond threat. The cautious experiments at building an alliance with the Commons and controlling the military power of the nobility had come to nothing and his *rapprochement* with France had been watched with disquiet by several nobles whom Richard in any case mistrusted. His reaction was to base his power in the last years of his reign on a group of men whom he thought he could rely on implicitly, on institutions he had seen work effectively in the early 1390s, and upon military force. Thus, he hoped, the security of his rule might at last be established; yet while seeking security he showed, now as earlier, a certain insensitivity towards the political consequences of his actions and created a climate of opinion in which few men were prepared, when it came to the test, to stand by him.

It is very difficult to perceive in Richard's policy any new theory of kingship or any attempt to introduce into England the ideas of continental writers such as Giles of Rome.[1] Nor is it necessary to see in the thoroughness and all-pervasiveness of his attack upon his opponents any sign of incipient insanity.[2] His actions are explicable in terms of his political experiences in the years up to 1397. In quelling opposition, Richard used the institutions he had at hand, whose political potential he had come to appreciate in the early 1390s. Parliament, if effectively managed, would give him no trouble, and in any case the Commons' willingness to support political opposition by the nobility had sharply diminished after their experience of the incompetence of the Appellant administration. The council and the Court of Chivalry were completely reliable and were run by men whose loyalty to the king was not, at this stage, in question. The fact that they used civil law procedure in judicial matters was, for Richard, coincidental. There is no evidence that he had much appreciation of the authoritarian principles of the civil law and, despite Fortescue's remarks, there is no reason to believe that he self-consciously sought to replace the common by the civil law. Richard's opponents, however, were more conscious of the theoretical implications of his measures than he was himself. They took the view

[1] R. H. Jones, *The Royal Policy of Richard II* (Oxford 1968).
[2] A. B. Steel, *Richard II* pp. 278-9.

that he was endangering the rights and liberties the common law gave
them, and which he himself had sworn to uphold at his coronation.
In 1399 the estate thought that they were approving the removal of a
king whose conduct had been contrary to law—and, by their standards, they were right.

Richard's search for freedom from restraints upon his power also
raised the question of the relationship between the law and the king's
will.[1] In 1387 the judges had expressed the view that the king's will
was superior to law, and that not only was it unlawful to force
measures on the king against his will, an unexceptionable doctrine, but
also those who did so should be punished as traitors. In the articles of
deposition in 1399 it was alleged that everyone's life, goods, and
chattels were at the king's will, contrary to law and custom, and that
the king had declared that the laws were in his own breast and that he
alone could change and establish the laws of his kingdom.[2] Whether
Richard ever actually said this is open to doubt, but as Professor
McKisack justly remarked,[3] he behaved as though he believed it was
true. Such a view of the relationship between law and will offered the
king a firm defence against aristocratic encroachment; yet it was a view
of government which no English king could hope to sustain, for it was
bound to seem a threat to the lives and property of his subjects, whose
security was founded upon the king's observance of due process of law
in his dealings with them. Whether Richard was justified in believing
that the aristocracy encroached too far on his power is another question.
The exceptional circumstances of Richard's minority make comparisons
with the immediately preceding reigns difficult, yet it is easy to understand how he came to hold his belief. Although the military and
financial problems which precipitated aristocratic intervention in
government were to some extent beyond Richard's control, it was
unnecessary to have an unusually high view of kingly dignity and
power to resent the constraints to which Richard was subjected
periodically in the first eleven years of his reign.

Richard's actions in the last two years of his reign created widespread
discontent, if the chroniclers are to be believed,[4] yet surprisingly little
open hostility. Although he was unpopular, he was not yet in serious

[1] There is an excellent short discussion of this subject in W. Ullmann, *Principles
of Government and Politics in the Middle Ages* (London 1961) pp. 182–92.
[2] *Rot. Parl.* Vol. III, p. 419.
[3] M. McKisack, *The Fourteenth Century* (Oxford 1959) p. 496.
[4] Walsingham, *Annales* pp. 239–40; Usk pp. 23–4.

danger of losing his throne. The removal of his most prominent aristocratic opponents and his terrorization of their associates gave him, for the moment, the security he needed. Rebellion could not hope to succeed without aristocratic leadership, and in 1398 it was hard to see whence such leadership might come. Richard, however, was still frightened of those nobles who were not closely identified with the new order created in September 1397, and frightened too of the power which Hereford would have at his disposal when Gaunt died, an event which could hardly be more than a few years away. Richard had already arranged close supervision of both the Earl of Northumberland and the Earl of Westmorland. By the autumn of 1398 Richard's treatment of three of the nobility whom he felt he could no longer trust (March, Norfolk, and Hereford) gave further point to the accusations of illegality and tyranny that were being made, and created a situation in which Richard's deposition became possible.

Richard's relationship with the Earl of March has generally been regarded as cordial, and although Tout disposed of the myth that he was actually proclaimed Richard's heir, it is sometimes suggested that Richard intended March to succeed him if he died childless.[1] Yet this interpretation is hard to sustain. Although March would succeed Richard if the crown were to descend according to strict hereditary right, the law of succession to the English crown had never been so precisely defined, and the precedent of John's succession suggested that strict hereditary right did not necessarily apply. In every other way, Gaunt was a more plausible candidate. He had been closely identified with the crown in the reign of his father as well as in Richard's reign; his children had married into European royal houses; and he had extensive experience of government in England. None of these considerations applied to March. He had spent much of his adult life in Ireland, even to the point of adopting Irish dress;[2] he had little experience of English political life, and no close or continuing association with the king. Relations between the king and Gaunt, however, and between the royal and Lancastrian followings, had become so close in the 1390s that had Richard died childless perhaps even Gloucester would not have been able to prevent Gaunt becoming king. No doubt this was one reason why Gloucester wanted to see Gaunt established in Aquitaine,

---

[1] Tout, *Chapters* Vol. III, p. 396; A. B. Steel, *Richard II* pp. 214, 217, 275.
[2] *Monasticon Anglicanum* by Sir William Dugdale, Vol. VI, pt 1, ed. Caley *et al.* (London 1830) p. 354. There is no evidence that he left Ireland between 1394 and 1398, when he came to the Shrewsbury session of parliament.

yet even this might not have disqualified Gaunt from the throne. Had anyone foreseen that Richard would die childless, the possibility of Gaunt's succession to the English throne might have taken some of the heat out of the proposals for Aquitaine. It is quite possible that Gaunt intended his three spheres of interest to be divided between the children of his three marriages: his Lancastrian inheritance to his eldest son, Hereford; his Spanish interests to his children by Catalina (as his diplomacy had already secured); and his duchy of Aquitaine to the Beauforts, a pale shadow of this scheme surviving in the appointment of John Beaufort, Marquis of Dorset, as lieutenant in Aquitaine on the 2nd of September 1398.[1] The family's French title perhaps presaged a French future for them.

March, then, was neither the accepted nor the obvious heir. His claim was strong in law but looked much weaker in reality. Nor is there much evidence for cordiality between him and the king. In 1397 Richard suspected him of harbouring his illegitimate uncle, Sir Thomas Mortimer, who was wanted in connection with the events of 1387–8, and Richard ordered him to hunt Sir Thomas down and deliver him to justice in England, though he never had much hope that March would comply.[2] This, however, cannot have been the only ground for Richard's distrust of the earl. After Lancaster, he was the greatest land-owner in the country, and in addition to his enormous territorial power he had a good enough claim to the throne to make him a possible focus for discontent and disaffection. To ensure his loyalty, therefore, Richard summoned him to England, to the Shrewsbury session of parliament, and required him to take an oath to uphold the work of the parliament.[3] He arrived at Shrewsbury, very close to his own lands in the Welsh marches, and according to Adam of Usk he was received with great joy by the people, who hoped 'through him for deliverance from the grievous evil of such a king'.[4] Usk goes on to say that Richard was alarmed at Mortimer's popularity, though it was only to be expected in that part of England, and 'did ever seek occasion to destroy him', the pretext being his protection of Sir Thomas Mortimer. Richard and his courtiers therefore 'sent into Ireland, as their lieutenant, to take him, my lord of Surrey',[5] but before Surrey reached Ireland, March (who had returned there at the conclusion of parliament) was killed by the Irish at Kells, county Kilkenny, on the 20th of July 1398.

[1] PRO Gascon Rolls C.61/105 m. 9.
[2] *CPR* 1396–9, p. 160; *Usk* p. 15; *Rot. Parl.* Vol. III, pp. 351–2.
[3] *Usk* p. 18.   [4] *ibid.* p. 19.   [5] *ibid.*

Usk owed his advancement to the Mortimer family,[1] and his account should not be accepted at its face value without independent confirmation. But in fact, on the 27th of July 1398, before Richard received news of March's death, he dismissed him as lieutenant in Ireland and replaced him by Surrey, ordering March to have nothing to do with the office after Surrey's arrival in Ireland.[2] Usk's account may represent no more than a highly coloured account of March's dismissal, yet the dismissal itself calls for explanation. It may be that Richard was angry at March's warlike attitude towards the Irish, which may have seemed to threaten the settlement he had reached in 1394–5. But in the battle in which March died he was trying in fact to enforce the settlement and dislodge MacMurrough from Leinster. It is more likely that in the circumstances of 1398 Richard distrusted March, was alarmed at his apparent popularity, and wanted to ensure that Ireland, like Wales and Chester, was in completely reliable hands. March's death came at a very fortunate moment for the king; it is impossible to say what future he intended for him after he had ceased to be lieutenant in Ireland, but it is unlikely to have been a very pleasant one. March's heir, Edmund, was still a child, so the power of the Mortimer inheritance was effectively nullified. The custody of the Mortimer lands in England was entrusted to the Duke of Albemarle, those in Ireland to the Duke of Surrey, those in South Wales to the Duke of Exeter, and those in North Wales to that ubiquitous agent of the royal will, William Lescrope Earl of Wiltshire.[3]

The king's dealings with the Duke of Norfolk and the Duke of Hereford are more difficult to understand. Both had apparently returned to favour in the 1390s, and Norfolk had shared in the distribution of lands and offices after the fall of his former Appellant colleagues in 1397. To all outward appearance, Norfolk was as fully a part of the court circle as Albemarle or Exeter, and if Bushy could be forgiven his part in the 'ridings and assemblies' of 1387, and York his membership of the 1386 commission there was no reason why Norfolk should feel insecure. Hereford's position, however, was different. He had not benefited to anything like the same extent as Norfolk from the fall of Gloucester, Arundel, and Warwick. Unlike Norfolk he had not been one of the Appellants who brought the charges against Gloucester, Arundel, and Warwick in the 1397 parliament, though according to

[1] *ibid.* introduction pp. xi–xii.
[2] *CCR* 1396–9, p. 325.
[3] *CPR* 1396–9, p. 408.

Usk he had intervened against Arundel in his trial.[1] He was far less closely identified with the court than Norfolk had become, and with the prospect of succeeding in not too long a time to the Lancastrian inheritance, he had some reason to believe that the king might not entirely trust him. Hereford's version of his quarrel with Norfolk (which led to their exile) has much to commend it, though it has recently been impugned.[2] He maintained that when the two were riding together in December 1397, Norfolk warned him that both of them were about to suffer for their part in the Radcot Bridge campaign. Norfolk went on to say that a plot had been laid to kill Henry and his father, and that the four lords closest to the king (Surrey, Wiltshire, Salisbury, and Gloucester) intended to destroy Henry, his father, Norfolk, Albemarle, Exeter, and Dorset. Some of this is hard to credit, especially the suggestion that the king's most intimate friends intended to encompass the deaths of Albemarle and Exeter; but the existence of some kind of move against Gaunt and his family is given striking confirmation by two recognizances which Bagot entered into in March 1398.[3] The first (dated the 1st of March) provided that Bagot should pay the king £1000 if it were proved any time in the future that he had brought about the disinheritance of Gaunt, his wife, or any of his children; the second (dated two days later) laid down that Bagot should be put to death without any further judgement or process against him if at any time in the future he were to kill or put to death Gaunt, his wife, or any of his children. It is difficult to believe that such remarkable documents would have been drawn up and enrolled had there not been rumours current of a plot against Gaunt and his family, and Norfolk may have been warning Henry of court gossip against both of them, with the implication that they should save themselves by flight or counter-plot. Norfolk failed to attend the Shrewsbury session of parliament, either because he was afraid the plot might succeed or because he thought the king might hear of his conversation and move against him. In fact Henry repeated the conversation to Richard, who was perhaps embarrassed by his relevations. This may explain why the session of parliament concluded abruptly on the 31st of January, leaving a committee to attend to unfinished business, and why Bagot was required to enter into the two bonds. Richard could not allow rumours of a conspiracy against Gaunt to flourish unchecked.

[1] *Usk* p. 14.
[2] K. B. McFarlane, *Lancastrian Kings and Lollard Knights* (Oxford 1972) pp. 43–7.
[3] PRO Close Roll 21 RII part 2 C.54/241 m. 15d.

Henry's account was formalized into a charge of treason against Norfolk, and the committee met at least twice to consider the charge. It held that there was insufficient evidence and that trial should therefore take place by battle in the Court of Chivalry at Coventry on the 16th of September 1398.[1] The sequel is well known: the king stopped the combat, and sentenced both parties to exile—Henry for ten years (soon reduced to six) and Norfolk for life. The king had been criticized both by contemporary chroniclers and modern historians for spoiling what had promised to be the social event of the year,[2] but according to the procedure of the Court of Chivalry he was entitled if he wished to take the quarrel into his own hands and settle it without letting the combatants fight to a finish.[3] There was no suggestion at the time even from hostile chroniclers that the decision was contrary to martial law.[4]

The event which precipitated Richard's downfall, however, was not the abortive duel at Coventry, but Gaunt's death on the 3rd of February 1399. The crucial importance of this event has not always been appreciated. It was certainly expected, for Richard had given Henry leave to receive livery of his inheritance if his father died before he returned from exile.[5] But it removed Richard's principal political supporter. The whole weight of the Lancastrian inheritance had helped to sustain the king's position since 1389, and Gaunt's political support had helped to carry the king through the parliament of September 1397. There were very close relations between the two households, and some of the persons high in Richard's favour were clients of both the king and the duke. Yet now the inheritance was to pass under the control, albeit for the moment the remote control, of a lord whom Richard had never fully trusted and who now felt a strong sense of injustice as a result of the sentence at Coventry. Gaunt's death placed Richard in an impossible position. His whole regime would be endangered if Henry were eventually to return. He might become the focus for all who thought they had suffered injustice or oppression at Richard's hands, and he might attract to his service some at least of the men who had found it possible to serve both Richard and Gaunt. On the other hand, to deny Henry his inheritance was to take action

[1] *Rot. Parl.* Vol. III, pp. 382–4.
[2] *Traison* pp. 18–21; *Usk* pp. 23–4; A. B. Steel, *Richard II* pp. 252–3.
[3] *The Black Book of the Admiralty* Vol. I, ed. Sir Travers Twiss, Rolls Series. (London 1871) p. 326.
[4] Walsingham, *Annales* p. 226; Usk p. 24.
[5] *CPR* 1396–9, p. 417.

more flagrantly contrary to the laws and customs of the country, and more offensive to the deepest instincts of the landowning community, than anything he had hitherto done. He also, of course, ran the risk of provoking Henry's return to claim his inheritance. Richard decided to take the risk. He revoked the letters patent he had granted Henry allowing him to receive his inheritance, and altered the terms of reference of the parliamentary committee of 1398 to impose a sentence of perpetual banishment on Henry and to revoke the letters patent permitting him to receive livery of his inheritance during his absence, thus in effect confiscating the possessions of the house of Lancaster.[1] This especially bore out the accusation of dishonest and tyrannical behaviour brought against Richard in the articles of deposition, for to medieval men a tyrant was above all a man who arbitrarily disposed of the property of his subjects.[2] As the twenty-sixth article of deposition put it, 'although the lands and tenements, goods and chattels of every freeman, according to the laws of the realm used through all past times, ought not to be seized unless they have been lawfully forfeited; nevertheless, the king, proposing and determining to undo such laws, declared and affirmed . . . that the lives of every one of his lieges and their lands, tenements, goods and chattels are his at his pleasure.'[3]

The Lancastrian inheritance was granted out to the nobles whom Richard still trusted.[4] The keeping of the Lancaster lands in Wales was given to Exeter, the honours of Lancaster and Tutbury and the lordship of Kenilworth to Surrey, the honours of Leicester, Pontefract, and Bolingbroke to Albemarle, and the lordship of Pickering to Lescrope. Had Henry remained in exile, the keeper of each part of the inheritance would in all probability have introduced his own officials, and the sense of attachment to the house of Lancaster which existed throughout the inheritance would gradually have faded. But Exeter, Albemarle, Surrey, and Lescrope had no time to break Henry's strength at this level

---

[1] *Rot. Parl.* Vol. III, p. 372.

[2] Sir John Fortescue, *The Governance of England* ed. C. Plummer (Oxford 1885) p. 117; 'Ffor, as Seynt Thomas saith, whan a kynge rulith his reaume only to his owne profite, and not to the good off is subiectes, he is a tyrant.' Cf. Aquinas, *De Regimine Principum* I, 1, 3; Aristotle, *Politics* IV, 10: 'This third form of tyranny is bound to exist where a single person governs men . . . without any form of responsibility, and with a view to his own advantage rather than that of his subjects' (trans. Ernest Barker (Oxford 1947) p. 212). See Caroline Barron, 'Tyranny' p. 1.

[3] *Rot. Parl.* Vol. III, p. 420.

[4] *CFR* 1391–9, pp. 293–7, 303.

in his inheritance. For the most part, they appear to have neglected it while they attended to the government of England or accompanied the king to Ireland. They may have installed their own constables in certain key castles, for Pickering was only surrendered when Henry arrived before it and Knaresborough was momentarily held against him.[1] But from other parts of the inheritance there is evidence that the Lancastrian officials remained at their posts, and although some ministers did not receive their fees and some annuities were unpaid, many receivers eventually accounted to Henry for the period of the confiscation.[2] In effect, there was a hiatus in the ownership of the inheritance rather than a transfer, and one reason for Henry's return in July 1399 must have been to take advantage of the failure of his inheritance's new masters to establish their authority effectively at the local level.

Another reason, of course, was Richard's departure for Ireland at the end of May 1399. Most authorities have agreed that the murder of March in 1398 provided the occasion for the expedition: 'he came in anger, burning for revenge.'[3] But Richard's removal of March from the lieutenancy of Ireland does not suggest that he regarded him so highly that he would mount a full-scale campaign to avenge him. In any case he had been contemplating another expedition since the winter of 1397.[4] He went, in fact, to save the 1394–5 settlement which had been almost entirely destroyed by MacMurrough's refusal to leave Leinster and by the revival of war in Ulster. Richard was certainly correct in thinking that another royal expedition was necessary if the colony was to be saved from extinction, and it has even been suggested that the confiscation of the Lancastrian inheritance was made necessary by the need to raise money for the expedition.[5] The recovery of Ireland was still one of Richard's main preoccupations, but to leave England when he did was a misjudgement of the first magnitude, and inevitably raises questions about his mental state.[6] But it is not unknown for rulers who suppress criticism and surround themselves with men whom they trust partly because they offer no criticism, to be out of touch with the true feeling of the country they rule and to misjudge the

[1] *Kirkstall Chronicle* p. 121.
[2] PRO Duchy of Lancaster Miscellaneous Books, DL.42/15 f. 61; Duchy of Lancaster Ministers' Accounts DL.29/728/11987.
[3] J. F. Lydon, 'Richard II's Expeditions to Ireland', *Journal of the Royal Society of Antiquaries of Ireland* XCIII (1963) p. 147.
[4] See p. 265 above.
[5] A. B. Steel, *Richard II* pp. 260–1.
[6] Tout, for instance, criticizes 'the fatuous king's' timing of the expedition (*Chapters* Vol. IV, p. 53).

strength of opposition to them, not through any mental abnormality but because they are in a position where no one will tell them the truth. The stories told by the chroniclers suggest that the style of Richard's court was highly formal and that those round him either had no judgement themselves or were simply flatterers. Furthermore, the king's use of the council as a means of political discipline and the control he sought to impose upon local government may have created a situation where men were afraid to use the usual channels through which grievances could be made known to the king and his councillors. It is impossible to be sure how much the king and those round him knew of the feeling of the country; it may well have been less than is commonly assumed, and this may go some way towards explaining Richard's decision to leave the country in May 1399.

In the spring of 1399, furthermore, Richard perhaps felt that an invasion by Henry was unlikely. His exile in France had been honourable: Richard had allowed him to retire to the French court and Charles VI had provided him with the Hotel de Clisson for his residence.[1] He received substantial sums of money from England, some of which came from the revenues of the duchy of Lancaster.[2] In the autumn of 1398 Henry apparently began negotiations for the marriage of the Comtesse d'Eu, daughter of the Duke of Berry.[3] Richard heard of this proposal and made strong representations against it, sending the Earl of Salisbury to France in the spring of 1399 to express his displeasure.[4] Charles VI and the Duke of Burgundy were also opposed to it, and even Berry himself seems to have been lukewarm. Neither Charles nor Burgundy wished to support a marriage to which Richard was opposed, and the project fell through.[5] Richard had every reason to believe that his interests were being carefully safeguarded by his friends in France.

It is clear, however, that Henry received some backing for his marriage plans from the Duke of Orléans, who went so far as to arrange an interview between Henry and the Comtesse at Asnières in April 1399.[6] It was Orléans' object to undermine the authority which Burgundy enjoyed at court and to obtain royal support for an invasion of northern Italy, where he hoped to carve out a kingdom for himself.[7]

---

[1] *Chronique du Religieux de Saint Denys* Vol. II, ed. M. Bellaguet (Paris 1839) pp. 674–5; Froissart, *Oeuvres* Vol. XVI, pp. 141–51.
[2] PRO Exchequer Issue Rolls E.403/559 m. 14; E.403/561 m. 4.
[3] F. Lehoux, *Jean de France Duc de Berry* Vol. II (Paris 1966) pp. 406–7.
[4] *ibid.*   [5] *ibid.*   [6] *ibid.*
[7] J. J. N. Palmer, *England, France and Christendom* (London 1971) p. 222.

Such a policy was bound to bring him into conflict with England, whose intention now was to oppose French expansion into Italy. A breach of the Anglo-French *entente* was a necessary precondition for his Italian adventure. Orléans also had ambitions in Aquitaine. His own lands lay close to those of the Count of Périgord,[1] and his expansionist policy was certain to bring him into conflict sooner or later with the English in Aquitaine. Here too he stood to gain from a renewal of Anglo-French hostility.

As long as Burgundy was in control, Richard had little to fear from either Henry or Orléans; but as Richard sailed for Ireland, plague raged in France and kept Burgundy in Artois.[2] With Burgundy out of the way, Orléans reinstated himself in Charles VI's favour, and Berry left court to spend the summer at Bicêtre.[3] Orléans was in control from late May onwards, and on the 17th of June he entered into an alliance with Henry.[4] The alliance excluded the kings of England and France and the Duke of York, keeper of England during Richard's absence; but it is hard to resist the conclusion that Orléans gave Henry some help in the preparations which he now began for the invasion of England. Orléans also received two grants which increased his authority in Aquitaine.[5] The Count of Périgord was disinherited and Charles promised to give Orléans his lands, while he also gave him the keeping of 'the fortresses and castles in Angoulême which are on the military frontier'. Orléans' supremacy guaranteed Henry freedom to organize a force. Without it, he probably could not have gone ahead when he did, for Burgundy would almost certainly have done his best to keep Henry in France and preserve the *entente*. Events in France in the summer of 1399 created the essential preconditions for the success of the invasion: in a very real sense, Orléans' behaviour was crucial in bringing about Richard's downfall. Burgundy, for his part, was horrified when he heard of Richard's deposition. He wrote to Berry saying that the news was 'une grant pitié, et me doubte que ceste chose ne soit bien taillée de venir à un très grant mal pour cest royaume. Car vous savez que le Duc de Lancastre gouverne par la voix du commun d'Angleterre, et le commun ne demande que la guerre.'[6]

The English government, meanwhile, under York's control, kept

[1] F. Lehoux, *Jean de France* p. 416.
[2] *ibid*. pp. 417–18.   [3] *ibid*. p. 416.
[4] *ibid; Chronique . . . de Saint Denys* ed. Bellaguet, p. 702.
[5] F. Lehoux, *Jean de France* p. 416.   [6] *ibid*. p. 420.

itself well informed of Henry's movements. It believed initially that Henry's force intended to split into two parts, one taking Calais and the other invading England.[1] It was credible that Henry should seek to take Calais and use it as a base from which troops could cross the Channel to back up the first invasion force. But in the event, Henry embarked with only a small force and made for the north of England, where he hoped to rally his retainers. The exact date of his arrival at Ravenspur is unknown; Walsingham said it was about the 4th of July; the Kirkstall chronicler said it was actually on the 4th of July; Usk named the 28th of June as the date; Evesham said he left France about the 24th of June.[2] Henry's voyage must have taken several days, for he put in at various ports, presumably for food and information, but there is evidence that Dunstanburgh Castle was garrisoned for Henry from the 1st of July[3] and Kenilworth from the 2nd of July.[4] The keepers who held these two castles for Henry were said to have done so 'at his first arrival in England', and it seems unlikely that they would have declared for Henry until they knew that he was in the country. Perhaps, therefore, his arrival took place in the last days of June, as Usk suggests. Usk also records that Robert Waterton, chief forester of Knaresborough Forest, was the first to meet Henry on his arrival, and brought with him two hundred foresters.[5] He may have obtained such detailed information from someone who was with Henry when he landed, and who was also in a position to give Usk the correct date of the landing. Henry's receiver-general, John Leventhorpe, also met him when he landed, and he was soon joined by thirty-seven other knights and esquires, mostly from Yorkshire and Lancashire, who brought companies of men with them.[6]

To secure his northern flank, Henry made first for Pickering, and the keeper of the castle whom Lescrope had installed surrendered it to him

[1] PRO Exchequer Accounts, various, E.101/42/12 m. 4.

[2] Walsingham, *Annales* p. 244; *Kirkstall Chronicle* p. 121; Usk p. 25; *Evesham* p. 151.

[3] PRO Duchy of Lancaster Miscellaneous Books DL.42/15 f. 74.

[4] *ibid.* f. 69ᵛ, which gives the date as the 2nd of June; but the auditors' accounts for the north parts give it as the 2nd of July: PRO Duchy of Lancaster Ministers' Accounts DL.29/728/11987. The entry in DL.42/15 was probably copied from this or another account, and the copyist may well have written 'Junii' for 'Julii'. Cf. R. Somerville, *History of the Duchy of Lancaster* (London 1953) p. 136.

[5] Usk p. 25.

[6] R. Somerville, *Duchy of Lancaster* p. 137; for names of those who came to Henry at his first landing, with wages paid to them, see PRO Duchy of Lancaster Miscellaneous Books DL. 42/15 ff. 70–71; Duchy of Lancaster Ministers' Accounts DL.29/728/11987.

without resistance.[1] He then made for Knaresborough, which he took with rather more difficulty, and from there he went on to Pontefract (his principal castle in Yorkshire) where there came to him 'a great multitude of gentlemen, knights, and esquires of Lancashire and York-shire with their their men, some of their own free will and others for fear of future events'—an interesting indication that at least some who joined Henry were opportunists. So far, Henry's supporters were in all probability drawn from his own extensive estates in Lancashire and Yorkshire, but a few days later at Doncaster, the Earl of Northumber-land, his son Hotspur, the Earl of Westmorland, and Lord Willoughby (an important landowner in Lincolnshire) joined Henry with their retinues, and thus the whole of the north of England was now secure for him.[2] This in itself probably gave him an important psychological advantage in gaining the south of England, for the fear generated by a large army marching down from the north probably did as much as the widespread dislike of Richard's rule to bring about the rapid collapse of morale in the south.

York meanwhile had begun to muster an army as soon as Henry's movements in Picardy had become known. He ordered the sheriffs to call out the *posse comitatus*, and received a good response from some of the southern counties.[3] The sheriffs of Hertfordshire, Bedfordshire, and Buckinghamshire, Northamptonshire, Rutland, Wiltshire, Cam-bridgeshire, and Huntingdonshire, Oxfordshire and Berkshire, Hamp-shire, and Gloucestershire all sent forces. But some of these sheriffs had close personal connections with the royal household, and all of them had had their terms of office prolonged in 1398. It is therefore not surprising that they answered York's call, and in this respect at least Richard's efforts to ensure the reliability of the sheriffs proved to have some value. The sheriff of Yorkshire, on the other hand, declined to send troops on the ground that he had to defend the country against the Scots,[4] but since Henry had already landed when he made his reply it was in fact remarkably diplomatic. A few lords brought out their retinues to fight with York: the Marquess of Dorset, the Earl of Suffolk, the Bishop of Norwich, and Robert Lord Ferrers. A handful of knights and esquires also answered the call, although they were a pitifully small proportion of the numbers available in the south and

---

[1] This account of his movements is based on the *Kirkstall Chronicle* p. 132.
[2] *ibid.*
[3] PRO Exchequer Accounts, various, E.101/42/12; Issue Rolls E.403/562 m. 14.
[4] PRO Exchequer Accounts, various, E.101/42/12.

east of England.[1] Some pressure was brought to bear on ordinary people to pay for troops to fight for Richard. In one area of southern Lincolnshire, William Driby ordered the constables of nine vills to levy money to pay for soldiers under threat of distraint, and he raised enough to be able to contribute six men-at-arms and thirty archers to York's army. Driby's action was unwise, however, for the most powerful lord in that part of Lincolnshire, William Lord Willoughby, had thrown in his lot with Henry, and afterwards Willoughby petitioned the council to order the repayment of the money if Driby could not show a warrant for his levy.[2]

York managed to assemble an army which numbered upwards of 3000 men,[3] and both he and Henry made for Bristol. Henry's march south is reported by the chroniclers as something of a triumphal progress.[4] York had sufficient forces to offer resistance if he had wished to do so, but only the Bishop of Norwich actually engaged a part of Henry's army, and was repulsed in the only fighting of the campaign.[5] York, in fact, declined to use his army against Henry, and with his defection Richard's only hope of serious resistance in England collapsed. Walsingham attributed York's defection to his belief that Henry's cause was just and his reluctance to stand in the way of one who came to claim his rightful inheritance.[6] This may be true, but York also realized that, despite his own forces, Henry enjoyed such obvious support that resistance would have been politically unwise and the military outcome uncertain. After York's defection, the constable of Bristol Castle, Sir Peter Courtenay, surrendered to Henry, and Lescrope, Bushy, and Green, who had fled there from Oxford, were trapped. Henry had no hesitation in executing all three of them, to the delight of the people.[7] Bagot had already fled to Cheshire, where he was eventually captured but later pardoned, perhaps on the strength of his earlier associations with the House of Lancaster.

The greater part of England had thus fallen to Henry with scarcely a hand raised against him; but there remained Cheshire, the principal source of Richard's military strength and the county likely to show the

1 PRO Exchequer Accounts, various, E.403/562 m. 14.
2 PRO Ancient Petitions SC.8/150/7454; Issue Rolls E.403/562 m. 14.
3 PRO Issue Rolls E.403/562, 563; J. L. Kirby, *Henry IV of England* (London 1970) p. 50.
4 *Usk* pp. 25–6; Walsingham, *Annales* pp. 246–7; *Kirkstall Chronicle* pp. 132–3.
5 *Kirkstall Chronicle* p. 133; Walsingham, *Annales* p. 246, who adds the name of Sir William Elmham.
6 Walsingham, *Annales* p. 244; *Traison* p. 39.
7 Walsingham, *Annales* pp. 246–7.

greatest loyalty to him. Having secured Bristol and thus erected a barrier across one of the two routes Richard might take from Ireland to London, Henry marched north to secure Cheshire and bar the other route. To give a stern warning to Richard's supporters he devastated the county as he entered it, and he took Chester without meeting any serious resistance.[1] At Chester he executed Sir Piers de Legh, whom Usk describes as 'a great evil-doer',[2] and this served to deter anyone who might have contemplated making a last stand for the king. All England was now Henry's, and he acted in such a way that it is difficult to believe that he aimed at anything less than the throne. He granted offices in the north to Northumberland and Westmorland under his duchy seal (and the two earls did not hesitate to recognize the authority of his seal[3]) while his summary executions at Bristol and Chester were the acts of one who considers himself the supreme authority in the country.

Yet there is evidence, too strong to be ignored, that Henry took an oath some time after he landed that he came only to claim his inheritance. The chronicler Hardyng states that Henry took an oath at Doncaster, in the presence of the Percies, and the *Dieulacres Chronicle* states that Henry swore that he did not have designs on the crown.[4] The case is further strengthened by the suggestion in the *Kirkstall Chronicle*[5] that it was Henry himself, not the Earl of Northumberland, who treated Richard as a captive once he had been brought to Flint, and the *Dieulacres Chronicle* says that Hotspur probably did not consent to Richard's deposition and that he declined to attend Henry's coronation banquet. This version of events cannot easily be dismissed as propaganda put forward by the Percies at the time of their rebellion against Henry IV in 1403.[6] On the other hand Northumberland's

---

[1] *Usk* pp. 25–7.   [2] *ibid.* p. 27.

[3] R. L. Storey, 'The Wardens of the Marches of England towards Scotland, 1377–1489', *EHR* LXXII (1957) p. 603; J. M. W. Bean, 'Henry IV and the Percies', *History* XLIV (1959) p. 219; R. Somerville, *Duchy of Lancaster* p. 138.

[4] *The Chronicle of John Hardyng* ed. H. F. Ellis (London 1812) p. 352; *Dieulacres Chronicle* ed. M. V. Clarke and V. H. Galbraith, *BJRL* Vol. XIV (1930) p. 179. This subject has generated an important body of literature. See especially B. Wilkinson, 'The Deposition of Richard II and the Accession of Henry IV', *EHR* LIV (1939) pp. 215–20; idem, *Constitutional History of England in the Fifteenth Century* (London 1964) pp. 2–4; J. M. W. Bean, 'Henry IV and the Percies' pp. 216–21.

[5] *Kirkstall Chronicle* p. 134. The same impression is given by the Whalley Abbey Chronicle: M. V. Clarke and V. H. Galbraith, 'The Deposition of Richard II', *BJRL* XIV (1930) p. 144.

[6] Cf. J. M. W. Bean, 'Henry IV and the Percies' pp. 216–21.

H

ready acceptance of grants from Henry and the leading part he played in persuading Richard to leave the safety of Conway, when he can hardly have been so naive as to suppose that even if Henry had sworn an oath Richard would be in no danger of being held as a captive or even deposed, suggest that by August he at least was prepared to accept that Henry might make himself king. For his own part, Henry might well have thought it expedient to take an oath, shortly after he landed and before he had time to assess the political situation in England, that he did not have designs on the crown; but as he advanced south the extent of his popularity became clearer. The letters which Henry circulated to his fellow nobles and to the Londoners (if the versions given by the author of the *Traison* are genuine) were notably vague about his intentions.[1] Henry had sufficient experience of Richard to realize that he could not expect to hold his inheritance safely so long as Richard was still king, and even if he had thought at the time of his landing that he might simply rule as Richard's chief counsellor, the extent of popular support for him perhaps convinced him that the throne could be his.

Richard meanwhile had divided his forces in Ireland into two groups and he had sent the first on ahead of him to North Wales under the command of the Earl of Salisbury. Jean Creton, author of 'A Metrical History of the Deposition and Death of Richard II' travelled with Salisbury 'for the sake of merriment and song', and provides an important eye-witness account of what happened in North Wales.[2] The king's intention was that Salisbury should rally forces there, while the king came on afterwards to South Wales. This was not an entirely unreasonable strategy, and if it is true that Albemarle suggested it (against the advice of others of Richard's council), there is no reason to believe Creton's story that his intention at this stage was treasonable.[3] The king's forces in Ireland were dispersed, and it made some sense to rally them at Waterford before crossing to England—hence the delay in Richard's return. The strategy broke down, however, when Salisbury failed to hold together the army he had assembled in North Wales. The Welsh were demoralized by fear of Henry and rumours that Richard was already dead. They would not fight for Salisbury, and they simply melted away.[4] When Richard landed at Haverfordwest after leaving Waterford on the 27th of July, his own army deserted him,

[1] *Traison* pp. 35–7.
[2] Ed. J. Webb, *Archaeologia* XX (1824) p. 314.
[3] *ibid.* pp. 312–13.   [4] *ibid.* pp. 317–18.

and Albemarle and Worcester, who was the Earl of Northumberland's brother, went over to Henry. The collapse of his forces left Richard no alternative but to go north to Conway and join Salisbury.[1] The fear generated by Henry's control of England was enough to bring about a collapse of Richard's military position, for no one believed that the king could recover his authority once England was lost.

Northumberland and Archbishop Arundel came to the king at Conway and persuaded him to go to meet Henry at Flint.[2] Northumberland and Arundel swore before Richard that Henry had come only to claim his inheritance; but it is hard to believe that they were entirely honest, and the *Traison* is firmly of the view that Richard was tricked into leaving Conway.[3] When Richard arrived at Flint, Henry treated him as a captive. He was taken from Flint to Chester and thence to London, where he was placed in the Tower. Men from Cheshire made an attempt to rescue him near Lichfield on the way to London,[4] but no one else showed any open support for him. It is improbable that fear was the only reason for the widespread acquiescence in Henry's *coup*: Richard's own unpopularity made men unwilling to fight for him.

While at Chester on the 19th of August Henry had issued writs in Richard's name calling a parliament for the 30th of September, and the sheriffs had been instructed to restore order in their counties:[5] there is some evidence that the justices had stopped holding their sessions when they heard of Henry's arrival. Henry's intention now was to restore normal administration as quickly as possible, making grants and appointments in Richard's name, though with the assent or advice of the Duke of Lancaster formally recorded.[6] Henry now recalled those whom Richard had exiled. Norfolk died at Venice in September, but the Earl of Warwick and Sir John Cobham, whom Richard had exiled to Jersey in 1397 for his part in the events of 1387–8, returned, and Archbishop Arundel was restored to Canterbury. Henry also sent for his own eldest son, Henry, afterwards Henry V, and the Duke of Gloucester's son Humphrey, both of whom Richard had taken to Ireland with him and lodged in Trim Castle. It is not clear that they were being treated as prisoners or hostages, but there was much to be

---

[1] *ibid.* p. 322.
[2] M. V. Clarke and V. H. Galbraith, 'Deposition' pp. 125–55. Most subsequent writers have broadly accepted their version of events.
[3] *Traison* pp. 55–60; M. V. Clarke and V. H. Galbraith, 'Deposition'.
[4] *Traison* p. 61.   [5] *CCR 1396–9*, p. 522.
[6] *CPR 1396–9*, pp. 592–6.

said, from the point of view of Richard's own security, for keeping both boys under close surveillance. Humphrey, however, failed to survive the journey back to England, and the Duke of Gloucester's family thus became extinct in the male line.

Meanwhile, Henry had to decide how to proceed when parliament met. Whatever he had thought or promised earlier, he had by this time almost certainly decided to take the throne, and, sometime in mid-September, he set up a committee to advise on the best way of deposing Richard and making himself king. Adam of Usk sat on this committee, and his evidence is of crucial importance.[1] He states that the committee reached the conclusion that Richard could be deposed 'by the authority of the clergy and people': not, it should be noted, by parliament. The committee was probably aware of the precedent of 1327, when Edward II had been set aside by the same authority; but according to Usk the precedent most in mind was that of the deposition of the Emperor Frederick II by Pope Innocent IV in 1245. Civil and canon lawyers on the committee, such as Usk himself, were likely to be as conscious of this precedent as of the one which seems much more obvious in modern eyes.[2]

On the question of Henry's title to the throne, however, the committee's view was much less clear cut. It sifted through a considerable quantity of chronicle evidence to see whether there was any basis for the belief that Edmund Crouchback, Henry's ancestor through his mother Blanche of Lancaster, had been the elder son of Henry III but had been set aside in favour of his brother Edward because of a deformity. The committee could find no basis for such a belief,[3] and did not offer any other suggestion. Henry himself apparently considered claiming the throne by right of conquest, but was discouraged from doing so by Sir William Thirning, chief justice of the king's bench since 1396, who argued that to do so would create insecurity in men's minds about their property.[4] Such a move would have been most inopportune after the events of the previous two years, and in his speech after his declaration as king Henry said that it was not his will that anyone should think that 'be waye of conquest I wold disherit any man of his heritage, franches, or other ryghtes that hym aght to have, ne put hym out of that that he has and has had by the gude lawes and custumes of the Rewme except thos persons that has ben agan the gude

---

[1] *Usk* pp. 29–30.
[2] *ibid.*; B. Wilkinson, 'The Deposition of Richard II and the Accession of Henry IV' p. 231.   [3] *Usk* pp. 31–2.   [4] Walsingham, *Annales* p. 282.

purpose and the commune profyt of the Rewme'.[1] In the event, Henry's speech claiming the throne reflected the ambiguity that was evidently felt about his title.

The committee's advice about how to depose Richard, however, appears to have been in general accepted. On the 30th of September those summoned to parliament by virtue of the writs issued on the 19th of August met in Westminster Hall. There had been much dispute about whether this assembly was a parliament or not,[2] and the debate among historians reflects the doubt that was probably felt at the time in some circles about the precise nature of the assembly. It would be well to allow for some imprecision of language on the part of some of those associated with the proceedings which ensued, but the central figure, Sir William Thirning, and the central document, the 'record and process' of Richard's deposition, were clear that the assembly consisted of 'the estates', and that Richard was deposed by the 'status et populus'. Both Thirning himself and the record of the proceedings took care to avoid creating the impression that Richard had been deposed by parliament, and the official view was that the assembly did not constitute a parliament.[3]

The official account[4] of the process of deposition suggests that all proceeded smoothly, with co-operation by the king and acquiescence by the assembled estates. But this account cannot be accepted in its entirety. When the assembly met, it was told that on the previous day, the 29th of September, a deputation which consisted, among others, of the Earl of Northumberland and Sir William Thirning went to the Tower and reminded Richard that he had promised at Conway to give up the throne. It is impossible to accept that he ever made such a promise: only Walsingham repeats the story, and his account is heavily indebted to the official version. It is much more probable, as the *Traison*[5] suggests, that Richard threatened to 'flay some of these men alive' than that he promised 'with a cheerful countenance'[6] to abdicate. None the less, the official record goes on to say that Henry himself and

---

[1] *Rot. Parl.* Vol. III, p. 423.

[2] G. Lapsley, 'The Parliamentary Title of Henry IV', *EHR* XLIX (1934), pp. 423–49, 577–606; *idem*, 'Richard II's "Last Parliament"', *EHR* LIII (1938) pp. 53–78; H. G. Richardson, 'Richard II's Last Parliament', *EHR* LII (1937) pp. 39–47; B. Wilkinson, 'Deposition' p. 231; H. G. Wright, 'The Protestation of Richard II in the Tower in September 1399', *BJRL* XXIII (1943) pp. 151–66.

[3] One of the strongest points in Lapsley's argument is the evident care taken over the precise wording of the 'record and process'.

[4] *Rot. Parl.* Vol. III, 416–24.

[5] *Traison* p. 56.   [6] *Rot. Parl.* Vol. III, p. 417.

Archbishop Arundel then joined the deputation in the Tower, and Richard agreed to resign in favour of Henry. As a token of his goodwill he gave Henry his signet ring. Again, it is straining credulity to accept that all proceeded so harmoniously. Adam of Usk, who had visited Richard in the Tower on the 21st of September, found him railing at a country that had betrayed so many kings and lamenting his own downfall,[1] while the *Dieulacres Chronicle* states that Richard placed his crown on the ground and resigned his right to God.[2] The Chronicle gives the impression of a king resigned to his fate but not in the least disposed to co-operate with his supplanter. Indeed, had he been happy to abdicate it is not clear why he could not have been brought before the assembly to say so.[3]

The following day, Richard's renunciation was read to the assembly, and this was followed by a recital of thirty-two articles which formed an indictment of his rule.[4] The articles were prefaced by a recital of his coronation oath, and the essence of the charges against him was that he had violated his oath to rule in accordance with the laws and customs of the realm, and had sought instead to rule according to his own will. This view of the king's relationship to law recalls, in its general approach, the speech which Gloucester and Archbishop Arundel made to the king at Eltham in October 1386, and it is perhaps worth speculating that although Sir William Thirning acted as chief spokesman during the deposition proceedings Archbishop Arundel may have had something to do with the drawing up of the articles of deposition themselves.

The official record goes on to say that the estates agreed by acclamation to accept Richard's renunciation, and 'for greater security' it was declared by the 'status'[5] that the charges against Richard were sufficient to warrant deposition. A commission representing the 'status et populus' then formally declared him deposed. But here too the official

---

[1] *Usk* p. 30; cf. Shakespeare, *Richard II*, Act III, Scene ii:

> For God's sake, let us sit upon the ground
> And tell sad stories of the death of kings:
> How some have been deposed . . .

[2] *Dieulacres Chronicle* ed. Clarke and Galbraith, p. 173.

[3] As the Bishop of Carlisle implied (p. 223 below) and as has been pointed out by modern writers, e.g. J. L. Kirby, *Henry IV* p. 69.

[4] *Rot. Parl.* Vol. III, pp. 417–21.

[5] Wilkinson suggests ('Deposition') that the term 'status' refers only to the lords present in the assembly, and that it was they alone who judged Richard worthy of deposition. In view of the care taken over the wording of the record, his suggestion should be taken very seriously.

record implies a smoothness and unanimity in procedure that cannot be accepted. The Bishop of Carlisle, Thomas Marke, stood up and declared that Richard should not be condemned unheard[1] and should be allowed to speak in his own defence and state his own will on the question of resignation. Marke received no support, however, and was handed over to the custody of the Abbot of St Albans for his temerity in speaking out. Marke's protest ruffled the proceedings but did not long impede them. After the formal declaration of deposition, Henry claimed the vacant throne, saying:

> In the name of Fadir, Son and Holy Gost, I, Henry of Lancastre, chalenge this Rewme of Yngland, and the Corone, with all the membres and appurtenances als I that am disendit be right lyne of the blode comyng fro the gude lorde Kyng Henry therde and thorghe that ryght that God of his grace hath sent me, with helpe of my kyn and of my frendes to recover it; the which Rewme was in poynt to be undone for defaut of governance and undoyng of the gode lawes.[2]

Henry's claim was couched in terms that were in all probability deliberately ambiguous. The hereditary element in the claim should not necessarily be taken as an appeal to the Crouchback legend, for the committee had found the legend baseless and Henry was unlikely to fly in the face of its opinion so soon. The words he used need mean no more than that he had royal blood on both his father's and his mother's side, arguably a better claim than that of the Earl of March, whose royal blood came only through his grandmother, the daughter of Lionel Duke of Clarence. Henry was perhaps saying no more than that he had a good hereditary title to the throne. His statement that he had come to 'recover' the realm is a veiled hint at a claim by conquest; and he also relies for his title on designation by God. There was no suggestion, however, that he was being made king by parliament. Finally, Archbishop Arundel preached a sermon after Henry's acceptance as king on the theme 'vir dominabitur populo', the clear implication of which was that Henry was a man and thus fit to rule, whereas another plausible candidate for the throne, the Earl of March, was only a child.[3] The following day news of his deposition was brought to Richard in the Tower by Thirning and a fellow judge John Markham, and here, for once, the official version of events records a credible

---

[1] *Traison* pp. 70-71.
[2] *Rot. Parl.* Vol. III, pp. 422-3.   [3] *ibid.* p. 423.

reaction by the former king. He said on receiving the news that 'he looked not hereafter, but hoped that his cousin would be a good lord to him'.[1]

Henry now called parliament on his own authority as king for the 6th of October, and in his opening address Archbishop Arundel reinforced the point made in the articles of deposition about the relationship between the king and the law. He declared that the new king would not be ruled 'de son purpos voluntaire, singulere opinione, mais par commune advis, conseil et assent'. He went on to say that the doing of justice and the upholding of the laws were essential to the government of the realm, and that it was the king's intention to give justice and equity to all.[2] There then followed the repeal of the acts of the parliament of 1397–8 and the restoration to lands and honours of all those who had suffered by its judgments. Those who had received dukedoms or earldoms at that time were, with the exception of the Earls of Westmorland and Worcester, required to resume the rank they had previously held.

The official record of the deposition proceedings in all probability misrepresents Richard's attitude and suppresses at least one protest about the manner in which the deposition was carried out. Richard's attitude seems to have developed from one of rage when the extent of Henry's success became clear and during the first month of his captivity to one of resignation when it became clear that Henry was determined to supplant him and that virtually no one would stand in his way. Yet even during the last weeks of his reign the evidence from Adam of Usk, the Dieulacres Chronicle, and in the end from the parliament roll, is insufficient to permit an assumption that Richard had lost his mental balance. He sometimes during his reign misjudged both events and people, and in the last two years of his reign his search for security made him insensitive to the wider political consequences of his actions; but a diagnosis of insanity is difficult to make on the evidence now available. In the last weeks of his reign his behaviour was understandable enough in view of the circumstances in which he found himself, and too little is known of the last months of his life or the circumstances of his death, probably at Pontefract Castle early in 1400, to make a judgement about the development of his personality after his deposition.

Despite the Bishop of Carlisle's intervention in the assembly of the 30th of September, there is little sign of any widespread opposition

[1] *Rot. Parl.* Vol. III, p. 425.   [2] *ibid.* p. 415.

either to the removal of Richard or to his replacement by Henry. Hotspur may have had doubts,[1] but he was not a member of the assembly or of the subsequent parliament, and his father the Earl of Northumberland seems to have gone along willingly with the proceedings. The claim of the Earl of March was not canvassed at all, so far as is known, until it became in the Percies' interest to do so in 1403. Nor do the subsequent revolts suggest that Richard enjoyed much popular sympathy. They came from Richard's inmost group of aristocratic supporters, Exeter, Salisbury, Surrey, and Thomas Despenser lately Earl of Gloucester; from the men of Cheshire; and from a few Franciscan friars.[2] The ease with which Henry gained the country, and the virtual unanimity with which Richard was set aside, is explicable only in terms of the deep unpopularity and the fears he had aroused in men of property. Throughout almost all England, men were not prepared to risk their necks for Richard. In 1387 Sir Ralph Basset had said that he was not prepared to have his head broken for the sake of the Duke of Ireland; in 1399, whatever their private doubts, men felt the same about Richard himself. They thought that law should protect their lives and their property, and that Richard had overridden law and custom and was ruling by his will alone. The articles of deposition are informed by this view of the king's relationship to law, and condemned his rule both in substance and in principle.

Yet Richard's deposition is not explicable solely in terms of the character of his rule in his last two years. In the 1380s Richard's government had aroused similar, though less violent fears, and his enemies had resorted to coercion, first constitutional and then military. Coercion, however, had turned out to be at best a short-term solution, and the king and his court had displayed great resilience in the face of aristocratic opposition. For the nobility expected the king to take the initiative in government, though they also expected him to pay due regard to their interests and prejudices. Their idea of monarchy was still essentially personal, and the acceptance of personal monarchy by the political community gave the king, in normal times, great strength and freedom. The nobility could not make their will prevail for long if the king was determined not to co-operate, and in the end the only effective alternative was to remove the king. Perhaps, therefore, paradoxically, the two depositions of the fourteenth century suggest not the weakness but the strength of the English medieval monarchy.

[1] See p. 323 above.
[2] *Traison* pp. 77–91; E. F. Jacob, *The Fifteenth Century* (Oxford 1961) pp. 27–9.

Appendix

Richard II's Itinerary in 1387

February	9	Left Westminster (Westminster p. 90)
	15	Beaumanoir, Leics. (*Knighton* Vol. II, p. 233)
	21–6	Nottingham (C.81/495/4214, 4222)
March	25	Royston, near Barnsley (C.81/495/4237)
	27	Lincoln (J. W. F. Hill, *Medieval Lincoln* (Cambridge 1948) p. 258)
April	3–8	Nottingham (C.81/495/4243–57)
	23	Windsor (C.81/495/4269)
	27–9	Easthampstead (C.81/495/4278, 4284)
May	8–13	Reading (C.81/496/4310–25)
	22	Woodstock (KB.145/10/1)
June	10–13	Coventry (KB.27/505 m. 1; *Knighton* Vol. II, p. 235)
	14	Banbury (KB.145/10/1)
	16	Banbury (*ibid*)
	26–7	Drayton Basset (*ibid*)
	29–30	Lichfield (*ibid*)
July	3	Stafford (*ibid*)
	4	Stone (*ibid*)
	12–16	Chester (Chester 2/59 mm. 3,4; C.81/497/4412; E.28/1/28)
	26	Malpas (Chester 2/59 m.4d.)
	28	Blakemere (*ibid*, m. 7d.)
August	1–5	Shrewsbury (*ibid*, mm. 6–9) *or* Worcester (C.81/497/4428)
	6	Acton Burnell (Chester 2/59 m. 7d)

August	9–12	Worcester (C.81/497/4433–51)
	14	Alvechurch. (C.81/1354/1) *or* Worcester (*CPR* 1385–9 p. 350)
	20	Groby, Leics. (*Knighton* Vol. II, p. 231)
	25–9	Nottingham. (C.81/497/4470–02; *Rot. Parl.* Vol. III, p. 233–4)
September	2	Clipstone, Notts. (Chester 2/59 m. 7)
	8	Clipstone (*ibid*)
	9–11	Nottingham (Chester 2/59 m. 7; C.81/497/4480)
	16–17	Leicester (*Knighton* Vol. II, p. 240; C.81/497/4482)
	20	Woodstock (*CPR* 1385–89, p. 349)
	22–30	Woodstock (C.81/497/4483–4500)
October	6–15	Woodstock (C.81/498/4516–33)
	30	Windsor (C.81/498/4562)
November	2	Windsor (C.81/498/4564)
	10	Return to London (Westminster p. 104)

This itinerary has been compiled from three principal sources: the Privy Seal warrants to the chancellor (C.81); the Chester Recognizance Rolls (Chester 2); and the common law writs and returns (KB.145).[1] The majority of the documents used in the two latter classes are signet letters, and it has been assumed for the purpose of constructing the itinerary that the secretary was with the king. In the case of Privy Seal letters dated away from Westminster during Richard's progress a problem arises, for the keeper of the Privy Seal did not travel with the king, though he or his clerks may have travelled to the king to seal writs drawn up at the places where they are dated. An alternative explanation is that they were drawn up by clerks with the king, and sent to London to be sealed. The former explanation is perhaps the more probable. The king's presence at a number of the places named in the dating clauses is, however, confirmed by other sources, and the series of Privy Seal warrants has accordingly been taken as a reliable guide to the king's itinerary. It is possible that on some occasions he was separated from his clerks, but in all probability his clerks either went ahead of the king or followed behind him on the same route, or stayed in a town close to a royal hunting-lodge.

[1] See p. 109 n. 6

Bibliography

A Manuscript Sources

I PUBLIC RECORD OFFICE (LONDON)

C.47	Chancery Miscellanea
C.53	Charter Rolls
C.54	Close Rolls
C.61	Gascon Rolls
C.66	Patent Rolls
C.76	Treaty Rolls
C.81	Chancery Warrants
C.135	Chancery Inquisitions *post mortem*
C.219	Parliamentary Writs and Returns
Chester 2	Chester Recognizance Rolls
DL.28	Duchy of Lancaster Accounts, various
DL.29	Duchy of Lancaster Ministers' Accounts
DL.30	Duchy of Lancaster Court Rolls
DL.41	Duchy of Lancaster Miscellanea
DL.42	Duchy of Lancaster Miscellaneous Books
E.28	Exchequer Treasury of Receipt Council and Privy Seal Records
E.34	Exchequer Treasury of Receipt Privy Seals and Patents for Loans
E.101	Exchequer King's Remembrancer Accounts, various
E.157	Exchequer King's Remembrancer Memoranda Rolls
E.163	Exchequer King's Remembrancer Miscellanea
E.179	Exchequer King's Remembrancer Lay Subsidy Rolls
E.207	Exchequer King's Remembrancer Bille
E.208	Exchequer King's Remembrancer Brevia Baronibus
E.356	Exchequer Lord Treasurer's Remembrancer Enrolled Customs Accounts

E.368   Exchequer Lord Treasurer's Remembrancer Memoranda Rolls
E.401   Exchequer Receipt Rolls
E.403   Exchequer Issue Rolls
E.404   Exchequer Warrants for Issues
KB.27   Coram Rege Rolls
PSO.1   Privy Seal Office, Warrants for the Privy Seal
SC.1   Ancient Correspondence
SC.6   Ministers' Accounts
SC.8   Ancient Petitions

II BRITISH MUSEUM
Add. Mss. 40859A
Cotton Titus B XI
Cotton Vespasian F VII
Harleian Ms. 565

III CARLISLE RECORD OFFICE
DRC.1/2   *Register of Bishop Appleby*

IV NATIONAL LIBRARY OF IRELAND
Harris Mss.

V PUBLIC RECORD OFFICE, DUBLIN
Ferguson Collectanea

VI EDINBURGH UNIVERSITY LIBRARY
Ms. 183 (formerly Laing Ms. 351)

VII SHROPSHIRE RECORD OFFICE
Acton of Aldenham Collection

B Printed Primary Sources

I PUBLISHED AND CALENDARED DOCUMENTS
Anglo-Norman Letters and Petitions from All Souls Ms. 182, ed.
M. D. Legge, Anglo-Norman Text Society III (Oxford 1941)
Calendar of Charter Rolls
Calendar of Close Rolls

Calendar of Documents Relating to Scotland Vol. IV, ed. J. Bain (Edinburgh 1888)

Calendar of Fine Rolls

Calendar of Inquisitions Post Mortem

Calendar of Letter Books of the City of London: H ed. R. R. Sharpe (London 1907)

Calendar of Miscellaneous Inquisitions

Calendar of Ormond Deeds II 1350–1413 ed. E. Curtis, Irish Manuscripts Commission (Dublin 1934)

Calendar of Papal Registers

Calendar of Patent Rolls

Codex Diplomaticus Prussicus ed. J. Voigt (Kaliningrad (Königsberg) 1853)

Diplomatic Correspondence of Richard II ed. E. Perroy, Camden Third Series XLVIII (London 1933)

Early Statutes of Ireland ed. H. F. Berry (Dublin 1907)

Exchequer Rolls of Scotland Vol. III (Edinburgh 1880)

Expeditions to Prussia and the Holy Land Made by Henry Earl of Derby ed. L. Toulmin-Smith, Camden New Series LII (London 1894)

Feet of Fines for the County of Sussex Vol. III ed. L. F. Salzman, Sussex Record Society XXIII (1916)

Issues of the Exchequer ed. F. Devon (London 1837)

John of Gaunt's Register 1372–76 ed. S. Armitage-Smith, Camden Third Series XXI (London 1911)

John of Gaunt's Register 1379–83 ed. E. C. Lodge and R. Somerville, Camden Third Series LVI (London 1937)

Liber Regie Capelle ed. W. Ullmann (London, for the Henry Bradshaw Society, 1961)

Monasticon Anglicanum Vol. VI, part 1) by Sir William Dugdale, ed J. Caley *et al.*, (London 1830)

Monumenta de Insula Manniae ed. J. R. Oliver, *Manx Society Publications* IV (Douglas 1860)

'The Ordenaunce and Fourme of Fightyng within Listes' in *The Black Book of the Admiralty* Vol. I, ed. Sir Travers Twiss, Rolls Series (London 1871)

The Pension Book of Clement's Inn ed. E. Carr, Selden Society LXXVIII (London 1960)

Political Poems and Songs Vol. I, ed. T. Wright, Rolls Series (London 1859)

Proceedings and Ordinances of the Privy Council of England ed. N.H. Nicolas (London 1834)

Proceedings Before the Justices of the Peace in the 14th and 15th Centuries ed. B. H. Putnam, Ames Foundation (London 1938)

The Ransom of John I King of France ed. D. M. Broome, Camden Miscellany XIV (London 1926)

Registrum Magni Sigilli Regum Scottorum Vol. I (Edinburgh 1912)

Reports from the Lords Committees Touching the Dignity of a Peer of the Realm 5 Volumes (London 1829)

Reports of the Royal Commission on Historical Manuscripts

Rogeri Dymmok Liber Contra XII Errores et Hereses Lollardorum ed. H. S. Cronin, Wycliffe Society (London 1922)

Rolls of the Warwickshire and Coventry Sessions of the Peace 1377–97, ed. E. G. Kimball, Dugdale Society XVI (London 1939)

Rotuli Parliamentorum 4 volumes (London 1783)

Rotuli Scotiae 2 volumes (London 1814–19)

Rotulorum Patentium et Clausarum Cancellariae Hiberniae Calendarium ed. E. Tresham (Dublin 1828)

Royal Wills ed. J. Nichols (London 1780)

Rymer, *Foedera Conventiones Litterae etc.* 2nd edition, ed. G. Holmes, 20 volumes (London 1704–35)

Select Cases Before the King's Council 1243–1482 ed. I. S. Leadam and J. F. Baldwin, Selden Society XXXV (Cambridge Mass., 1918)

Select Cases in the Court of King's Bench Vol. VII, ed. G. O. Sayles, Selden Society LXXXVIII (London 1971)

Select Pleas in the Court of Admiralty ed. R. G. Marsden, Selden Society VI (London 1892)

Some Sessions of the Peace in Lincolnshire ed. E. G. Kimball, Lincoln Record Society XLIX (1955)

Statutes of the Realm, 11 volumes (1810–28)

Two Early Tours in Ireland ed. J. P. Mahaffy, *Hermathena* XVIII (Dublin 1914)

Unpublished Letters from Richard II in Ireland ed. E. Curtis, Proceedings of the Royal Irish Academy XXXVII (1927)

II CHRONICLES

Annales Ricardi Secundi et Henrici Quarti in J. de Trokelowe et Anon., *Chronica et Annales* ed. H. T. Riley, Rolls Series (London 1866)

Annals of the Four Masters Vol. IV, ed. J. O'Donovan (Dublin 1851)

The Anonimalle Chronicle 1333–81 ed. V. H. Galbraith (Manchester 1927)

The Chronicle of John Hardyng ed. H. Ellis (London 1812)

Chronicon Adae de Usk ed. E. M. Thompson (London 1904)

Chronicon Angliae auctore monacho quodam Sancti Albani ed. E. M. Thompson, Rolls Series (London 1874)

Chronicon Henrici Knighton ed. J. R. Lumby, 2 volumes, Rolls Series (London 1895)

Chronique de la Traison et Mort de Richard II ed. B. Williams (London 1846)

Chronique du Religieux de Saint Denys ed. M. Bellaguet (Paris 1839)

Eulogium Historiarum sive Temporis Vol. III, ed. F. S. Haydon, Rolls Series (London 1863)

Froissart, *Oeuvres* ed. K. de Lettenhove, 25 volumes (Brussels 1867–77)

Historia sive Narracio Mirabilis Parliamenti attributed to Thomas Favent, ed. M. McKisack, Camden Third Series XXXVII (London 1926)

Historia Vitae et Regni Ricardi II a monacho quodam de Evesham ed. T. Hearne (Oxford 1729)

The Kirkstall Chronicle 1355–1400 ed. M. V. Clarke and N. Den-holm-Young, *BJRL* XV (1931)

A Metrical History of the Deposition of Richard II attributed to Jean Creton, ed. J. Webb, *Archaeologia* XX (1814)

Polychronicon Ranulphi Higden Vol. IX, ed. J. R. Lumby, Rolls Series (London 1886)

Scalacronica of Sir Thomas Grey of Heton ed. J. Stevenson (Edinburgh 1836)

Thomas Walsingham, *Historia Anglicana* ed. H. T. Riley, 2 volumes Rolls Series (London 1863–4)

III TEXTS

Sir John Fortescue, *De Laudibus Legum Angliae* ed. S. B. Chrimes (Cambridge 1942)

Sir John Fortescue, *The Governance of England* ed. C. Plummer (Oxford 1885)

The Libelle of Englyshe Polycye ed. G. Warner (Oxford 1926)

H*

Richard the Redeless attributed to William Langland, ed. W. W. Skeat (London 1886)

J. Wycliffe, *De Officio Regis* ed. A. W. Pollard and C. Sayle, Wycliffe Society (London 1887)

C Secondary Works

Armitage-Smith, S. *John of Gaunt* (London 1904)

Aston, Margaret, 'The Impeachment of Bishop Despenser', *BIHR* XXXVIII (1965)

Thomas Arundel (Oxford 1967)

Atkinson, R. L., 'Richard II and the Death of the Duke of Gloucester', *EHR* XXXVIII (1923)

Atiya, A. S., *The Crusade of Nicopolis* (London 1934)

Baldwin, J. F., *The King's Council in England during the Middle Ages* (Oxford 1913)

Barron, Caroline, 'The Tyranny of Richard II', *BIHR* XLI (1968)

Bayley, G. C., 'The Campaign of 1375 and the Good Parliament', *EHR* LV (1940)

Bean, J. M. W., 'The Percies and their Estates in Scotland', *Archaeologia Aeliana* 4th series XXXV (1957)

'Henry IV and the Percies', *History* XLIV (1959)

The Decline of English Feudalism 1215–1540 (Manchester 1968)

Bellamy, J. G., 'The Coterel Gang', *EHR* LXXIX (1964) pp. 698–717

'The Northern Rebellions in the Later Years of Richard II', *BJRL* XLVII (1964–5)

The Law of Treason in England in the later Middle Ages (Cambridge 1970)

Bird, Ruth, *The Turbulent London of Richard II* (London 1949)

Broome, D. M., 'The Ransom of John I King of France', *Camden Third Series* XXXVII (1926)

Brown, A. L., *The Early History of the Clerkship of the Council* (Glasgow 1969)

'The Latin Letters in All Souls Ms. 182', *EHR* LXXXVII (1972)

Brown, R. A., Colvin, H. M. and Taylor, A. J., *The History of the King's Works* Vol. II (London 1963)

Bueno de Mesquita, D. M., 'The Foreign Policy of Richard II in 1397: Some Italian Letters', *EHR* LVI (1941)

Carus-Wilson, E. M. and Coleman, Olive, *England's Export Trade 1275–1547* (Oxford 1963)

Chrimes, S. B., 'Richard II's Questions to the Judges, 1387', *Law Quarterly Review* LXII (1956)

Clarke, M. V., *Fourteenth Century Studies* (Oxford 1937)

Clarke, M. V. and Galbraith, V. H., 'The Deposition of Richard II', *BJRL* XIV (1930) pp. 125–55

Clementi, D., 'Richard II's Ninth Question to the Judges', *EHR* LXXXVI (1971)

Clowes, W. L. *A History of the Royal Navy* Vol. I (London 1897)

Cobban, A. B., *The King's Hall in the University of Cambridge in the Later Middle Ages* (Cambridge 1969)

The Complete Peerage, by G. E. C. ed. V. Gibbs *et al.*, 12 volumes (London 1910–59)

Curtis, E., *A History of Medieval Ireland* (London 1923)
  Richard II in Ireland (Oxford 1927)
  'Unpublished Letters from Richard II in Ireland', *Proceedings of the Royal Irish Academy* XXXVII (1927) pp. 276–303
  'The Barons of Norragh, Co. Kildare, 1171–1660', *Journal of the Royal Society of Antiquaries of Ireland* LXV (1935)

Davies, R. G., 'Some notes from the Register of Henry de Wakefield, Bishop of Worcester, on the Political Crisis of 1386–88', *EHR* LXXXVI (1971)

Davies, R. R., 'Owain Glyn Dŵr and the Welsh Squirearchy', *Transactions of the Honourable Society of Cymmrodorion* (1968)

Devon, F., *Issues of the Exchequer* (London 1837)

du Boulay, F. R. H. and Barron, Caroline (editors), *The Reign of Richard II: Essays in Honour of May McKisack* (London 1971)

Edwards, J. G., 'The Parliamentary Committee of 1398', *EHR* XL (1925)
  'Some Common Petitions in Richard II's first Parliament', *BIHR* XXVI (1935)
  'The Commons in Medieval English Parliaments', *Creighton Lecture* (London 1957)

Emden, A. B., *A Biographical Register of the University of Oxford* (Oxford 1959)
  A Biographical Register of the University of Cambridge (Cambridge 1963)

Fairbank, F. R., 'The Last Earl of Warenne and Surrey', *Yorkshire Archaeological Journal* XIX (1970)

Fryde, E. B., 'The Last Trials of Sir William de la Pole', *Economic History Review* 2nd Series XV (1962–3)

Galbraith, V. H., *Roger Wendover and Matthew Paris* (Glasgow 1944)

Gilbert, J. T., *The Viceroys of Ireland* (Dublin 1865)

Goodman, A., *The Loyal Conspiracy* (London 1971)

Griffiths, R. A., 'Gentlemen and Rebels in late medieval Cardiganshire', *Ceredigion* V (1964–7)

Harriss, G. L., 'Preference at the Medieval Exchequer', *BIHR* XXX (1957)

'Aids, Loans and Benevolences', *Historical Journal* VI (1963)

Harvey, Barbara, 'Draft Letters Patent of Manumission and Pardon for the Men of Somerset in 1381', *EHR* LXXX (1965)

Haslop, G. S., 'Two Entries from the Register of John de Shirburn, Abbot of Selby 1369–1408', *Yorkshire Archaeological Journal* XLI (1964)

Hatcher, J., *Rural Economy and Society in the Duchy of Cornwall 1300–1500* (Cambridge 1970)

Hay, D., 'Booty in Border Warfare', *Transactions of the Dumfriesshire and Galloway Natural History and Antiquarian Society* 3rd series XXXI (1954)

Hewitt, H. J., *Medieval Cheshire* (Manchester 1929)

The Black Prince's Expedition of 1355–57 (Manchester 1958)

The Organization of War under Edward III (Manchester 1966)

Hill, J. W. F., *Medieval Lincoln* (Cambridge 1948)

Hobsbawm, E. J., *Bandits* (London 1969)

Holmes, G. A., *The Estates of the Higher Nobility in Fourteenth Century England* (Cambridge 1957)

Holmes, G. A., *The Nobility under Edward III* (unpublished Ph.D. Thesis, Cambridge 1952)

Hurnard, N. D., *The King's Pardon for Homicide before 1307* (Oxford 1969)

Jacob, E. F., *The Fifteenth Century* (Oxford 1961)

Jones, M. C. E., *Ducal Brittany 1364–1399* (Oxford 1970)

'The Ransom of Jean de Bretagne, Count of Penthièvre: an Aspect of English Foreign Policy 1386–88', *BIHR* XLV (1972)

Jones, R. H., *The Royal Policy of Richard II* (Oxford 1968)

Keen, M. H., *The Outlaws of Medieval Legend* (London 1961)

The Laws of War in the Late Middle Ages (London 1965)

'Treason Trials and the Law of Arms', *TRHS* 5th series XII (1962)

Kirby, J. L., *Henry IV of England* (London 1970)

Langland, W., *Richard the Redeless* Vol. I, ed. W. W. Skeat (London 1886)

Lapsley, G., 'The Parliamentary Title of Henry IV', *EHR* XLIX (1934) pp. 423–49, 577–606

'Richard II's "Last Parliament" ', *EHR* LIII (1938) pp. 53–78

Leach, A. F., 'A Clerical Strike at Beverley Minster in the Fourteenth Century', *Archaeologia* LV (1896)

Lehoux, F., *Jean de France, Duc de Berry* Vol. II (Paris 1966)

Lewis, N. B., 'Article VII of the Impeachment of Michael de la Pole', *EHR* XLII (1927)

'Re-election to Parliament in the Reign of Richard II', *EHR* XLVIII (1933)

'Simon Burley and Baldwin of Raddington', *EHR* LII (1937)

'The "Continual Council" in the early years of Richard II', *EHR* XLI (1926)

'The Last Summons of the English Feudal Levy, 13 June 1385', *EHR* LXXIII (1958)

List of Sheriffs of England and Wales from the Earliest Times to 1831 PRO Lists and Indexes IX (1898)

Lydon, J. F., 'Richard II's Expeditions to Ireland', *Journal of the Royal Society of Antiquaries of Ireland* XCIII (1963)

McFarlane, K. B., 'Bastard Feudalism', *BIHR* XX (1947)

'Loans to the Lancastrian Kings: the Problem of Inducement', *Cambridge Historical Journal* IX (1947)

John Wycliffe and the Beginnings of English Nonconformity (London 1952)

'The Investment of Sir John Fastolf's Profits of War', *TRHS* 5th series VII (1957)

'England and the Hundred Years War', *Past & Present* XXII (1962)

'The English Nobility in the Later Middle Ages', *12th International Congress of Historical Sciences* (1965)

Lancastrian Kings and Lollard Knights (Oxford 1972)

McKerral, A., 'West Highland Mercenaries in Ireland', *Sc.HR* XXX (1951)

McKisack, May, *The Fourteenth Century* (Oxford 1959)

Mahaffy, J. P., 'Two Early Tours in Ireland', *Hermathena* XVIII (Dublin 1914) pp. 1–9

Moorman, J. R. H., *The Grey Friars in Cambridge* (Cambridge 1952)

Murray, K. M. E., *Constitutional History of the Cinque Ports* (Manchester 1935)

Myres, J. N. L., 'The Campaign of Radcot Bridge in December 1387', *EHR* XLII (1927)

Nicholls, K., *Gaelic and Gaelicised Ireland in the Middle Ages* (Dublin 1972)

Nicholson, R. A., *Edward III and the Scots* (Oxford 1965)

'David II, the Historians and the Chroniclers', *Sc.HR* XLV (1966)

Otway-Ruthven, Jocelyn, *The King's Secretary and the Signet Office in the Fifteenth Century* (Cambridge 1939)

A History of Medieval Ireland (London 1968)

Palais, H., 'England's First Attempt to Break the Commercial Monopoly of the Hanseatic League', *American Historical Review* LXIV (1969)

Palmer, J. J. N., 'The Anglo-French Peace Negotiations, 1390–96', *TRHS* 5th series XVI (1966)

'The Last Summons of the Feudal Army in England', *EHR* LXXXIII (1968)

'The Impeachment of Michael de la Pole in 1386', *BIHR* XLIII (1970)

'The Parliament of 1385 and the Constitutional Crisis of 1386', *Speculum* XLVI (1971)

England, France and Christendom (London 1971)

Perroy, E., *L'Angleterre et le Grand Schisme d'Occident* (Paris 1933)

The Hundred Years War (London 1951)

Pike, L. O., *Constitutional History of the House of Lords* (London 1894)

Plucknett, T. F., 'The Impeachments of 1376', *TRHS* 5th series I (1951)

'Impeachment and Attainder', *TRHS* 5th series III (1953)

Postan, M. M., 'The Costs of the Hundred Years War', *Past & Present* XXVII 1964

Powell, E., *The Rising in East Anglia in 1381* (Cambridge 1896)

Quinn, D. B., *The Elizabethans and the Irish* (New York 1966)

Rayner, D., 'The Form and Machinery of the "Commune Petition" in the Fourteenth Century', *EHR* LVI (1941)

Return of Members of Parliament, Part I: Parliaments of England 1213–1702 (London 1878)

Reville, A., *Le Soulèvement des Travailleurs d'Angleterre en 1381* (Paris 1898)

Richardson, H. G., 'Richard II's Last Parliament', *EHR* LII (1937) pp. 39–47

'John of Gaunt and the Parliamentary Representation of Lancashire', *BJRL* XXII (1938)

Robson, J. A. *Wyclif and the Oxford Schools* (Cambridge 1961)

Roskell, J. S., 'The Problem of the Attendance of the Lords in Medieval English Parliaments', *BIHR XXIX* (1956)

  The Commons and their Speakers in English Parliaments, 1376–1523 (Manchester 1965)

Ross, C. D., 'Forfeiture for Treason in the Reign of Richard II', *EHR LXXI* (1956)

Russell, P. E., *The English Intervention in Spain and Portugal in the Time of Edward III and Richard II* (Oxford 1955)

Sayles, G. O., 'The Rebellious First Earl of Desmond', in *Medieval Studies Presented to Aubrey Gwynn* (Dublin 1961)

Sherborne, J. W., 'The Battle of La Rochelle and the War at Sea, 1372–1375', *BIHR XLII* (1969)

Somerville, R., *History of the Duchy of Lancaster* Vol. I (London 1953)

Squibb, G. D., *The High Court of Chivalry* (Oxford 1959)

Stamp, A. E., 'Richard II and the Death of the Duke of Gloucester', *EHR XXXVIII* (1923)

Steel, A. B., 'Sheriffs of Cambridgeshire and Huntingdonshire in the Time of Richard II' (typescript in Cambridge University Library 1934)

  Richard II (Cambridge 1941)

  The Receipt of the Exchequer 1377–1485 (Cambridge 1954)

Stones, E. L. G., 'The Folvilles of Ashby de la Zouch', *TRHS* 5th series VII (1957) pp. 117–36

Storey, R. L., 'The Wardens of the Marches of England towards Scotland 1377–1489', *EHR LXXII* (1957)

Suarez Fernandez, L., *Navegación y Comercio en el Golfo de Vizcaya: Un estudio sobre la Politica Marinera de la Casa de Trastámara* (Madrid 1958)

  Historia de España (Madrid 1966)

Tait, J., 'Did Richard II Murder the Duke of Gloucester?' in *Historical Essays* ed. T. F. Tout and J. Tait (Manchester 1907)

Thrupp, Sylvia, *The Merchant Class of Medieval London* (Ann Arbor 1962)

Tout, T. F., 'The Earldoms under Edward I', *TRHS* new series VIII (1894) pp. 129–55

  Chapters in the Administrative History of Medieval England 6 volumes (Manchester 1923–35)

Tuck, J. A., *The Baronial Opposition to Richard II 1377–89* (unpublished Ph.D. thesis, Cambridge 1966)

  'Richard II and the Border Magnates', *Northern History* III (1968)

'The Cambridge Parliament 1388', *EHR* LXXIV (1969)

'Anglo-Irish Relations 1382–1393', *Proceedings of the Royal Irish Academy* LXIX (1970)

'Some Evidence for Anglo-Scandinavian Relations in the Fourteenth Century', *Medieval Scandinavia* V (1972)

Ullmann, W., *Principles of Government and Politics in the Middle Ages* (London 1961)

Vicens Vives, J., *Historia Económica de España* (Madrid 1966)

Victoria History of the Counties of England (in progress)

Warren, W. L., 'A Reappraisal of Simon Sudbury', *Journal of Ecclesiastical History* X (1959)

Wedgwood, J. C., 'John of Gaunt and the Packing of Parliament', *EHR* XLV (1930)

Wilkinson, B., 'The Deposition of Richard II and the Accession of Henry IV', *EHR* LIV (1939) pp. 215–39

Constitutional History of England in the Fifteenth Century (London 1964)

Wolffe, B. P., *The Royal Demesne in English History* (London 1971)

Wright, H. G., 'Richard II and the Death of the Duke of Gloucester', *EHR* XLVII (1932)

'The Protestation of Richard II in the Tower in September 1399', *BJRL* XXIII (1943) pp. 151–66

Index